The Syrian Social Nationalist Party

Its Ideology and History

Salim Mujais

The Syrian Social Nationalist Party
Its Ideology and History

Salim Mujais

Copyright © 2019 Black House Publishing Ltd

All rights reserved. No part of this book may be reproduced in any form by any electronic or mechanical means including photocopying, recording, or information storage and retrieval without permission in writing from the publisher.

ISBN 13: 978-1-912759-14-9

Black House Publishing Ltd
Kemp House
152 City Road
London
United Kingdom
EC1V 2NX

www.blackhousepublishing.com
Email: info@blackhousepublishing.com

Dedication

To Syria, the Phoenix Land

Acknowledgment

My daughter has been my guardian against infelicities of content, style, and grammar. She has my love and gratitude.

I also owe a debt of gratitude to Mr. Karl Winn, who offered thoughtful comments and criticism that helped enhance the clarity and coverage of this work.

Contents

Preface	1
The Ideology of the SSNP	11
The National Landscape	11
The Nation Concept	20
National Identity and Sovereignty	26
Syria Defined	32
Social Justice And Human Rights	41
Political Discipline and Party Organization	50
Case study: Palestine	56
The Aim of the SSNP	63
The Early History of the SSNP	67
Clandestine Beginnings (1932-1936)	67
Infiltration by French Informants	74
A Historical Trial	78
Visibility and Widespread Involvement (1936-1938)	84
The Franco-Syrian Treaties	87
The Second Arrest	90
Memorandum to the League of Nations	92
Strengthening the Ideological Base	94
Direct Dialogue with the Mandate	98
The Question of Alexandretta	101
Northern Outreach	105
Lebanese Confrontations	109
The Question of Palestine	114
Lebanese Politics	117

The Case of May Ziadeh	130
Confronting a Religious Bastion	134
The First of March 1938	140
Seeking International Support	145
Exile and Repression (1938-1947)	155
Political Accommodations	175
Re-Establishing Contact	177
The "National Party"	180
Return Preparations and Challenges	182
Cairo Interlude	185
Saadeh Returns From Exile	187
Parliamentary Elections	193
The Battle For Leadership	195
Palestine in Peril	196
Rebuilding the SSNP	199
The Zaim Coup	204
The Uprising	209
Treachery, Trial and Martyrdom	212
Epilogue	215
Appendix	229
The Principles and Aim of the SSNP	229
Bibliography	249
About the Author	255

Preface

In the fall of 1932, five young men met in a modest room in Beirut and took an oath of membership to a new political organization. They were mostly students of the American University in Beirut and their leader, Antoun Saadeh, taught German privately at the University and Arabic to members of the British and American diplomatic corps in Beirut. Three years later, at dawn on November 16, 1935, the security forces of the French Mandatory authority raided that same room and arrested Saadeh and a number of his lieutenants on the charge of forming an illegal clandestine political party. In the interim, the new political organization had grown from the initial five to over a thousand members spread along the Syrian coast from Jaffa to Latakia, into the Lebanon range, and in the hinterland from Jerusalem to Amman, Damascus, Homs and Hama. As the date of the original meeting had not been recorded, the date of the arrest was accepted as a symbolic substitute and November 16, 1932 became the official date of the founding of the Syrian Social Nationalist Party (SSNP).[1]

The SSNP is sometimes referred to in the Western press by the French mistranslation of its name: "Parti Populaire Syrien", or the Syrian Popular Party, abbreviated as PPS. In the Middle East, the Party is commonly referred to simply as the Nationalist Party (*al-Hizb al-Qawmi*) attesting to the characteristic link between the term nationalism and the perception of the Party by the people of the Fertile Crescent. For the first decade of its existence, the party was known as the Syrian National Party (in Arabic *al-Hizb as-Suri al-Qawmi*). In the early years of WWII, its founder added the term "Social" (*al-Ijtima'i*) to the name

---

1 Syria as used in SSNP literature refers to the entire Fertile Crescent including Lebanon, the present Syrian Republic, Palestine, Jordan, Iraq, Kuwait and the district of Alexandretta.

The Syrian Social Nationalist Party

Antoun Saadeh - Founder of the Syrian Social Nationalist Party

Preface

of the party to characterize its national ideology more clearly, and henceforth the party became known as the Syrian Social Nationalist Party (SSNP, *al-Hizb as-Suri al-Qawmi al-Ijtima'i*).

Over the following decades, the SSNP was subjected to ferocious attempts by colonial powers and local governments aimed at eradicating it from political life in the Middle East. Nevertheless, after every onslaught, the SSNP seems to rise from the ashes, and earned the name of the Syrian Phoenix from its determined enemies.[2] Commenting on the resilience of the SSNP in the face of persecution during the French Mandate period, Albert Hourani maintained that the SSNP was able to hold its own because of several significant factors: "First, it made a more determined effort than any other organization to think out the whole national problem in all its aspects, and to formulate a programme in the light of clear and valid political principles. Again, it was rigidly organized on the membership principle, with a hierarchy, a logical division of functions and a strict discipline. Finally, its leader was a man of courage, decision and powerful intellect."[3]

The Syrian Social Nationalist Party is indeed the first organized party in the Middle East to have a definite national doctrine and a well-structured ideology. The Pan-Arab theorist Sati' al-Husri, no friend of the SSNP, wrote in the early 1950's: "Until now, there has appeared no party in the Arab world that can compete with the SSNP for the quality of its propaganda, which addresses both reason and emotion, or for the strength of its organization, which is effective both overtly and covertly. By virtue of its organization, this party succeeded in creating a very powerful intellectual current in Syria and Lebanon."[4]

---

[2] Eyal Zisser: The Syrian Phoenix: The Revival of the Syrian Social National Party in Syria, Die Welt des Islams, New Series, *Volume*. 47, Issue 2 (2007), pp. 188-206.

[3] Albert Hourani, *Syria and Lebanon: A Political Essay*, Oxford University Press, London, 1946, p.197.

[4] Sati al-Husari: *al-Uruba bayn Du'atiha wa Mu'aridiha* (Arabism between its proponents and opponents), Complete Works, part 1, Center of Arab Unity Studies, Beirut, 1990.

The Syrian Social Nationalist Party

The SSNP has played a prominent role in shaping the make-up of the political and intellectual environment of the Middle East through its intimate involvement in political events and its influence on political and cultural discourses in the area. Knowledge of the Party in the Western Hemisphere, however, has remained for a long time limited and distorted, predominantly because of the lack of publications that expound the ideology of the Party and its history. Except for an academic study by an ex-party member,[5] and the occasional pamphlet published by the SSNP, knowledge of the Party in the West was limited to the incomplete and often misguided opinions of political commentators[6] or general historians.[7] Recently, however, authors affiliated with the Party have undertaken to remedy the knowledge gap and several worthy publications have appeared in English tackling a variety of topics related to the ideology of the SSNP and various aspects of its history.[8] There remains a need,

---

5   Labib Zuwiyya Yamak: *The Syrian Social Nationalist Party: An Ideological Analysis*. Harvard Middle Eastern Monograph Series, Harvard University Press. Cambridge MA, 1969. The author of this monograph was a member of the SSNP in the late forties. Surprisingly, his writings reflect little insight into the details of the ideology and history of the SSNP expected from someone who had been a member. In addition to its documentary shortcomings, the work suffers from a rigid methodology aiming at projecting preformed western judgement completely oblivious to the social and historical conditions of the Near East.

6   A representative sample along those lines is the naive and grossly inaccurate article by Daniel Pipes titled "Radical politics and the Syrian Social Nationalist Party", which appeared in *International Journal of Middle Eastern Studies* 20: 303-324, 1988.

7   The otherwise reliable historian Kamal Salibi perpetuates in his book *A House of Many Mansions: The History of Lebanon Reconsidered* (University of California Press, 1988) a common misrepresentation of the SSNP as a political outlet for the Orthodox Christians of the Fertile Crescent. Other examples include: Mackey, Sandra, *Lebanon: death of a nation*, Anchor Books, NY, 1991; Mansfield, Peter, *The Arabs*, Harmondsworth, New York, 1978; Karpat, Kemal, *Political and social thought in the contemporary Middle East*, Praeger, NY, 1982; Spyer, Jonathan, *The rise of nationalism: the Arab World, Turkey, and Iran*, Mason Crest Publishers, Philadelphia, 2008; Bogle, Emory, *The modern Middle East: from imperialism to freedom*, 1800-1958, Prentice Hall, NJ, 1996

8   Safia Antoun Saadeh, *Antun Saadeh and democracy in geographic Syria*, London, Folios, 2000; Adel Beshara, *Antun Saadeh the man, his thought: an*

Preface

however, for an integrated overview that presents a systematic examination of the ideology of the SSNP and its early history, which is the aim of the present work.

Antoun Saadeh, the founder and leader of the SSNP, was born in the village of Shweir (Mount Lebanon) on March 1, 1904.[9] His father, Dr. Khalil Saadeh, was a physician and a leading national militant. Because of the oppressive conditions under Ottoman rule in Syria before World War I, Dr. Saadeh emigrated first to Egypt and then to South America where he became a political and civic leader in the Syrian community championing the cause of the motherland.[10] Antoun Saadeh spent the war years in Mount Lebanon suffering from famine, oppression, and the desolation of his country.

In 1920, Antoun Saadeh travelled to the United States escorting his younger siblings to join his maternal uncle and worked briefly as a railroad inspector before moving to Brazil to join his father. In Brazil, Saadeh assisted his father in publishing a daily paper (*al-Jarida*) and then a monthly journal (*al-Majalla*) where he expressed his early and passionate involvement in

---

anthology, Reading, UK, Ithaca Press, 2007; Adel Beshara, *Syrian nationalism: an inquiry into the political philosophy of Antun Sa'adeh*, Melbourne phoenix Publishing, 2011; Adel Beshara, *Outright assassination: the trial and execution of Antun Sa'adeh*, 1949, Reading, U.K., Ithaca Press, 2012; Adel Beshara, *The Intellectual Legacy of Antun Sa'adeh: Philosophy, Culture And Society*, Beirut, Lebanon, Kutub, 2017; Edmond Melhem, *Antun Saadeh, National Philosopher: an Introduction to his Philosophical Thought*, Beirut, Dar Fikr, 2011.

9   For a detailed biography of Antoun Saadeh see Salim Mujais: *Antoun Saadeh: a Biography*, Kutub Publishing, Beirut, volume 1 (2004), volume 2 (2009), volume 3 (2018).

10   Dr. Khalil Saadeh (1857-1934) studied medicine at the Syrian Protestant College (currently American University of Beirut) and led a life of intense intellectual productivity and nationalist militancy. In addition to his medical writings, he was a novelist (in English his novels include *Caesar and Cleopatra*, and *Anthony and Cleopatra*; In Arabic: *Secrets of the Russian Revolution*, and *Mystery of the Bastille*, in addition to his translations of his own English novels), a linguist (his was the first major English-Arabic dictionary) and a political activist. The collected works of Dr. Khalil Saadeh in eight volumes have been recently edited by Badr el-Hage and Salim Mujais and published by Kutub, Beirut.

the issues of nationalism, the destiny of Syria, and its future. During his stay in Brazil, Saadeh was intensely involved in the cultural and political affairs of the Syrian community. He studied independently and learned Portuguese, German, and Russian in addition to French, which he had learned in Cairo before the First World War, and English which he had acquired in Syria before he emigrated. He was widely read in history and the social and political sciences, and taught Arabic language and literature in one of the Syrian communities' private colleges.

In 1930, Saadeh returned to Syria determined to bring into existence a political movement that aimed at transforming Syria into a modern viable polity. He acquainted himself with the political and social conditions of the country and expressed his views on national revival and sovereignty in the press and in public lectures. In the fall of 1932, Saadeh founded the SSNP as a secret organization and the Party grew in secret until November 16, 1935, when the French authorities alerted to the presence of the political organization apprehended Saadeh and his lieutenants and imprisoned them. While in prison awaiting trial, Saadeh wrote on December 10, 1935, a statement at the request of his lawyer in which he expounded his reasons for founding the SSNP:

> "I was an adolescent when World War I broke out, but I had become cognizant of, and sensitive to, the conditions of my people. As I witnessed the woeful condition in which my people were and as I suffered the misery rampant among them, the first question that came to my mind was: What was it that brought all this woe on my people.
>
> "After the end of the war, I began looking for the answer to this question and for the solution to the chronic political problems that kept pushing my people into one adversity after another. Obviously, I was not seeking an answer to that question to satisfy a scientific or intellectual curiosity, but rather to discover the most effective means to eliminate the causes of this woe. After an organized preliminary study, I

concluded that the absence of national sovereignty was the primary cause of what had befell and what was ailing my nation. This led me to pursue the study of nationalism and societal rights and their genesis. In the process of my study and research I became keenly aware of the importance of the idea of a nation, its meaning and the complexity of the factors from which it emanates."[11]

The interest of Saadeh in the national cause was the culmination of a period of contemplation and study of the causes of Syrian decadence, and a commitment to revive his ailing nation. The central issue was not political independence per se, but the independence that followed national integration of the Syrian people whose unity was fragmented. As national unity could not be achieved without instilling in the consciousness of the people that they exist as a distinct national group, Saadeh focused his attention primarily on the issue of national identity and defined it in the basic principles of the SSNP. This focus on the primordial issue of national identity distinguished his ideological formulations from all other thinkers in the Fertile Crescent and influenced profoundly the course of the Party. By making national identity and its definition primordial, Saadeh was aiming for clarity of national goals.

In Saadeh's writings, the concept of nationalism is distinct from the beliefs and views prevalent in the West in the 19th and most of the 20th centuries. He articulated his views in a seminal work titled *Nushu' al-Umam* (The Emergence of Nations). In the final chapter, he examines the meaning of nationhood and nationalism:

> "The nation is above all a social community... (it) is a human group leading a life of united interests, united destiny, united spiritual-physical elements in a particular country

---

[11] Letter from Antoun Saadeh to Hamid Frangieh. Antoun Saadeh: *Complete Works*, Saadeh Cultural Foundation, Beirut, 2001, volume 2, pp 9-12. All quotations from the writings of Antoun Saadeh are from this edition of his works in 12 volumes and translated from the Arabic by the present author.

with which it interacts in the course of development to acquire characteristics and features that distinguish it from other groups.

> Nationalism... is the nation's awakening and alertness to the unity of its life, to its personality, characteristics, and the unity of its destiny... It is sometimes confused with patriotism which is the love of the fatherland, because patriotism is part of nationalism and because the fatherland is the strongest factor in the genesis of a nation and the most important constituting element."[12]

Saadeh was aware of the 'politicization' of the concept of nationalism and the pitfalls of political theories of nationhood. "Every nation feels the need for sovereignty and for protecting its interests against encroachment and aggression by other nations. In this contention, which is often violent, the nation's politicians and thinkers resort to theories that suit the circumstances of their nation and raise its morale. Some go out in search of historical pretext or some religious or racial propensity."[13]

Saadeh's objective was to define the national identity of the Syrians and to set in motion a movement that would revive the Syrian nation and make it possible for Syria to become a modern and viable entity. This movement would aim to change the pattern of the social, political, and economic life in Syria. The SSNP is, therefore, "an idea and a movement concerned with the total life of the nation." The SSNP was conceived as an agent of change and represents the first concrete effort in Syria towards the total modernization of society. The change that the Party envisages is a comprehensive one that seeks to rebuild society in accordance with a distinct social philosophy. The tenets of this philosophy are embodied in the principles of the SSNP.

---

12 Antoun Saadeh: The Emergence of Nations, *Complete Works*, volume 3, pp 1-159.

13 *Ibid.*

Preface

In the present work, the basic and reform principles of the SSNP are presented based on the writings of Saadeh and his teachings. The text of the fourth edition of the "Exposition of Principles" is used as the primary document and is offered in its entirety in the appendix. There are four editions of the "Exposition of Principles". The first edition was written hastily by Saadeh when he was in jail in 1936 to provide the Party constituency with a document for ideological reference. He later returned to the work and expanded it in 1939 while in Brazil, and again in 1946 in Argentina. The final edition was published in Beirut in 1947 and has remained the standard core text of the ideology of the Party. The discussion of the ideology is followed by an overview of the early history of the Party from its founding in 1932 to the martyrdom of Saadeh in 1949, which will serve to illustrate the actualization of the ideology of the SSNP in the details of national and political struggle.

The Saadeh family featuring Dr. Khalil Saadeh and his wife Nayfeh along with their six sons in 1912. Their daughter Grace would be born after the date of this picture. Antoun Saadeh, the fourth son, is standing in the middle row next to his mother.

The Ideology of the SSNP

THE NATIONAL LANDSCAPE

The ideology of the Syrian Social Nationalist Party (SSNP) was formulated to redress the conditions responsible for Syria's decadence and suffering, to define a desired future state, and to chart and execute the course toward that future state. The ailments of Syria were myriad: divisions along sectarian and ethnic lines, a corrupt political class, and an absence of a unifying national consciousness, all complicated by colonial intervention. When Saadeh returned to Syria in 1930 to found the SSNP, he encountered a country truncated by colonial interventions and burdened by the accretion of social ills of historic proportions. The *Allied Conference* at San Remo on April 24, 1920 had partitioned the former Ottoman territory into British and French mandates, in effect, formalizing the "secret" Sykes-Picot Agreements of 1916.[1] The delineations of territory between British and French spheres of influence, as well as within their respective allocations, was the subject of compromise and constant change. The Franco-British Convention of December 23, 1920 defined the general boundary for Syria, Lebanon, Palestine and Iraq, but the agreed upon boundaries were arbitrary and subject to the interests of the negotiating parties. The most contentious demarcations were understandably those between

---

1 The Sykes-Picot agreement negotiated in 1916 between the French Francois George Picot and the British Sir Mark Sykes is a famous example of such colonial schemes. The Fertile Crescent was to be divided into five sectors. France was to have the northwest sector that included coastal Syria extending north into Anatolia. Great Britain was to have the southeast sector constituted by the vilayets of Basra and Baghdad. Between these were areas A and B which would be respectively, French and British spheres of interest. The fifth sector was Palestine from Acre to Gaza and from the coast to the Jordan where an international administration would be established. (R. Sanders: *The High Walls of Jerusalem: A History of the Balfour Declaration and the Birth of the British Mandate for Palestine*, Holt, Rinehart and Winston, New York, 1983, pp 305-307 and Saadeh, Collected Works, Volume XIV, pp 158-171).

the French and British areas of dominion.[2] The story of the boundaries between the French and British areas is instructive as one contemplates the narratives that will later emerge in support of the artificial proto-states. Between Lebanon and Palestine, the British proposed a boundary from Sidon eastward to include the lower Litani valley. The French counter-proposals remained close to the Sykes-Picot boundary (which ran close to Safad). The final agreement placed the boundary a few miles north of the Sykes-Picot line. Hence, the demarcation between Lebanon and Palestine was not the natural outcome of a historical evolution of two distinct national identities, but rather subject to colonial whim that emerges as the major arbitror of the new artificial national identities. Similar considerations were operative in the delineation of the artificial boundaries between other neighboring states. This colonial behavior created artificial proto-states that challenge the development of a unified national consciousness and fractionate national efforts at liberation.

The imprint of colonial intent in the demarcation of the artificial states in the Near East is illustrated best by the case of the district of Mosul.[3] On December 1, 1918, Lloyd George struck a deal with Clemenceau during the latter's visit to London. Against a concession that Palestine would pass into British control and Mosul attached to Mesopotamia, Lloyd George promised his support for a French Mandate of Syria, which included not only the littoral, but also the hinterland. The agreement survived

---

2 On the demarcation of the northern boundaries of Palestine, see: Gideon Biger: *The Boundaries of Modern Palestine, 1840-1947*. Routledge, NY, 2004. Review of the various boundaries can be found in a series of specific boundary papers prepared by *The Geographer*, Office of Strategic and Functional Research, Bureau of Intelligence and Research, Department of State, USA. International Boundary Study No. 75 – February 15, 1967 Israel – Lebanon Boundary. International Boundary Study No. 94 – December 30, 1969 Jordan – Syria Boundary. In addition, International Boundary Study No. 98 – April 15, 1970 Iraq – Jordan Boundary.

3 A most peculiar component is the request of delegates of the Assyro-Chaldean community to the Peace Conference in Versailles to have their own state in the upper curvature of the Fertile Crescent. According to the *Revue du Monde Musulman* (Paris, 1920, Volumes XL-XLI, p 155).

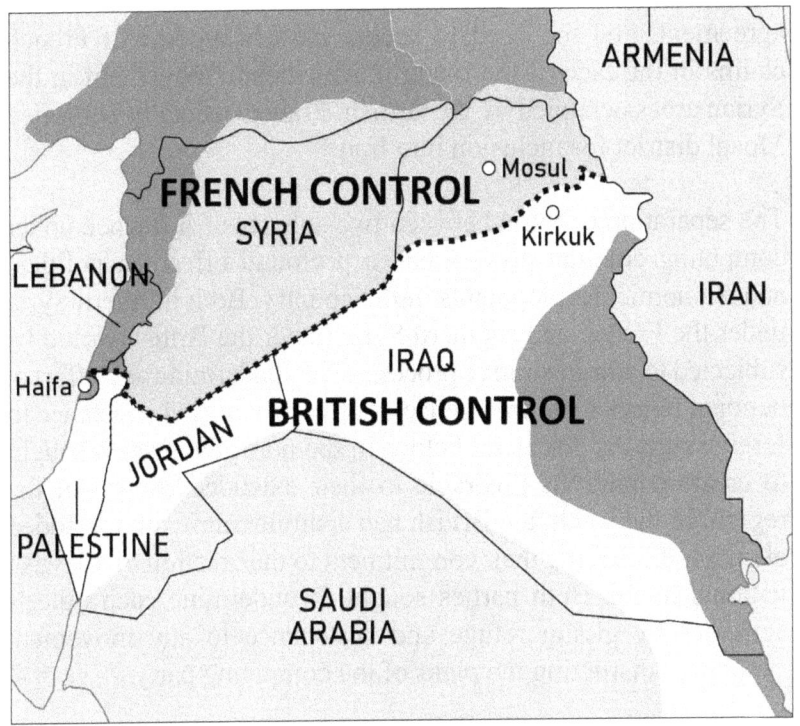

Sykes-Picot division of Syria

the subsequent squabbles during the Paris Peace Conference and served as a model for the arrangements at the San Remo conference.[4] The allocation of the Mosul Vilayet in the San Remo agreements was a significant departure from the 1916 Sykes-Picot agreement that had assigned the district to France. At San Remo, the interests of the two Powers in the oilfields of Iraq influenced the decisions of partition of lands. The British Government agreed to grant France a share in the crude oil or in development of the oilfields. Arrangements were made to transport oil from Iraq and Iran through the French sphere of influence in the Eastern Mediterranean. In consideration of this

---

4   Friedman, Isaiah: *Palestine, a Twice-Promised Land*. Transaction Publishers, New Brunswick, NJ, 2000, page 73. Sicker, Martin: *Reshaping Palestine: From Muhammad Ali to the British Mandate, 1831-1922*. Praeger/Greenwood publishers, Westport, CT, 1999, page 142. Paris, Timothy: *Britain, the Hashemites and Arab Rule, 1920-1925*. Routledge, London, 2003, page 60.

agreement, and the need to secure British support of French claims in the face of the rising independence movement in the Syrian areas occupied by the British, France officially conceded Mosul district for inclusion into Iraq.[5]

The separation of Syria between two spheres of influence under competing colonial powers had a profound effect on political and economic developments in the country. Both northern Syria under the French and southern Syria under the British would be subjected to administrative processes that undermine any effort at national unity or the emergence of effective unified resistance to foreign rule. As discussed below, in the north the French sought to create conditions favorable to their extended control of the region. In the south, the British had a similar aim with the added element of fulfilling their commitment to the creation of a Jewish national home. Both parties sought to undermine each other's activities by giving refuge and sustenance to any movement capable of disrupting the plans of the competing party.

Two major phases can be discerned in the French mandate and the political and administrative organizations of the states under France's tutelage prior to the founding of the SSNP. The first phase extends from General Gouraud's arrival in Beirut on November 21, 1919 to the insurrection of 1925. The second phase, inaugurated by the appointment of Henry de Jouvenel as High Commissioner, ends with the defining of the *Statut Organique* in May of 1930.

In the first phase, two major developments took place: the territory under French mandate was "organized" into separate states, and each of these states was given a "representative" government. The French determined that as a policy Syria should be divided into segments with an indigenous façade behind which the French acted at will. This is explicitly stated

---

5 International Boundary Study No. 100 – May 15, 1970 Iraq – Syria Boundary, *The Geographer*, Office of Strategic and Functional Research, Bureau of Intelligence and Research, Department of State, USA.

by a diplomat at the Quai d'Orsay in May of 1920: "From now onwards it is necessary to consider the regime which will follow our occupation and that will allow us to maintain our position with reduced military resources... The need is for an indigenous façade which is reasonably consistent, behind which we can operate without direct responsibility and in the way and under the circumstances which we judge useful... The possibility of an Arab dynasty reigning over a united Syria being excluded, it would seem that there would be no danger in leaving the various ethnic groups, by themselves or with help requested from us, to establish the framework of their national autonomy... It will therefore be essential to make a study of those ethnic groups which may as soon as possible constitute the first regional autonomous units." [6]

The architect of this administrative reshaping of geographic Syria was General Henri Gouraud (1867-1946), an experienced colonialist and a battle hardened military commander. At the end of his stay in Syria, French prime Minister Poincare celebrated him as *"Le pacificateur et l'organisateur de la Syrie!"* From August 31, 1920 to December 20 of the same year, General Gouraud created and organized the separate states of Grand-Liban, Damascus, Aleppo, and the Alawites. The state of Jabal el-Druze was not constituted until October 24, 1922. To maintain stability, the French created "representative" governments, initially by appointment and subsequently by a combination of limited elections and appointments. While Gouraud was the executor of this policy of fragmentation, the colonial formulation was fiercely advanced by all levels of French government.

The insurrection of 1925 inaugurated the second phase, and while the aim of the insurrection was never to transform the political landscape, it did accelerate the transformation of political institutions. The French continued to have challenges in securing cooperative local politicians in some parts of the

---

6   Quoted in David Kenneth Fieldhouse: *Western Imperialism in the Middle East 1914-1958*, Oxford University Press, Oxford, 2006, p254.

country even after the brutal suppression of the insurrection of 1925. In the recently created states of the *Grand Liban* and the Alawites region, cooperation was relatively easy to secure. The new High Commissioner Henry de Jouvenel signed the Lebanese Constitution on May 23, 1926. He attempted to call for elections of a constitutional assembly in the Syrian State, but a general boycott of the elections put an end to this endeavor. It took 2 years until April 1928 before the High Commissioner Henri Ponsot called new elections.

The Assembly met first on June 9 and after two months of deliberations adopted a constitution to establish a parliamentary regime. However, the articles of the constitution were incompatible with the existence of the Mandate and the High Commissioner consequently dissolved the Assembly. After another lapse of two years, Henri Ponsot issued in May 1930 the organizational framework for all the states under French Mandate. To the 115 articles of the constitution prepared by the suspended Constitutional Assembly of the Syria State, he added Article 116 defining the role of the Mandatory authorities vis-à-vis local rule and safeguarding full French privileges![7] The so-called *"Statut Organique"*[8] enshrined the separate political and administrative organizations of the states of Lebanon, Syria (Damascus-Aleppo), Jabal el-Druze, Alawites, and the district of Alexandretta. While not allowing for any federal umbrella for these distinct political and administrative units, (a French

---

7   See the text of the letter in *Revue Générale de Droit Internationale Public*, volume IV, 1930, pp 671-672.

8   Article 1 of the Mandate issued on 24 July 1922 states: "The Mandatory shall frame, within a period of three years from the coming into force of this mandate, an organic law for Syria and Lebanon. This organic law shall be framed in agreement with the native authorities and shall take into account the rights, interests, and wishes of the population inhabiting the said territory. The Mandatory shall further enact measures to facilitate the progressive development of Syria and the Lebanon as independent states. Pending the coming into effect of the organic law, the Government of Syria and Lebanon shall be conducted in accordance with the spirit of this mandate". Stephen Hemsley Longrigg: *Syria and Lebanon under French Mandate*. Oxford University Press, London, 1958, p109.

commentator judged such an endeavor "premature!")[9] the French nevertheless created a semblance of an economic unity by instituting the *"Conférence des intérêts commun"* with the aim of enhancing commerce and encouraging an economic revival. All of these permutations illustrate the perpetual determination of the French to maintain quasi-permanent control over the lands under Mandate.

In Palestine, the effects of collusion between the mandatory authority and the Zionist initiative were operative at various levels.[10] The political, colonial and demographic aspects of this collusion have been amply documented.[11] The demographic geography of southern Syria was being modified and the ability of the Southern Syrians (Palestinians) to resist this transformation was being systematically undermined. The British were keen to prevent the development of any para-state organizations that would allow the Palestinians to protect their very existence and the fabric of their communities.[12] Unlike other parts of

---

9 See article by P. Pic: "L'Evolution du Mandat Français en Syrie et du Mandat Anglais en Palestine de 1924 à 1931», in *Revue Générale de Droit Internationale Public*, volume V, 1931, pp 428-465.

10 Article 2 of the Palestine Mandate officially approved by the League of Nations on July 24, 1922 states: "The Mandatory shall be responsible for placing the country under such political, administrative, and economic conditions as will secure the establishment of the Jewish national home, as laid down in the Preamble, and the development of self-governing institutions, and also for the safeguarding the civil and religious rights of all inhabitants of Palestine, irrespective of race and religion". Quoted in: Ronald Sanders: *The High Walls of Jerusalem: a history of the Balfour declaration and the birth of the British Mandate for Palestine*. Holt, Rinehart and Winston, NY, 1983, p 658.

11 Moshe Mossek: *Palestine Immigration Policy Under Sir Herbert Samuel: British, Zionist and Arab Attitudes*, Routledge (UK) 1978; Sami Hadawi: *Bitter Harvest; Palestine Between 1914-1967*, New World Press, 1967; May Seikaly: *Haifa: transformation of a Palestinian Arab society 1918-1939*, I.B.Tauris, London, 2002; Selwyn Ilan Troen: *Imagining Zion: dreams, designs, and realities in a century of Jewish settlement*, Yale University Press, New Haven, 2003.

12 On the policies of the British mandate in Palestine and the bankruptcy of the Palestinian leadership, see Rashid Khalidi: *The Iron Cage: The Story of Palestinian Struggle for Statehood*. Beacon Press, Boston, 2006.

French colonial troops in Beirut, Lebanon 1930

Syria (Lebanon, the hinterland, Jordan) where a semblance of a national state was established and Syrians participated to various degrees in their affairs and had a *de facto* apprenticeship in self-rule and state organization, the Syrians of Palestine were totally prevented from these pursuits. In contrast, Jewish para-state organizations were given free rein.

The British resorted to partitioning of Southern Syria to suit their colonial need. Like other states in Geographic Syria, Trans-Jordan was an artificial creation. The ephemeral Syrian Kingdom of Faysal was inclusive of Trans-Jordan. With the defeat of Syrian forces in Maysaloun in July 1920, the region came under the control of the British. The British shied from direct rule and established several governing authorities (at least six) based on tribal-regional affiliations with British officers posted to each. These local governments were scrapped in favor of a unified region called Trans-Jordan under Emir Abdallah in March 1921. The borders of the region were established by agreements with the French who relinquished al-Ramtha to Trans-Jordan[13] and with the triumphant Saudi government who had overthrown Abdallah's father King Hussein of the Hejaz.[14]

When on March 27, 1921, the British recognized Emir Abdallah as provisional ruler of the district of Trans-Jordan, they did so to dissuade King Hussein's impetuous son from executing his threat to take military action against the French in Syria. London feared that this attempt might provide an excuse for French forces to move into the British claimed zone. The draft of the Palestine Mandate was revised in August of 1921 to exclude Trans-Jordan from said mandate. Later, a distinction between Palestine and Trans-Jordan was made to limit the commitment of the British to the Jewish National Home. For the next decade, close supervisory control by the Mandate was exercised through a variety of means. The constant of the arrangement, however, was the alignment of Trans-Jordanian policy and activity with the aims of the Mandate to avoid any exacerbation of relations with the French. It is in this light that one needs to understand the efforts of Emir Abdallah to eliminate all anti-French activities originating in his region, in effect in the words of Churchill, Abdallah *"has been asked to execute a complete volte-face and to take active steps to nullify the effects of his previous policy."*[15]

The British were not ready to allow Trans-Jordan to remain a hotbed of nationalist activity against the French. This meant a progressive "purge" of all elements from local government and armed forces that were anti-French and their replacement with regional representatives with allegiance to the Emir. Tribal chiefs as well as urban intellectuals argued, *"Trans-Jordan was for the Trans-Jordanians,"* creating a new separatist mentality

---

13 Michael R. Fischbach: *State, Society and Land in Jordan*. Brill, Leiden, 2000, pp 65-66.

14 Randall Baker: *King Husain and the Kingdom of Hejaz*. The Oleander Press, 1979, pp 187-189.

15 Efraim Karsh and Inari Karsh: *Empires of the Sand: The Struggle for Mastery in the Middle East*. Harvard University Press, 2001, pp 314-326.

under the firm control of an ambitious ruler.[16] In this national landscape, the mere existence of Syria as a viable national entity was seriously jeopardized, hence the primordial importance of the definition of nationhood in the ideology of the SSNP.

THE NATION CONCEPT

The First Basic Principle of the SSNP states: *"Syria is for the Syrians and the Syrians are a complete nation."* The first clause of the principle is an assertion of national sovereignty. The second clause is an affirmation of nationhood, and the two clauses together form a declaration of national identity. Since nationhood is a prerequisite and basis of national sovereignty, it would have been logical to assume that the order of the two clauses should have been reversed. It is likely, however, that Saadeh chose the order based on two considerations. The statement "Syria is for the Syrians" was very commonly used in the nationalist literature of the time and had become the rallying cry for national liberation efforts in the homeland and the diaspora.[17] Incorporation of the statement as the first clause of the first basic principle would resonate in the minds of Syrians and elicit by its familiarity immediate recognition and acceptance. The second consideration is that the order of the two clauses recapitulates the ontogeny of Saadeh's nationalist thinking. As he relates in his writings, the primordial element triggering his nationalist direction was pondering the causes of woe that befell Syria during and after the First World War. His initial conclusion was that the absence of national sovereignty was the originator of all calamities he and his compatriots experienced and continued to suffer. This identification of the absence of national sovereignty as the causal factor led him to study the question of nationhood and to the formulation of the principles of Syrian nationalism.[18]

---

16 Kamal S. Salibi: *The Modern History of Jordan*. I.B. Tauris publisher, 1998, pp 113-140.

17 Katibah, Habib Ibrahim. *Syria for the Syrians, under the guardianship of the United States*. Boston, Syrian National Society, 1919. In Egypt, nationalists of that period used the slogan "Egypt for the Egyptians!"

18 Letter to Hamid Frangieh, November, 1935. *Complete Works*, Volume 2, pp. 9-12.

Irrespective of the order of the two clauses, like all nationalist thinkers of all times, Saadeh recognized that nationhood provided the legal basis for sovereignty and was irrevocably linked to national identity. Hence, formulating a clear concept of the nation was a necessary and fundamental step for the construction of a national ideology. It is the formulation of the concept of the nation, its nature, and the elements leading to its emergence that separates Saadeh from the common linkage of nationhood and sovereignty in the writings of other nationalist theorists. Examining his nation concept is therefore essential prior to continuing the overview of the principles of Syrian nationalism.

Saadeh undertook to expound the findings of his study and contemplations of the question of nationhood in his seminal book *Nushu' al-Umam* (The Emergence of Nations)[19] written between 1935 and 1936, and published in Beirut in 1938. While he tackled the issue in other works, the systematic treatment that he offers in his book should take primacy in the elucidation of his ideas. In the introduction to the book, Saadeh defined the purpose of its writing: "National consciousness is the greatest social phenomenon of our time... For every group that rises to the level of national consciousness, the level of awareness of group personality, it becomes necessary for the individual members of that group to understand social reality, its conditions and the nature of the resultant relations. . ... A study of this nature that clarifies human social reality, its stages, conditions, and nature is necessary for every society that seeks survival. ... Any nation lacking scientific social studies will inevitably fall into ideological anarchy and intellectual confusion." [20]

---

19 Saadeh, Antoun: *Nushu' al-Umam, Complete Works*, volume 3, pp. 1-159.

20 Originally, Saadeh had intended to write two books: *The Emergence of Nations*, and *The Emergence of the Syrian Nation*, but the notes and research for the second book were confiscated at the time of his first arrest in November of 1935 and never returned to him. He subsequently prepared them again, only to have them lost after his arrest and execution in July of 1949.

An inquiry into the nature of a nation is necessary to safeguard the vitality of a national endeavor and avoid the pitfalls of division and conflict engendered by a confused understanding and definition of nationhood. It can have a profound effect on political theories and principles and consequently can influence the course of political events and actions.[21] Saadeh was aware of the potential politicization of the concept of nationhood. "Every nation feels the need for sovereignty over itself and the protection of its interests from the transgressions of other nations. In this often violent conflict, the politicians and intellectuals of a nation resort to theories that agree with the conditions of their nations and can elicit a strong sense of solidarity and hope. Some will seek a historical precedent, a real or imagined example of history, or of a religious or ethnic argument."[22] This politicization is operative internally as well as externally. "Conflicting theories are not confined to the conflict among nations, but can also affect approaches within a single nation to serve the interests and ambitions of different groups."[23] He gives as an example the varying theories of French nationalism, but the example of Syria would be as apt. Muslims in Syria adopt Pan-Arabism as a front for Pan-Islamism and their theorists expound on Arab nationalism, whereas Christians in Syria invoke a Phoenician history as a front for Christian separatism. Theorists of nationalism are often influenced by their particular historical conditions that color their perspective. He cites Renan (1823-1892) as an example and the influence of the Capetian Dynasty on his definition of the nature of a Nation.[24]

To guard against politicized definitions, Saadeh undertakes an examination of the various theories of nationalism.[25] This critical analysis is important to review as the SSNP has frequently been

---

21 *Ibid.*, p. 5.
22 *Ibid.*, p. 130.
23 *Ibid.*
24 *Ibid.*, p. 132.
25 *Ibid.*, pp. 133-147.

accused of espousing theories it clearly refutes. He addresses racial theories stating, "The fact is that no modern nation has a single racial or ethnic origin... if we examine the history of the formation of the Italian nation, the only constant is the land of Italy whereas multiple ethnic origins can be discerned."[26] Just like Italy has mixed ethnic origins (Etruscans, Romans, Lombards, Ligurians etc.), so does France (Gauls, Latins, Iberians, Franks, Alamans and Norsemen) and England (Celts, Romans, Anglo-Saxons, Norse and Normans). Saadeh quotes Tennyson declaiming: "Saxon and Norman and Dane are we."[27] So is Germany despite all the rhetoric on Aryan blood. In debunking racial theories, Saadeh was aware of their great influence and emotional appeal because of their associations with select status and arrogant pride. "People are enamored with the concept of "race" and consider it the source of all good deeds and virtues, provided it is pure. Thus, we find individuals and groups that cling to the purity of their race and each claim theirs to be the best and most noble breed... and one of the strangest beliefs advanced by some is that humans are predisposed to yearn for a racial belief and that it is futile to attempt to negate such a natural tendency."[28] He surveys the spread of such racial theories in France and how it has been usurped to serve in the cause of conflict with Germany and in the latter as a prop for aristocratic rule. He asserts that racist theories cannot be supported by objective science and are susceptible to manipulations to serve the goals of the political elites that formulate them.

Linguistic theories of nationhood are clearly relevant to the definition of Syrian nationhood in the face of Pan-Arab considerations. Such theories are witnessing a revival in Europe at the hands of some nationalist theorist such as in the definition of Croatian and Catalan nationalisms, German expansionism,

---

26   Ibid., p. 139.
27   From the poem *A Welcome to Alexandra* by Alfred, Lord Tennyson (1809–1892) on the occasion of the marriage of the Prince of Wales to Princess Alexandra of Denmark, on March 10, 1863.
28   Ibid., p. 16.

and others. The importance of language is magnified when it is considered in a national context as a carrier of a cultural heritage. A single nation benefits from a single language that carries its culture, ideals, and spirit, but the language need not be unique to that nation for the value of a language is not its technical form which can be common among multiple nations, but what it carries of the nation's cultural heritage. The unity of language does not define a nation, but is useful for the cohesion of a nation. Saadeh cites how Ireland is not defined by the English language that was imposed on it, yet it retained its nationhood.[29] When language is invoked as a basis for nationhood, it is frequently to validate other motives. The use of language in the Pan-Arab national formulation is as a front for minimalist Pan-Islamism.

Religion based concepts of the nation have always existed within some religions. In Islam, the community of believers is referred to as "ummah," literally "nation." The inherent incompatibility between religion and nationalism is obvious. The universalism of religion is contrary to the formation of nations.[30] There are instances, however, where religion becomes a rallying cry for nationalism such as in the religious wars in Europe that had the goal of making the state's territory congruous with the religious creed of rulers, or the role of Catholicism in Irish nationalism, Shi'ism in Iranian nationalism, Lutherism in German nationalism, etc. Saadeh, however, considered the permanence of religious influence in the definition of the nation and in the mobilization of national effort as a nefarious element because of the heterogeneity of the religious composition in Syria and on philosophical grounds since he considered the rigidity of religion as an obstacle to progress. We will return to the question of religion and nationality below during the discussion of the reform principles of the SSNP.

While recognizing that the political elites in a nation can politicize the concept of nationhood and manipulate it, Saadeh

---

29 *Ibid.*, p. 143.
30 *Ibid.*, p. 143.

does not push this critique of this phenomenon to the point of considering nations as constructed imaginary communities. For Saadeh, nations are objectively differentiated realities with a collective identity and a common national interest. This reality underlies the observation that nationalism is the most universal phenomenon in contemporary history. On the basis of this concept of the nation as a group of human beings living a life of unified interests, unified destiny, in a particular geography, and distinguishable from other groups, Saadeh proceeds to define the nationalism that the SSNP espouses.

Saadeh considered national consciousness as the greatest social phenomenon of the time requiring the individual to add to his sense of "self" a sense of the character of his nation, the latter eliciting in him a heightened degree of altruism and devotion.[31] The emergence of nationalism had a transformative effect on political theory and institutions, and governed the development of democracy. Indeed, Saadeh links the emergence of nationalism with the strengthening of democratic ideals.[32] Taking the emergence of nationalism in Western Europe as a model, he argues that nationalism did not halt its march with the abolition of feudalism and strengthening of royalty, but went beyond it to the assertion that the people are the source of sovereignty, and that the state is for the people and not the converse. Democracy is thus an essential component of nationalism and a manifestation of the common will. The state was transformed from a tool of oppression and authoritarian rule, to an expression of self-rule by the people.

At the end of his book, Saadeh describes nationalism thusly: "Nationalism is the awakening of the nation and its consciousness of the unity of its life, of its personality and characteristics, and of its destiny. It is the nation's bond. It may sometimes be confused with patriotism, which is the love of the homeland,

---

31 *Ibid.*, p. 5.
32 *Ibid.*, pp. 110-112.

because patriotism a component of nationalism, and because the homeland is the most powerful factor in the emergence of the nation and its most important element. It is a deep, living conscience that appreciates the common good, fostering love of the homeland and internal cooperation to avert the dangers that may beset the nation... nurturing the feeling of the unity of interests, the sustenance of life and its betterment by being loyal to this common life... Nationalism is the spirit or feeling emanating from the nation, from the unity of life in the course of time. Nationalism is not an irrational fanaticism born from primitive or religious causes. It is not a kind of totemic or a racial delusion, but a genuine feeling, an honest emotion and determined caring for the common life. Its elements spring from the bonds of social life... In its moments of weakness, it may be corrupted and ruled by political propaganda and beliefs, but its true nature will awaken in the silence of the night, in the hours of contemplation and in the remembrance of the homeland."[33]

Saadeh's view that nationalism is the awakening of nations to self-consciousness is evidently contrary to the generalized assertions of some contemporary theorists that nationalism always invents nations where they do not exist. Saadeh recognized that some nationalisms are indeed linked to imagined and invented nations, to wit his critique of Lebanese nationalism and Pan-Arab nationalism. He maintained, however, that nations are true social entities and not merely ideological constructs as some theorists would claim.

NATIONAL IDENTITY AND SOVEREIGNTY

While the principles of Syrian nationalism were formulated in 1932, they are nevertheless informed by the conclusions expressed in *Nushu' al-Umam*. Indeed, the central document that contains the basic and reform principles of the SSNP and the elaboration of their implications was originally written by

---

33 *Ibid.*, p. 149.

NATIONAL IDENTITY AND SOVEREIGNTY

Saadeh in 1936 after he completed the writing of *Nushu' al-Umam*.

The principles of the SSNP are classified into two broad categories: the basic principles of which there are eight and the five reform principles. The eight basic principles of the SSNP embody the doctrine of Syrian nationalism. They proceed in a logical order from a declaration of the existence and nature of the Syrian nation (first principle), to an identification of the character of its cause (second and third principles), to a clarification of its genesis (the fourth principle) and its homeland (fifth principle). The basis of national unity (sixth principle), the sources of national character and consciousness (seventh principle), and the guiding principles of national militancy (eighth principle) are then defined.

The SSNP considered that the most urgent issue was the determination of national identity, which is the only viable basis of national consciousness and the starting point of national revival. Religious and ethnic tendencies had led to the proliferation of "invented identities." Christian separatists had advocated for a Lebanese identity harking to Phoenician roots. Muslim pan-Arab theorists dreamed of a more subdued Islamic entity limited to Arab-speakers. Minorities reeling from past oppression looked for relief in their own states. The confusion was further aggravated by the proto-states created by colonial intervention. The SSNP posits that all these disparate identities are the product of historical grievances, religious fanaticism, and interests of corrupt political elites in collusion with colonial designs. The only true distinct national entity is embodied in the formulation of a Syrian nationhood, hence the First Basic Principle stating: *Syria is for the Syrians and the Syrians are a complete nation*. In the explanation of this principle, Saadeh states: "Thus, the assertion that the Syrians constitute a nation complete in itself is a fundamental doctrine, which should put an end to ambiguity and place the national effort on the basis of clarity without which no national revival in Syria is possible.

The realization of the complete nationhood of the Syrians and the active consciousness of this nationhood are two essential prerequisites for the vindication of the principle of national sovereignty. For, were the Syrians not a complete nation having right to sovereignty and to the establishment of an independent state, Syria would not be for the Syrians in the full sense, but might fall an easy prey to the intrigues of some other sovereign power pursuing interests conflicting with, or that might conflict with, the interests of the Syrian people."[34] In this principle lies the legal basis of national sovereignty. Nationhood is the legitimating principle in the modern international system. In essence, this principle announces the illegitimacy in the eyes of the SSNP of all international treaties, alliances or schemes that may affect the Syrian homeland in a fashion contrary to the real interests and wishes of the Syrian nation. "The Syrians are a nation upon whom alone devolves the right to own, dispose of, and make decisions concerning every inch of Syrian territory. The homeland belongs to the nation as a whole and no one, not even individual Syrian citizens, may dispose of any part of its territory in such a way as to destroy or endanger the integrity of the country, which integrity is a necessary condition for preserving the unity of the Syrian nation."

This principle is a resounding refusal of the right of Britain to issue the Balfour declaration promising to facilitate the settlement of Zionists in southern Syria (Palestine) and the creation of a Jewish homeland, and a rejection of the presumed rights of Jews to such a homeland in southern Syria.[35] This principle further

---

34 All quotes in this section are from the exposition of the principles of the SSNP by Antoun Saadeh (Fourth Edition, 1947), a translation of which can be found in the Appendix.

35 The Balfour declaration came in the form of a letter that Arthur James Balfour addressed on November 2 to Lord Rothschild. Balfour's letter stated: "I have much pleasure in conveying to you, on behalf of His Majesty's Government, the following declaration of sympathy with Jewish Zionist aspirations which has been submitted to and approved by, the Cabinet: 'His Majesty's Government views with favour the establishment in Palestine of a national home for the Jewish people, and will use their best endeavors to facilitate the achievement

asserts the permanence of national sovereignty in the face of the temporary political arrangements and separate states that arose in Syria under the influence of foreign colonial powers and separatist movements. It affirms the primacy of the integrity of the nation and its homeland over the temporary political forms that may arise during periods of national disintegration and foreign occupation. Since sovereignty over the homeland is national, no individuals, or groups within Syria have the right to forfeit or to allow the permanent loss of sovereignty over any part of the Syrian homeland.

A distinctive aspect of this principle is the necessary interconnection of its two clauses. A requisite that Syria the homeland belong to the Syrians is that the latter form a complete nation. This interdependence between the nation and the homeland is a primary axiom of Syrian Nationalism. The integrity of the Syrian nation is the safeguard of the integrity of the Syrian homeland and vice versa. Thus, all attempts leading to a loss of Syrian national integrity threaten the loss of homeland. Saadeh often stressed that national disintegration was a main reason for the loss of the district of Alexandretta in the north, and Palestine in the south. Separatism is thus a danger to the integrity of the homeland. Conversely, the Syrian nation cannot prosper when valuable portions of the homeland are lost. The integrity of the homeland is vital to the survival and prosperity of the nation.

In its apparent simple structure, this principle is the most valuable guide to the understanding of Syrian nationalism and to the elucidation of the plan for national struggle. It is a call to the constituency of the Party to fight separatism, to resist

---

of this object, it being clearly understood that nothing shall be done which may prejudice the civil and religious rights of existing non-Jewish communities in Palestine, or the rights and political status enjoyed by Jews in any other country.' I should be grateful if you would bring this declaration to the knowledge of the Zionist Federation." (R. Sanders: *The High Walls of Jerusalem: A History of the Balfour Declaration and the Birth of the British Mandate for Palestine*, Holt, Rinehart and Winston, New York, 1983, pp 623).

factional tendencies, to reject colonialism, and to re-establish Syrian possession of the entire homeland. Based on this principle, the SSNP does not recognize the right of Zionists to establish a belligerent religious state in the southern part of Syria (Palestine) with clear intentions of engulfing larger sections of the Syrian homeland. Furthermore, the SSNP does not abide by any international agreements that would deprive the Syrians of their national integrity or the integrity of their homeland. Finally, the independence of Syria in deciding its national interests and the course of its life in its homeland is an immutable right that the SSNP does not allow to be jeopardized or abrogated.

The question of sovereignty is further affirmed in the Second Basic Principle: *The Syrian cause is an integral national cause completely distinct from any other cause.* Saadeh explained: "This principle signifies that all the legal and political questions that relate to any portion of Syrian territory, or to any Syrian group, are part of one indivisible cause distinct from, and unmixed with, any other external matter which may nullify the conception of the unity of Syrian interests and of the Syrian will. This principle follows from and is complementary to the first principle. Since Syria is for the Syrians and the Syrians are a complete nation endowed with the right to sovereignty, it follows that this nation's cause, that is its life and destiny, belongs to her alone and is independent from any other cause that involves interests other than those of the Syrian people. This principle reserves to the Syrians alone the right to expound their own cause and to be their sole representatives, determine their own interests and shape their own destiny. It renders theirs an all-inclusive and indivisible cause.

The *cause célèbre* for this principle is the long-held attitude rampant among Syrians before the advent of the SSNP that the destiny of Syria is inextricably linked to the destiny and will of the foreign colonial power in control. While under Ottoman rule, many Syrian thinkers thought of the destiny of Syria as part of the Ottoman Empire and fought for Ottoman nationalism.

Even the early resistance to Jewish settlements in southern Syria was formulated in the context of loyalty to the Ottoman state.[36] Subsequently, the separatist Christian leaders in Lebanon sought to link the destiny of Lebanon to France.[37] By proclaiming the integral and independent framework for the Syrian national cause, Saadeh was establishing the guiding principle for the struggle of the Party. The SSNP does not view the life and destiny of Syria as fundamentally dependent on any non-Syrian issues and thus the pursuit of the interests of Syria by the Party is guided solely by those principles independent of extraneous causes or struggles.

Another example to clarify the significance of this principle is the position of the Syrian Communist Party vis-à-vis the partition of Palestine. The Communist Party accepted the partition scheme in concordance with the position of Stalinist Russia, decried any efforts for the liberation of Palestine and called for the unity of Jewish and Palestinian workers against Arab bourgeoisie, at a time when Palestine was ethnically cleansed of Palestinian workers, peasants and bourgeoisie!

This principle also establishes the unifying direction in tackling the issues of the life and destiny of the nation. Thus, the occupation of southern Syria by Zionists is not a 'Palestinian issue' or a separate 'Palestinian cause,' but part of the Syrian cause. By establishing the wider appurtenance of the Palestinian issue, Saadeh commits the entire Syrian nation to the struggle for the return of Palestine to full Syrian sovereignty. It is clear that abandonment of this principle has been largely responsible for the defeat of the efforts of Palestinians in keeping and recuperating southern Syria. It is only with a unified Syrian

---

36 N.J. Mandel: *The Arabs and Zionism before World War I*, University of California Press, Berkley, 1976.

37 The collaboration between the separatist groups and French imperialism are illustrated in: W. Shorrock: *French imperialism in the Middle East*, The University of Wisconsin Press, Madison 1976; and Meir Zamir: *The formation of Modern Lebanon*, Cornell University Press, Ithaca, N.Y., 1985.

effort that southern Syria can be liberated. The assumption by the entire Syrian nation of the responsibility for issues affecting some of its regions assures vigilance in all national matters. The exemplification of this principle lies in the thousands of SSNP members whose struggle, sacrifices and martyrdom has transcended regional affiliations.

The emphasis on the national framework for the Syrian cause and its integral character establishes a unity of effort in the struggle for achieving Syrian goals. It is a guardian against regionalism, sectarianism and individualism in attending to issues related to the life and destiny of the nation. In accordance with this principle, the SSNP "does not recognize the right of any non-Syrian person or organization to speak on behalf of Syria and its interests either in internal or international matters. The Party does not recognize the right of anybody to make the interests of Syria contingent on the interests of other nations."

SYRIA DEFINED

The definition of the Syrian nation and homeland expounded in the SSNP principles is clearly different from the various definitions of Syria common in historical and literary works in Syria and abroad. While historical research unceasingly uncovers evidence of unifying tendencies in the civilization of the Fertile Crescent. "A large number of historians have confined their definition of Syria to Byzantine or late Hellenistic Syria, whose boundaries extended from the Taurus range and the Euphrates to the Suez thus excluding the Assyrians and Chaldeans from Syrian History. Other historians have further confined this definition to the region between Cilicia and Palestine, thus leaving out Palestine." The Third, Fourth and Fifth basis principles of the SSNP are concerned with this definition. The Third Basic Principle: *The Syrian cause is the cause of the Syrian nation and the Syrian homeland*, lays the framework derived from the concept of nation defined above. "This principle ... emphasizes the indissoluble bond between the nation and its territory. Nations arise in distinct territories that sustain their lives and national character. The concept of the unity of the nation and its homeland ... frees the concept of nationhood from such historical, racial or religious misconceptions as are contrary to the nature of the nation and its vital interest." Hence, the definition of the Syrian nation in the fourth basic principle is a direct application of the nation concept formulated by Saadeh. In general, the doctrine states that nations formed because the geographical environment coupled with historical-economic and sociological events led to the formations of distinct human societies with distinct life cycles, character and history.

The Fourth Basic Principle: *The Syrian nation is the product of the ethnic unity of the Syrian people which developed throughout history*, clarifies that the Syrian nation is the product of a historical process that facilitated the emergence of unity through interaction and participation in national life. "Thus, the principle of Syrian nationhood is not based on race or blood, but rather on the natural social unity derived from homogeneous intermixing. Through this principle the interests, the aims, and the ideals of the Syrian nation are unified and the national cause is guarded against disharmony, disintegration, and strife that result from primitive loyalties to blood ties. The alleged racial purity of any nation is a groundless myth. It is found only in savage groups, and even there it is rare. The Syrian nation consists of a mixture of Canaanites, Akkadians, Chaldeans, Assyrians, Arameans, Hittites, and Mitanni as the French nation is a mixture of Gauls, Ligurians, Franks, etc... and the Italian nation of Romans, Latins, Etruscans, etc... the same being true of every other nation."

It also explicitly defines the basis of citizenship. "This principle would redeem Syria from the blood bigotries, which are apt to cause the neglect of national interests. For those Syrians who believe or feel that they are of Aramaic extraction would no longer be actuated to fan Aramaic blood loyalty, so long as the principle of Social Nationalist unity and the equality of civic, political and social rights and duties are guaranteed, and no ethnic or racial discrimination in Syria is made. Similarly, those Syrians who claim to descend from a Phoenician (Canaanite), Arab, or Crusader stock, would no longer have allegiance but to their Syrian community. Thus, would genuine national consciousness arise. The unity of the Syrian nation arose from the elements, which have formed in the course of history the Syrian people and the mental and spiritual traits of the Syrian nation." Assimilation of various ethnic elements through participation in national life has governed the emergence of the Syrian nation historically and determines the approach to new current or future elements. "There are large settlements of immigrants in Syria, such as the Armenians, Kurds, and Circassians, whose assimilation is possible given sufficient time. These elements may dissolve in the nation and lose their special loyalties." A critical pre-requisite for this assimilation is the adoption by these new groups of the principle of Syrian nationhood and unfettered participation in national life. Elements that maintain exclusive racial and/or ethnic loyalties would not fulfill the prerequisite for incorporation in Syrian nationhood.

Saadeh marshals in his writings various evidence in support of the development of unity of life within the confines of the Syrian homeland. He was to dedicate a specialized book *Nushu' al-Umma as-Suriya* (The Emergence of the Syrian Nation) for expounding the evidence in a systematic comprehensive work. The initial draft of the work was confiscated by the authorities during the second wave of arrests by the French Mandate in 1936 and never returned to its owner. Saadeh had resumed preparations to write the book in 1949, but his premature death intervened. His extant writings, however, are replete with information on the process and timeline of the emergence of the Syrian nation.

The unification tendencies in the confines of the Fertile Crescent became manifest in the development of economic ties, cultural interactions, and population mixing all antecedent to the earliest political forms of unity. The unity of the life cycle within the Fertile Crescent has preceded the political unity of the first territorial empire by the Akkadian rulers in the 24th to 23rd centuries BC. The unity of life has persisted when political unity was lacking. The territorial empires arising in Syria have contributed to the maintenance and promotion of the unity of life. Thus the Babylonian empire of Hammurabi, the Assyrian empire, the Neo-Babylonian state, the Seleucid rule etc... have given political and administrative facilitatory forms to the unity of life prevalent within the confines of the Syrian homeland. "The history of the ancient Syrian states (Akkadian, Chaldean, Assyrian, Hittite, Canaanite, Aramean, Amorite) point to one and the same trend: the political, economic, and social unity of the Syrian Fertile Crescent. This fact should enable us to view the Assyrian and Chaldean wars, aimed at dominating the whole of Syria, in a new light. These were internal wars, a struggle for supremacy among the powerful groups and dynasties within the nation which was still in the making and which later attained its maturity."

The Syrian territory is defined in the Fifth Basic Principle: *The Syrian homeland is that geographic environment in which the Syrian nation evolved. It has distinct natural boundaries and extends from the Taurus range in the northwest and the Zagros mountains in the northeast to the Suez canal and the Red Sea in the south and includes the Sinai peninsula and the gulf of Aqaba, and from the Syrian sea[38] in the west, including the island of Cyprus, to the arch of the Arabian desert and the Persian gulf in the east. (This region is also known as the Syrian Fertile Crescent).* "The secret of Syria's persistence as a distinct nation despite the numerous invasions to which it succumbed, lies in the geographic unity of its homeland. It was this geographic unity that ensured the political unity of this country even in ancient times when it was still divided among the Canaanites,

---

[38] The terminology 'Syrian sea' is not peculiar to the literature of the SSNP, but has been utilized by European geographers and cartographers. Indeed, a perusal of ancient maps reveals the term to have been used as early as the second century AD by Claudius Ptolemy (Mare Siriacum). The practice was continued in Renaissance and sixteenth century maps and by British, Dutch, German and French cartographers until the beginning of the 20th century. Kenneth Nebenzahl: *Maps of the Holy Land*. Abbeville Press, N.Y., 1986.

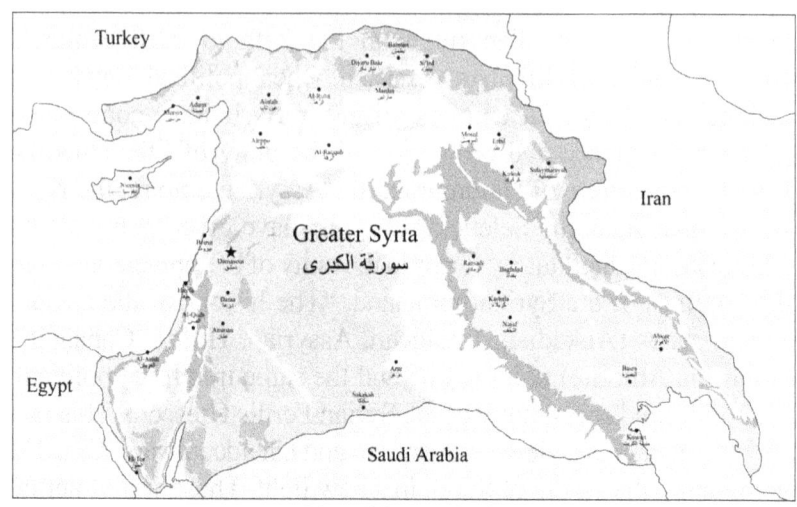

Map of Greater Syria

the Arameans, the Hittites, the Amorites, the Assyrians, and the Chaldeans..."

What are the reasons for the divergence in the definition of Syria among historians? In particular, if the name Syria is derived from Assyria,[39] why do many accounts of the expanse of Syrian territory exclude the land east of the Euphrates the original home to the Assyrians?

Saadeh ascribed the failure of historians in general to grasp the historical unity of Syria as defined in the principles of the SSNP to the enduring influence of Greek and Roman historians. A similar opinion has been independently advanced recently by the British historians Amelie Kuhrt and Susan Sherwin-White: "Traditional approaches to the study of the Hellenistic East after Alexander

---

39 Several theories have been advanced to explain the origin of the name Syria. It is, in form, a Greek name (Suria) first used by the Greek historian Herodotus (Herodotus: *The Histories*, Penguin Books, 1986, pp 466-467). He does not use a distinction between Syrian and Assyrian consistently and states: "These people used to be called Syrians by the Greeks, Assyrians being the name for them elsewhere." The Syrian writer Lucian, writing in Greek, referred to himself interchangeably as "Syrian" and "Assyrian". Lucian: *The Works of Lucian*, in eight volumes. Harvard University Press, Cambridge, MA, 1961.

SYRIA DEFINED

have been mainly hellenocentric and have selected as of prime importance the establishment and spread of Greek culture... This is a serious lack which stems from the overriding significance attached to the classical tradition in which most scholars of the ancient world have been educated. One of the results of this is that where there is no clear Greek evidence a political, social and cultural vacuum is assumed. Another distorting factor has been the preoccupations of Roman historians who have tended (not unnaturally) to concentrate almost exclusively on those regions of the Seleucid empire which by the first century B. C. had become part of the Roman empire. This approach has led them to [ignore] the central importance of the vast territories controlled by the Seleucid east of the Euphrates."[40]

The question of limiting the term 'Syria' to the western part of the Fertile Crescent has also intrigued the historian Fergus Millar: "By Syria I mean anywhere west of the Euphrates and south of the Amanus mountains — essentially therefore the area west of the Euphrates where Semitic languages were used. This begs a question about Asia Minor (and especially Cilicia), from which Aramaic documents are known, and a far more important one about northern Mesopotamia and about Babylonia. Should we not, that is, see the various Aramaic-speaking areas of the Fertile Crescent as representing a single culture, or at any rate closely connected cultures, and therefore not attempt to study the one area without the others?"[41]

Historical events may have also reinforced the lack of appreciation. "Syria's loss of sovereignty because of the major foreign invasions resulted in its partition into arbitrary political units. In the Perso-Byzantine period, the Byzantines extended their rule over western Syria and applied the name "Syria" to that

---

40　Ameli Kurht and Susan Sherwin-White (editors): *Hellenism in The East*. University of California Press, Berkley, CA, 1987.

41　Millar F: The problem of Hellenistic Syria. In Ameli Kurht and Susan Sherwin-White (editors): *Hellenism in the East*. University of California Press, Berkley, CA, 1987, pp 110-133.

part only, while the Persians dominated the eastern part, which they called "Irah", later Arabicized as Iraq... The partitioning of Syria between the Byzantines and the Persians into Eastern and Western Syria and the creation of barriers between them, retarded considerably, and for a long period, the national growth and the development of the social and economic life cycle of the country. This division resulted also in distorting the truth about the boundaries of Syria... Similarly, after the First World War the condominium of Great Britain and France over Syria resulted in the partition of the country according to their political aims and interests and gave rise to the present political designations: Palestine, Jordan, Lebanon, Syria, Cilicia, and Iraq. Natural Syria consists of all those regions, which constitute one geographic-economic-strategic unit. The Syrian Social Nationalist cause will not be fulfilled unless the unity of Syria is achieved."

The Syrian homeland has played a major role in the shaping of the Syrian nation and its character. The internal elements of the Syrian environment provide means of interaction between the various regions. Indeed, if one considers the waterways of Syria, its rivers and streams, one can view the contribution of the physical environment to the formation of one society. Considering that the major part of the history of any human society revolved until recently predominantly around agriculture, the continuity of agricultural space would inevitably invite lines of interaction between human elements within the environment. The courses of the great Syrian rivers, the Euphrates and the Tigris, are natural couriers of life between western and eastern Syria, and between the northern and southern regions of eastern Syria. The Orontes links the plains of central and northern regions of western Syria while the Litani and Jordan rivers link the central and southern parts. The Mediterranean littoral spreads without interruption over fertile coastal lands from the gulf of Alexandretta to the early shores of the Sinai Peninsula.

These internal elements favoring unity of life are paralleled by natural borders that define, albeit relatively, the confines of the society forming herein. The borders of the Syrian Fertile Crescent have limited the extension of continuous life and thus shaped the formation of the nation. These borders, however, were never exclusive. They were in various historical periods overrun in both directions. Syrian commercial colonies from the Assyrian periods have been identified in Anatolia and from the Phoenician periods over much of the Mediterranean. The military might of Assyria extended beyond the Zagros and Taurus mountains to the north and east, and over the Sinai into Egypt. Conversely, the Egyptians often coveted the Syrian coast and the intrusions of the Pharaonic state into western Syria were recurrent. The Gutians, the Kassites, and the Persians crossed the eastern borders when the military preparedness of eastern Syrian states faltered. The Hittites, the Greeks, the Romans and the Ottomans crossed the northern borders.

For the last two centuries, Syria had been the target of cultural colonialism by Christian missionaries as well as secular organizations from France, Britain, the United States and Russia. To combat this cultural colonialism, the SSNP Seventh Basic Principle holds that *The Syrian Social Nationalist movement derives its inspiration from the talents of the Syrian nation and its cultural political national history.* "This principle asserts the spiritual independence of the nation in which its national character, qualities, and aims are grounded. The Party believes that no Syrian revival can be effected save through the agency of the inborn and independent Syrian character." Like all national liberation movements, the SSNP imbues national consciousness with its national history, and in this context, Syrian cultural history. The literature of the SSNP is replete with material detailing the contributions of Syria to human cultural achievements. Strengthening the Syrian ethos is a necessary endeavor to resist cultural colonialism.

It is instructive to examine briefly the list of Syrians mentioned by Saadeh as illustrative of the contributions of Syria to human civilization. The first mentioned was Zeno of Citium (c. 334 –

c. 262 BC, founder of the Stoic school in philosophy). This is symbolic of the admiration Saadeh had for the philosophical school of stoicism, and the fact that a major school of 'Western' philosophy is a Syrian school. Bar Salibi (died 1171 AD, the great spokesman of the Jacobite church in the 12th century), St John Chrysostom (c. 349 – 407 AD), and Ephraim (c. 306 – 373 AD) are prominent Fathers of the Christian church. Ephraim Syrus (the Syrian) was the first great theologian of the Syrian church and a sacred poet instrumental in introducing monasticism. The two Fathers that represent the Aramaic element in the Syrian Church (Bar Salibi and Ephraim) flank the Father that represents the Hellenistic element (John Chrysostom).

Syrian thought in the Seleucid, Roman and early Byzantine periods found its expression in a polylinguistic form: Greek and Aramaic (Syriac). By choosing these prominent Syrians, Saadeh is illustrating the contributions of Syria to Christian thought. Next, Saadeh lists two poets of differing standing: al-Maari (December 973 – May 1057 AD), and Deek-el-Jin (777–849 AD) of Emessa. Considering the wealth of poets in Syria, the choice is intriguing yet instructive. Abu Al-Ala' al-Maari was a philosopher poet of great intellectual depth. The poetry of Deek-el-Jin of Emessa is sincere and esthetically refined. Saadeh was thus highlighting aspects of literary contributions that are of greater import than the popular "classical" Arabic poets. al-Kawakibi (1849-1902 AD) and Gibran (1883-1931 AD) are more modern writers notable for their involvement in social and political aspects of Syrian life and their adherence to principles of Syrian revival and renaissance. Four of the military leaders that Saadeh lists are direct descendants (Sargon 722-704 BC, Sennecharib 704-681 BC, Esarhaddon 680-669 BC, and Assurbanipal 669-627 BC) and represent the rulers of the Assyrian state at its best. It is a period of Syrian history notable for the crowning of the social, economic and cultural unity of Syria with political administrative unity.

Nebuchadnezzar (605-562 BC) and Tiglat-pilasser III (745-727 BC) are rulers that established major expansion and centralization in the government of Syria. There are several Hanno-named Carthaginian leaders, among them is the famous Hanno who was the first to sail around the western shores of Africa. It is easy to understand the choice of Hannibal to be included in this roster. Of equal significance is Yusuf Azmeh who as the defense minister of the Syrian state that arose in Damascus at the end of the First World War led the only organized armed resistance to French colonial forces in the battle of Maysaloun. It is clear that the choice of these notable Syrians is to illustrate aspects of Syrian history, in all the diverse ways in which a civilization can express itself, that are noteworthy of study and inspiration for modern Syrians.

The SSNP aims to show the Syrians that the realities of their history are reasons for pride, self-respect and eagerness to restore Syria to its creative role in human civilization. In his scientific, philosophical and ideological writings, Saadeh constantly illustrated doctrinal issues with examples from Syria's historical record. What is even more crucial is his directives to Party intellectuals to seek their inspiration in the events of this history. In a sense, Saadeh is responsible for the modern wave of intellectuals in Syria whose poetry, novels, and theater are imbued with topics and influences from Syria's cultural heritage.

The implication of this principle on national struggle is clear. A nation needs to be self-consistent, its civilization continuous, and its character preserved. A nation needs to be intellectually independent to contribute in a creative way to human development.

SOCIAL JUSTICE AND HUMAN RIGHTS

The Sixth Basic Principle: *The Syrian Nation is One Society*, is concerned with social justice and the essence of modern citizenship. Saadeh clearly states "Real independence and real sovereignty will not be fulfilled and will not endure unless they rest upon this genuine social unity which is the only sound basis for a national state and Social Nationalist civil legislation. This unity forms the basis for citizenship and the guarantee of the equality of rights for all citizens." On this principle are based the reform principles of the separation of church and state and the elimination of social barriers between the various sects and creeds. "This principle is the basis of genuine national unity, the mark of national consciousness, and the guarantee of the life and endurance of the Syrian character. One Nation-One Society. The unity of society is the basis of the community of interests and consequently the basis of the community of life. The absence of social unity entails the absence of common interests, and no resort to temporary expediency can make up for this loss. Through social unity, the conflict of loyalties and negative attitudes will disappear to be replaced by a single healthy national loyalty ensuring the revival of the nation. Similarly, all religious bigotries and their nefarious consequences will cease and in their stead national collaboration and toleration will prevail. Moreover, economic cooperation and a sense of national concord and unity will be fulfilled and pretexts for foreign intervention will be abolished."

This principle establishes the legal and legislative homogeneity of the society as a basis for a sound nationalist state. While the SSNP recognizes that in Syria today exist many religious and ethnic distinctions distributed over much of the Syrian homeland, these distinctions should not be brought into the realm of the legislation of the Syrian state. Furthermore, national loyalty should surpass and supersede religious and ethnic loyalties and affiliations. Generalized and absolute equality of rights is a basic principle of Syrian nationalism.

On a social level, Syria is currently divided along religious and ethnic lines. Religious and ethnic persecutions by sectarian rules whether indigenous to Syria or foreign, have contributed to this state. Persecution by other Christian sects led the Maronites to leave northern Syria and take refuge in the Lebanese mountains. This tendency to seek a geographical sanctuary was fostered by continuation of oppression by later rulers. A similar situation can be detailed for the Druze, the Assyrians, and the Alawites. Finally, the political associations of religious history continue to separate the Sunni and Shi'i Muslims in Syria.

Religious conflict and economic strife were major contributors to the disarray in Syria and national weakness. It is not surprising therefore to note that the majority of the Reform Principles of the SSNP are concerned with robust secularization of the state and society and the provision of the conditions for economic prosperity. A basic element that links the four reform principles in question (vide infra) is the question of justice and the fundamental belief in the preservation and advancement of human rights and the equality of rights for all citizens. In a society plagued by longstanding religious conflict, only radical secularization of the state and society can guarantee the equality of rights for all citizens.

The First Reform Principle reiterates the standard proposition of the *separation of religion and state*. In the West, the usual formulation is the separation of the Church and State, since Western nations are predominantly Christian and the term "Church" encompasses all religious institutions of whatever denominations. In Syria, however, the SSNP had to contend with multiple religions and myriad denominations within each religion. Further, the intent was not simply to separate the institutions of religion from the institutions of the state, but more importantly religion altogether from the state.

> "The greatest obstacle to our national unity and our national progress has been the association between our religious and political institutions and the pretension of ecclesiastical bodies to political power and their actual possession of such power in varying degrees. Theocracy or the religious state is incompatible with the concept of nationhood because it stands for the domination of the whole community of believers by an ecclesiastical authority. Religion recognizes

no national interests because it is concerned with a community of believers dominated by a central religious authority. The concept of a religious-political bond in lieu of the political is contrary to nationalism in general and to Syrian Social Nationalism in particular. The adherence of Syrian Christians to such a concept would set them apart from other religious groups within the nation and would expose their interests to the danger of being submerged in the interests of other groups with whom they happen to share a religious bond. Similarly, the adherence of Syrian Moslems to the concept of a religious bond would bring their interests also to possible conflict with those of their non-Muslim compatriots and would submerge those interests in those of the greater religious community. The inevitable outcome of the concept of a religious bond is the disintegration of the nation and the decline of national life. We cannot achieve national unity by making the state a religious one because in such a state rights and interests would be denominational in nature pertaining exclusively to the dominant religious group. Where such rights and interests are those of a religious group, common national rights and interests will not obtain. Without the community of interests and rights there can be no unity of duties and no unified national will. Based on this legal philosophy, the SSNP has succeeded in laying down the foundations of national unity and in actually realizing it within its ranks."

This Principle is based on several historical and theoretical imperatives. The first imperative is to remediate actual social problems in Syria as regards the divisiveness of religious sects when they take political and legal forms. The necessity of such a principle for national revival cannot be overstated. The tragedies perpetrated in Syria by the religiously motivated or contrived policies continue to sap the revival energies of the Syrian nation and retard its progress towards becoming a viable modern polity. The internecine massacres in Lebanon and the power struggles in Iraq and the Syrian Republic have clear religious undercurrents.

The recent resurgence of religious based and motivated militant political and armed organizations illustrates the fragility of the social order in Syria and the predisposition to greater calamities if application of this principle and its ramifications detailed below is further delayed.

Another imperative for the promulgation of this principle is to vindicate national sovereignty that has to reside in the entirety of the Syrian nation and not be limited to any denominational group however majoritarian. Unity of society is a necessary condition for safeguarding national sovereignty. Further, the unity of society is jeopardized by legal inequality and the latter usually obtains when a religious state emerges in multidenominational societies.

To leave no doubt about the extent of secularization intended, the Second Reform Principle, *Debarring the clergy from interference in political and judicial matters*, elaborates on the prohibition of involvement of the clergy of any religion in judicial and political matters of national character. "The rationale for setting forth this principle in a separate article is that religious bodies attempt to acquire or retain civil authority even where the separation of church and state has been conceded. This Principle puts an end to the indirect interference of ecclesiastical bodies in civil and political matters. This Principle defines precisely the meaning of the separation of the church from the state for reform must not be confined to the political sphere but must extend to the legal-judicial sphere as well. In a country where judicial function is not homogeneous owing to the diversity of religious sects, political rights and sound political institutions will not be possible nor will general national unity for the latter is conditional on the unity of laws. The state must have a uniform judiciary and a unified system of laws. Citizens must all be equal before the one law of the state. There can be no unity of character where the basis of life is in conflict with the unity of the nation."

Explicit in this formulation is that religion cannot be a source of jurisprudence for the national state for that would preclude equality of rights in a multidenominational society, and would be an impediment to progress and evolution of laws because of the inherent rigidity of religious doctrine. Saadeh was careful in clarifying that these prohibitions relate to judicial matters of national import. The SSNP, consequently, does not concern itself with denominational judiciary matters that individuals may choose to abide by in matters of personal affairs such as marriage, divorce, membership in the faith, or other, as long as all Syrians have a common secular option for the same, and as long as the religious forms do not supersede or impinge on national legislation. An individual Syrian may choose to have his or her marital status blessed by the judicial apparatus of their faith as long as it does not contravene or subvert the governance of that status by the civil laws of the state.

The Third Reform Principle concerns itself with the secularization of society. It states *"Removal of the barriers between the various sects and confessions"*. While respecting freedom of religion for individuals, the SSNP recognizes that traditions and customs emanating from historical religious processes have created barriers between citizens of different faith that undermine the emergence of a strong sense of national identity and free social intercourse. "There exists in Syria age-old barriers between the various sects and denominations that are not of the essence of religion. There are conflicting traditions derived from the structure of religious and denominational institutions that have exerted an enormous influence on the social and economic unity of the people, weakened it and delayed our national revival. As long as these barriers remain, our call for freedom and independence will remain futile. Every nation that seeks a free and independent life in which it can realize its ideals must possess real spiritual unity. Such spiritual unity is not possible in a country in which each group lives in isolation from other groups and has particular social and legal systems, which set it apart from other groups. This would result in diversity in character and disharmony in aims and aspirations. The socio-legal barriers separating the sects and denominations of the same nation constitute a major obstacle to the realization of the unity of the nation. The existence of the present social and legal barriers, which separate the various sects, entails the persistence of obnoxious religious bigotries."

While secularization of laws and the judiciary may eliminate contractual barriers, the nefarious effects of religious segregation may remain. This is particularly true in the question of group identity fostered by religious education. The institution of civil marriage for example may remove the procedural barrier to interdenominational marriage that is commonly barred or made exceedingly difficult by religious norms. However, if sectarian religious education continues to drum the prohibition, the avoidance of interdenominational marriage may be perpetuated even in the presence of permissive secular laws. A consequence of this principle, for example, is that religious education in non-public schools (parochial schools) should be monitored and broadly defined by the state.

The SSNP approach toward achieving national unity is linked to the establishment of justice in the judicial, social, and economic spheres. While the preceding Reform Principles address the former two spheres, the Fourth Reform Principle concerns itself with the basis for economic justice: *The abolition of feudalism, the organization of national economy on the basis of production and the protection of the rights of labour and the interests of the nation and the state.* When the Principles of the SSNP were first formulated, feudalism was rampant in Syria. Successive land reforms and economic changes have practically abolished the practice. Nevertheless, the Principles hold that the SSNP opposes any forms of economic injustice. This is delineated in the assertion regarding the 'protection of the rights of labour' as economic injustice is against the interests of the nation. "The organization of the national economy on the basis of production is the only means for the attainment of a sound balance between the distribution of labor and the distribution of wealth. Every citizen should be productive in one way or another. Moreover, production and producers must be classified in such a way to assure coordination, participation, and cooperativity in the widest extent possible and to regulate the just share of laborers in production and to insure their right to work and to receive just compensation for their labor. This Principle will put an end to absolute individualism in production because every form of production in society is genuinely a collective or a cooperative one. Grave injustices can be perpetrated against labor and laborers were individual capitalists to be given absolute control. The public wealth of the nation must be controlled in the national interest and under the superintendence of the national state. Progress and strength of the national state cannot be achieved save with this policy."

Critics of the SSNP, particularly Marxists, have often raised the issue of lack of extensive development and detail of the economic plan in the principles of the SSNP. The SSNP and Saadeh have delved frequently into the details of economic issues. Indeed, Saadeh has constantly addressed economic matters as they arose. While it is beyond the scope of the present essay to examine Saadeh's approach to these different economic issues, it is to be remembered that the principles were meant to define aspects and positions that the SSNP considered essential and immutable.

Equality in poverty is not a condition that the SSNP accepts for Syrians. The economic approach should embody the view of the SSNP for the future of Syria as a vibrant and viable polity. Equitable prosperity can be achieved only if the productive forces of the Syrian nation and the resources of its homeland are activated. The survival and success of the Syrian nation depend among other things on its economic strength and power.

Productivity is understood in a wide sense. It is agricultural, industrial, and intellectual productivity. This broad concept of productivity is a guard against the disasters frequently brought upon rising nations by an exclusive and a stubborn attempt at industrialization at the expense of other components of the economic life of the nation. While the SSNP recognizes the need for the Syrian nation to develop industry, the latter is viewed as but one component of economic growth and advancement.

The safeguarding of the rights of labor is not a call to unionism. SSNP members have been active in the union movement in Syria since the inception of unions in the early thirties. The Party has, at various stages in its history, supported the rights of workers when presented in the context of union struggle. The limitations of unionism, however, have also been considered. Unionism is usually based on a narrow view of economic life. It is frequently limited to a specific sector of the economy, and the demands are perceived in isolation of more general issues. The framework of the national character of the economy is absent from most union demands. A call for wage increase, for example, is a frequent union demand. The consequences of this event on the competiveness of the product in international markets is rarely considered.

While many political groups catered to the nascent labor movement in Syria by uncritical endorsement of unionism, and admittedly achieved political gain because of this endorsement, the SSNP had the political courage to assess objectively the benefits and drawbacks of unionism in Syria. The resistance to unbridled unionism is not only on the basis of the principle of safeguarding the interest of the entire nation, but also on the realization that unionism in Syria has frequently been exploited by political manipulators, duped by capitalists or controlled and emasculated by socialist governments. Based on these theoretical and observational factors, the SSNP calls for organization of productivity and labor based on specialization, but only as a means of improved productivity and streamlined management. The economic system, however, does not call for militant unionism because it presupposes the application of the economic view within the framework of a nationalist state.

Political Discipline and Party Organization

The SSNP brought strategic and organizational discipline to the political field in Syria that hitherto had been dominated by erratic initiatives and random alliances governed by personal and sectarian interests. Political amateurism and usurpation of the will of the people had been the norm. Strategic discipline is enshrined in the Eighth Basic Principle: *Syria's interest supersedes every other interest*. The text associated with this principle leaves no doubt as to its value and role: "This is the most important Principle in national activity for, in the first place, it provides the clue to the sincerity and integrity of national militants, and, in the second place, it directs their energies towards the interest of the Syrian nation and its welfare. It is the criterion by which all national movements and actions are judged. Through this criterion, the SSNP excels all other political factions in Syria, to say nothing of its obvious excellence in other respects. The SSNP aims at serving the concrete interests of the Syrians and at meeting their common needs and aims. There is no longer a need to seek in vain the definition of national endeavor in the domain of the abstract and the impracticable. This Principle centers all other principles round the interest of the nation so that Syrians are no longer misled by the teachings of those who would serve contrary interests. The life of the nation is a concrete reality and so are its interests. The success of the SSNP in bringing about this amazing national revival in our country is due, in great measure, to the fact that the Party seeks to serve the genuine interests of the Syrian nation and assert its will to life."

This is the central operational Principle that guides the struggle and militancy of the SSNP for the establishment of the new order and renaissance in Syria. It does not imply only complete devotion to the cause of the nation and homeland, but puts the onus of extreme care on the shoulders of the SSNP constituency. This Principle links extreme devotion with the responsibility of seeking the best for the Syrian nation. The romanticism of good-intended deeds is unacceptable in national struggle because the cause is too great not to be approached with great seriousness and careful planning. While laudable, devotion to the cause of the nation is insufficient. A serious and responsible preparation is necessary to safeguard the interests of Syria. Thus to serve the genuine interests of the Syrian nation, the SSNP does not offer only a devoted constituency, but also a well thought out doctrine and plan. The doctrine and plan embodied in the preceding Principles find their operational vehicle in this principle. The SSNP does not contend that it is the only party devoted to the Syrian nation, but it asserts that the vehicle of this devotion is what really affects the destiny of Syria.

Political amateurism and usurpation of representation were and continue to be very common in Syria. Mindful of the dangers on the national cause from such political behavior, Saadeh sought to establish within the organizational structure of the SSNP a system of control and accountability. The strict hierarchical structure and emphasis on discipline have led critics of the SSNP to accuse it of militarism. The best treatise on the necessity of this organizational structure was offered by one of Saadeh's closest early comrades and the leader of the organization for many years during Saadeh's exile in South America (1938-1947), Nehmeh Thabit. Thabit wrote this explanation in 1945 in response to an attack by the Communist Party.[42] The Communists had raised the easy libel of *fascist*[43] in attacking the SSNP. Because this allegation is used recurrently, it is useful to examine how a young colleague of Saadeh addressed the issue.

---

42 *Al-Hizb al-Qawmi yarud ala al-Hizb al-Shuyu'ee* (Memorandum of the SSNP to the Lebanese Parliament in rebuttal of the Communist Party Memorandum), April 10, 1945, pamphlet.

43 Many political commentators and writers, then and now used this label of fascist and proto-fascist, to characterize many of the political parties that were founded in the 1930's in the Near East because of their "militaristic" organizations and displays. While some similarities in appearance may have engendered this appellation, it has no ideological foundation and is in this author's opinion a manifestation of intellectual laziness and perpetuation of facile and useless labels.

"Alleging that the SSNP is a fascist organization is not unique to the Communist Party. The now defunct French Mandate had used the allegation. The Mandate and its collaborators found that the allegation would reduce the burden of fighting the SSNP because it would make them appear as safeguarding the "national" scene from foreign interference and not persecuting patriots for their involvement in a liberation movement. Further, the allegation would make the SSNP doubly dangerous for it was not only espousing a foreign system, but a system that was ideologically opposed to the principles of justice, democracy and humanity that the Mandate authorities endeavor to inculcate in us with devotion and unwavering compassion… Thus, it may appear that the fault lies with the SSNP and its "nefarious intent" for having chosen a robust centralized hierarchical system and not with the "noble intent" of the Mandate power. Why would the SSNP commit such an "error," adopt a centralized hierarchical system, and submit to the leadership of its Za'im with broad powers? It is obvious that the political means and methods of a particular party and its organizational structure are subject to the conditions surrounding the founding of the party and devolve of the need for these means and organizational aspects. Two fundamental factors dictate the choice of an organizational structure: First the aims and goals of the party; and Second, the obstacles encountered by the party. Based on this, we can now explore the special conditions of the emergence of the SSNP that have fostered the choice of a particular organizational and administrative character…

Under the oppressive conditions of the Mandate, it was necessary to oppose the modern means and methods of the Mandate with modern means and methods of our own. The truth is that the emergence of the SSNP with its strict centralized organization was in response to the heavy-handed Mandate organization. In the struggle between a

Mandate interested in perpetuating the status quo from which it benefited and nurturing our political and social ailments that it used to validate the indefinite extension of the Mandate, and the emerging renaissance rebelling against occupation and the abrogation of our national rights, and determined to lead the nation towards progress and freedom, in this struggle between the interests of the Mandate to maintain its hegemony and the interests of the SSNP as a national liberation movement, there was a need for serious preparedness.

Aware of the inevitable confrontation... the leader of the SSNP developed an innovative administrative system that makes the national liberation movement feasible under the conditions of the Mandate, and that guarantees that the SSNP would reach its goals despite the expected obstacles. To change the course of events in our country, Saadeh saw that it was necessary to abandon the archaic political methods and the bankrupt traditional maneuvers, and to adopt a modern organizational system concordant in its broad structure and detail with our special conditions under the Mandate and our unique circumstances. Moreover, the Mandate was equipped with specialized branches working tirelessly to establish its presence and execute its plans... and we had no institutions to safeguard our interests from the very effective interventions of the Mandate and the corruption it was spreading in our midst. Our fellow citizens did not mount against this network of Mandate influence except an anemic, fledgling political effort, inconsistent and poorly organized...

It is clear that the failure of all attempts at liberation initiated in our country was due in the first place to the sterility of the political methods used and the corruption. It is fatuous and criminally naïve in this century to oppose the organized and specialized Mandate effort with an impulsive unorganized political effort that becomes operative only when fed with popular dissent. The organization and discipline of the SSNP was an attempt to correct the miserable failures of the irrational politics of demonstrations and strikes... Indeed, it was not difficult for the Mandate power to manipulate and manage the tumultuous popular dissent that spent its energies with meager results...

These general considerations led the leader of the SSNP to give the party its paramilitary centralized hierarchical form... Further, the authority invested in the leader was not considered by the membership to impede in any way the respect of democratic principles for it is clear that in times of crisis, nations and societies do resort to consolidation of authority in a small number of trusted individuals who through their talents, devotion and sacrifice, help lead the nation out of crisis... Moreover, the constitutions of democratic nations have embedded in them the mechanisms of such investment of authority... Democratic virtues will not arise in any society by the mere fact of enshrining them in a written constitution... for these virtues are not realized in written words, but by real behavior of the citizenry. The success of all democratic systems is contingent on the establishment of ethical values without which the word democracy remains meaningless... The constitution of the SSNP allows a balance between the need to invest the leader with the authority necessary to fulfill the required reform and the upholding of the principles of nurturing democratic values in the members of the party and their training in shouldering the responsibilities of democracy...

So, while the SSNP resorted to the centralized hierarchical system out of necessity, and to protect itself and its members from the predatory Mandate authorities, the fascists adopted the centralized system as a matter of doctrine and a philosophical view of society making it a permanent system for social organization that defines social structure and individual responsibilities in a definitive way... In the final account the difference between the SSNP view of the centralized system and the fascist view of that system is that the SSNP uses this system as a means dictated by the conditions of its struggle whereas the fascists use it as a definitive doctrinarian and philosophical necessity for societal organization."

Colonialism being an act of violence perpetrated by aggressor nations, vanquished nations need to mount a counter array of strength to resist and end colonial aggression. In the first half of the 20th century, Syria witnessed directly two world wars, regional conflicts and colonial aggression. The SSNP had to confront the targeting of its nation by the traditional European colonial powers (France, England, and Germany), aggressive endeavors by neighboring states bent on territorial expansion (Turkey, Arabia, and Egypt), and an organized settler colonialism by a global Zionist organization. The inclusion of the formation of a strong military capability as a component of SSNP principles should come as no surprise. The SSNP considers that in the struggle of nations for advancement, survival, and control of natural resources, a nation's power, particularly military power, becomes a decisive factor in establishing and safeguarding national rights, sovereignty and independence. Nations expand their territory when strong and vibrant and relinquish parts of their homeland when feeble and in decline. Hence, the Fifth Reform Principle states: *Formation of strong armed forces that will be effective in determining the destiny of the country and the nation.* "In international competition of national interests, national right is recognized only to the extent it is supported by the power of the nation... Force is the decisive factor in affirming or denying national rights... it is incumbent upon us to be always in a state of complete military preparedness. The entire Syrian nation must be well armed and prepared. We have witnessed with distress parts of our country taken away and annexed to foreign countries because we have lost our military power. We are resolved not to let this state of helplessness continue. We are determined to turn the tide so that we may regain all our territory and recover the sources of our strength and vitality."

THE SYRIAN SOCIAL NATIONALIST PARTY

CASE STUDY: PALESTINE

The Palestinian question is among the most important political issues addressed by the political program for the SSNP. It can best be addressed by examining three inter-related aspects: First, The conflation of the Jewish question with the Palestinian question; Second, Legal basis for defending Syrian rights in Palestine; Third, Solutions acceptable to the SSNP to manage the ongoing situation in Palestine.

The SSNP draws a clear distinction between the Palestinian Question and the Jewish Question. The former relates to the rights of southern Syrians to self-determination and sovereignty in their own land, and the right to refuse and resist colonial settlers. The latter question is the need of the Jewish people for a haven to escape the anti-Semitism and persecution in European countries. The sacrifice of the rights of the Palestinians to provide a solution for the Jewish Question is what the British mandate in collusion with the Zionist organizations were endeavoring to achieve. In the SSNP perspective, Palestine is southern Syria. The division of Syria into two spheres of influence under British and French control after World War I and the creation of proto-states in each area has tended to obscure a reality long acknowledged that Palestine constitutes the southern part of Syria. Far from constituting a separate regional entity,[44] Palestine and the Palestinians are part of the Syrian homeland and the Syrian nation. As such, the issue of national rights devolves to the Syrian nation and not an 'Arab presence' after the Islamic conquest. Jews have no historical rights in Palestine. The Syrian nation antedates the first entry of Jews to Palestine (Land of Canaan) and their recent return is a recurrent foreign incursion

---

44 For a detailed discussion of these developments see: Muhammad Muslih: "The rise of Local Nationalism in the Arab East" in *The Origins of Arab Nationalism*. Reeva Spector Simon, Lisa Anderson, Muhammad Y Muslih, Rashid Khalidi (editors), Columbia University Press, NY, 1993, pp 189-203. Also, Muslih, Muhammad: *The Origins of Palestinian Nationalism*. Columbia University Press, NY, 1989, pp 131-154.

Case Study: Palestine

because of the precedence of Syrian (Canaanites) settlement in the land. In an open letter to Lloyd George Saadeh had explained: *"You say, Sir, that the achievements of Zionism to date prove that the land of milk and honey was not a myth, but you forget that the milk and honey flowed from the land thanks to the efforts of the nation that inhabited the land, and inhabits it still, prior to the advent of the Jews escaping bondage in Egypt."*[45] The claim to a *Promised Land* is a non-issue in international law, but rather a particularistic view of religion.

The magnitude and nature of the Zionist threat is beyond the immediate impact of land ownership and resources directly relevant to the residents of southern Syria. The view steeped in regionalism that was and remains prevalent, failed to elicit a broad national response to the grave Zionist threat, compounded by the preoccupation of politicians in other Syrian states with their own petty regional concerns. All the actors on the Palestinian stage were woefully ignorant or neglectful of the true national dimensions of the Palestinian question. Focus on the unity of national rights advanced by the SSNP is the sole guarantor of the coherence of national struggle against the Zionist incursion and any other threats to national security.

The proper legal rebuttal to the Balfour Declaration had first appeared in the *Blue Memorandum* of the SSNP published on June 15, 1936,[46] and in subsequent publications.[47] The Balfour Declaration is a political commitment that has no legal power in international law and contradicts Article 22 of the *League of Nations* charter. The SSNP considers the Balfour Declaration as a purely political declaration that binds only the British

---

45 *Complete Works*, volume 1, pp 241-244.

46 *Balagh ila ar-Ra'y al-Aam* (A Public Statement, otherwise known as the Blue Memorandum because of the color of the cover of the printed copy), *Complete Works*, Volume 2, pp. 31-36.

47 *Muzakirat al-Hizb as-Souri al-Qawmi ila al-Usbat al-Umamiya wa al-Umam al-Mutamadinat* (Memorandum of the Syrian National Party to the League of Nation and Civilized Nations), *ibid.*, pp. 133-37.

government. Further, the Balfour declaration contradicts Article 22 of the charter of the League of Nations that prohibits Mandate Powers from any action that may jeopardize, abrogate or infringe on the sovereignty of the countries under mandate. The Balfour declaration as a political pledge binds only to its originator, Great Britain, and should not affect the fundamental national rights of the people of Palestine. This is an important legal point that contemporary politicians in Palestine and the Arab east had ignored to the peril of their arguments. Traditional political leaders had mounted their defense of Palestinian rights by noting the contradiction between the promises made by Sir McMahon to King Hussein of Arabia and the Balfour declaration. They claimed that the correspondence between the British representative in Cairo and the Arabian potentate during the early part of World War I preceded the Balfour declaration and therefore should supersede it. They did not understand that they were by this argument accepting the right of Great Britain to make pledges about the land of Palestine. As to the assurances given by Britain to Sharif Hussein, they too should have had no bearing on determining national rights in Palestine as neither Britain nor Sharif Hussein had any rightful claims to Palestine. The labeling of Palestinians as Arabs did and does not confer on the ruler of Arabia the right to decide or dispose of their national patrimony, just as Britain and any other Arab country cannot decide upon the rights of, say, the Egyptians. As Sharif Hussein was an Ottoman appointee, he had no right legally to represent Palestinians despite the capricious argumentations of Pan-Arabists.

Zionist pamphleteers had an easy target with the traditional arguments. They stressed that the existence of ambiguous pledges to the Arab king *"could not in itself invalidate another set of pledges which are at least equally binding."* They highlighted the fact that the so called pledges made to King Hussein by Sir McMahon in 1915 were *"far from embodying any definite engagement even towards the Sherif"* and they quote the British Foreign Office characterization of the affair as *"a long and inconclusive correspondence."* The Zionist pamphleteers

CASE STUDY: PALESTINE

emphasized that *"Arab Palestine remained perfectly passive throughout the German-Turkish operations, while, on the other hand, Jewish colonists, whose services were afterwards publicly recognized by the military authorities, actively co-operated with the British forces at the risk of their lives."* [48] They also point to another weakness in the apposition of the Hussein-McMahon correspondence and the Balfour declaration: Hussein never disavowed or objected to the Balfour declaration. Further, they assert that Hussein's son, King Feisal of Syria and then of Iraq, had declared that he regarded the Zionist proposals at the Peace Conference in Versailles *"as moderate and proper"* and that *"there is room in Syria for us both."*

In concordance with its position on the rights of Jews to a national home in southern Syria and the Balfour declaration, the SSNP has opposed all partition plans proposed by the British (Peel Commission) and the United Nations. *There are no benefits imminent or delayed for the Syrians in a partition plan. Any partition plan carries critical and major benefits for the Jews and leads to the formation of an exclusively Jewish state.* The SSNP considered the issue of population transfer proposed by the Peel Commission and subsequently achieved by the Zionist establishment as *"forceful dispossession of land that will turn the Syrians into scattered refugees,"* an outcome that Ben Gurion welcomed: *"It allows the Jews to call their state a national home in the broadest sense of the term... and makes the constituency of the state exclusively Jewish."*

The participation of the SSNP in acts of resistance to Zionist settler colonialism is based on a distinct understanding of the Palestinian question and should not be conflated with other acts of resistance. Indeed, the SSNP has frequently criticized the political leadership in Palestine. As early as October 1937, Saadeh wrote:

---

48 See Leonard Stein: *The Truth about Palestine: A Reply to the Palestine Arab Delegation*. Zionist Organization, London, 1922.

"their arbitrary reactive politics have led to a series of erratic "patriotic" acts that have engendered only material and moral losses... The Committees in Palestine did not strive to develop a stable policy because political thinking in Palestine continues to be subject to arbitrary approaches. The outcome has been that events have determined political reaction and the national politics in Palestine have remained reactive... Shedding blood may be necessary in a robust defensive strategy with clear practical goals and validated objectives. Shedding blood with no consideration of outcomes is a waste of life and squandering of time and resources... Revolt is again afoot in Palestine. We can only hope it will be less harmful than the preceding one."[49]

He continued to offer a sharp critique of the activities of the political leaders in Palestine led by the Mufti of Jerusalem Hajj Amin al-Husseini.[50] Saadeh had met the Mufti when the latter escaped from Palestine to avoid arrest by the British and came to Beirut. "In the meeting between al-Zaim [Saadeh] and his Excellency the Mufti of Palestine in the home of Dr. Samih al-Khalidi in 1937 attended by a representative of the SSNP and the Arab Higher Committee, the most important question that al-Zaim asked was in relation to organization and planning. The absence of organization and planning in the Palestinian movement was responsible for the failure of the revolt of 1936. The armed guerilla activities were beneficial to the Jews and detrimental to the Syrians. These guerilla groups were active by arbitrary impulses with no wisdom or deliberation and cost the Syrians more than it cost the Jews. Indeed, it benefited the Jews where it meant to harm them."[51] The political amateurism of Palestinian leaderships has regrettably continued until the present

---

49 *Thawrat Filastin* (Rebellion in Palestine) *Complete Works*, volume 2, pp187-188.

50 The lack of organization and central leadership on the Palestinian side and the benefits the Jews accrued from the activities of the revolt of 1936 have been amply documented by historians. See Benny Morris: *Righteous Victims: A History of the Zionist-Arab Conflict, 1881-1999*, Knopf, 1999, pp 130-145.

51 *Complete Works*, volume 6, p 213.

CASE STUDY: PALESTINE

time and the critique offered in 1936 and 1948 could as well characterize the present. "Al-Hajj Amin al-Husseini struggled mightily against the Jews, but it was an arbitrary struggle devoid of political and organizational skill or understanding."[52]

The SSNP has a clear and objective view of the reasons responsible for the success of the Zionist endeavor. Zionist activities are logical, progressive steps in a well-organized program executed with rigor and precision despite all impediments. The overall program and its constituent parts represent a multipronged national threat that can be only vanquished and eradicated by a basic comprehensive opposing program supported by unified national strength. The theme that the Zionist plan can only be resisted and defeated by an equally comprehensive and robust Syrian plan is a constant in the SSNP's view of the question of Palestine.

Conciliatory formulations have recurrently plagued the Syrian efforts against Zionism. An example among Pan-Arabists are the views advanced by Zaki al-Arsuzi. Arsuzi advocated the dangerous notion that Arabs and Jews should achieve a common understanding to resurrect Semitic genius. The concept of Semitic ties is an old one in this context based on Bible genealogy. Of concern are modern formulations of alliance based on this antiquated concept. Arsuzi had called on the Jews to forego their work for a separate national home and to collaborate with the Arabs for the independence of Palestine within an Arab federation.[53] Such views would from time to time take organizational forms such as the *Semitic Union* in Jerusalem and Nablus that advocated Jewish-Arab association.[54] More recent conciliatory attempts invoke 'peace' as their modus

---

52 *Complete Works*, volume 6, pp140-141.

53 The article in which these comments figure is titled "*Falsafat al-Qawmiyah al-Usbawiyah*" (The National Philosophy of al-Usba). This article does not currently figure in the *Complete Works* published in 2001, but was included in previous compendia (See Antoun Saadeh: *al-Athar al-Kamilah*, Beirut, 1980, volume 4).

54 Hillel Cohen: *Army of Shadows: Palestinian Collaboration with Zionism, 1917-1948*, University of California Press, Berkley, 2008, p25.

operandi. The SSNP maintains that any conciliatory activity or advocacy is at best naïve and at worst detrimental to the national cause short of securing national rights.

It is clear that the SSNP is opposed to Jewish immigration to Palestine. The SSNP principles clearly called on all SSNP members to resist this immigration with all their strength, and they did. The question remains, however, on how to handle the Jewish immigrants already in the land. The SSNP addressed this issue in a memorandum on Palestine submitted by the SSNP to the *Congress of the Arab Front* in Jaffa scheduled for September 21, 1945.[55] The Memorandum listed several demands related to curtailing any further Jewish immigration to Palestine, the prohibition of land sales to non-Palestinian Jews, the prevention of the establishment of settlements for new immigrants, and the prevention of preferential treatments of Jewish institutions and individuals by the Mandate authorities. In the final segment, the Memorandum tackled the process of the progressive dissolution of the Jewish National Home. It called for the repatriation of Jews who had entered Palestine during the period of the British Mandate to their countries of origin under the auspices of an international committee of representatives of these said countries of origin. Such a process of repatriation was to be gradual but was not to exceed in duration the elapsed period of the Mandate.

---

55 The SSNP Political Bureau: *al-Qadiyyah al-Filistiniah* (The Palestinian Question), 1945. Memorandum presented to the Congress of the Arab Front in Jaffa September 21, 1945. The Congress was cancelled, but the memorandum was printed and circulated at the time. "We demand that the Mandate puts no obstacles in the way of the initiatives that an independent Palestinian state deems necessary to effect the departure of the Jews who came to Palestine during the period of the British mandate with the proviso that such departure be gradual, and under the supervision of an international committee with the membership of the countries of origin of the Jewish immigrants. This would need to be accomplished in a time span no longer than the duration of the Mandate."

The Aim of the SSNP

Saadeh's objective was not only to define the national identity of the Syrians but also to set in motion a movement that would revive the Syrian nation and make it possible for Syria to become a modern and viable entity. This meant the need to change the pattern of the social, political, and economic life of his people. The SSNP was thus conceived as an agent of change and represents the first concrete effort in Syria towards the total modernization of society. The change that the Party envisages is a comprehensive one that seeks to rebuild society in accordance with a distinct social philosophy. In the formulation of the text of the Aim of the SSNP, visionary and practical issues are juxtaposed:

> "The aim of the Syrian Social Nationalist Party is the creation of a Syrian Social Nationalist renaissance, which will fulfill its declared principles and return the Syrian nation to vitality and strength; the organization of a movement seeking the complete independence of the Syrian nation and the vindication of its sovereignty; the establishment of a new order to protect its interest and raise its standard of living; and the endeavor to form an Arab front."

National revival is the central theme in the program of the SSNP. The elements of this revival are embodied in the principles discussed above namely the establishment of the concept of nationhood, the guarantees for sovereignty and independence, and the assertion of social unity, judicial equality, and justice. The aim of the SSNP embraces all elements of national life and is not restricted to a political form of purpose. It is based on a new outlook to national life embodied in its principles.

The revival of the Syrian nation and the progress of its life are clearly linked with the unification of the nation. National unification is the primary objective on which political unification is built. Saadeh had clearly stated that the elimination of the separatist political forms is dependent on the will of the people. "As to the question of the political unification of Syria, my long-maintained unambiguous position is that its occurrence should be on the basis of the success and triumph of our principles and movement and not on the basis of the reactionary or arbitrary movements of any origin."[56]

There are multiple separatist movements in Syria based on the artificial states created by colonial powers and sustained by the interests of ruling elites and factions. Some of the separatist movements are based on ethnic and religious tendencies. The prototype for the latter is Lebanese separatism and the position of the SSNP toward it can illustrate the general approach. The SSNP considers the origin of Lebanese separatism to represent the collusion of French colonial interests with the interests of leaders of Christian sects chafing from past persecution under an Islamic majority rule. The genesis of the Lebanese state found its impetus in the inequalities in rights among the religious sects, and its promoters among the clergy and reactionary politicians in collusion with colonialists.[57]

The French Mandate created a political framework for this separatism in the guise of the state of the *Grand Liban*. This separatism was further perpetuated by other colonial interests. The separatists strived to formulate an alternate narrative in the form of an invented Lebanese nationalism. They contrived to create a nationalism based on Phoenician particularism and the administrative quasi-independence during the feudal period (the emirates of Fakhreddine and Shehab respectively) and the period of the *Mutasarrifyat*. The SSNP acknowledges that Lebanese separatism and other ethnic religious separatisms are

---

56 Letter to Ghassan Tueini 13 Dec 1946, *Complete Works*, Volume 11, pp. 285-88.

57 Saadeh, A: *Ikhtiraa al-Qawmiyat al-Lubnaniyat* (The Invention of Lebanese Nationalism), *Complete Works*, volume 6, pp. 161-67. *Mehzelat Istiqlal Lubnan* (The Farce of Lebanese Independence), *ibid.*, pp. 180-82. *Awham Ba'd al-Mutalabninine* (The Illusions of Some Lebanese), *ibid.*, pp. 232-35.

The Aim of the SSNP

based on objective grievances, but such grievances would have their reasons eliminated with the applications of the principles of Syrian nationalism as promulgated by the SSNP principles.

While the SSNP opposed Pan-Arabism, it maintained the adherence and inclusion of Syria in the Arab World. "As regards the Arab World, the Party favors recourse to conferences and voluntary alliances, as the only practical way to cooperation between Arab nations. ... As a matter of foreign policy, the SSNP aims to create an Arab Front from the Arab nations. This front should serve as a bulwark against foreign imperialistic ambitions and prove of considerable moment in deciding major political questions." National sovereignty, however, should not be surrendered in such pacts and alliances.

Place des Martyrs at Night - Beirut, Lebanon, 1932.

French miltary forces in Beirut, Lebanon, 1930.

The Early History of the SSNP

The early history of the SSNP will illustrate how this ideologically based political organization undertook to transform the political, intellectual, and cultural framework of Syrian society. We will examine the challenges it faced from a rapacious constellation of enemies, foreign and domestic, how it had the strength to challenge and confront them, and the high price it paid in suffering and sacrifices towards its goal. The resilience of the SSNP came from two sources: its principled outlook and the commitment and devotion of its leadership and ranks. Its trajectory over the first two decades of its existence was dotted by spectacular events, but it mostly consists of assiduous preparation and building towards grand achievements that are recurrently thwarted by enemies that are more powerful.

CLANDESTINE BEGINNINGS (1932-1936)

During the First World War, Saadeh witnessed the horrendous conditions that engulfed his homeland and brought woe and misery to his people. Reunification of his family after the war brought him to Sao Paulo, where under the tutelage and example of his father his political views took a sharp focus between 1920 and 1924 as reflected in his writings in *al-Majalla* and *al-Jarida*, two publications edited by his father Dr. Khalil Saadeh in Brazil. In 1924, he founded in collaboration with other young Syrians in Brazil a secret political group named *The Syrian Patriotic League* dedicated to the independence of geographical Syria. The *League* became public in 1925. However, the manner of its unveiling and the deviation from organizational efforts to ostentatious publicity led him to withdraw from its ranks. He later founded *The Free Syrians Party* in the latter part of 1926 and in 1927 initiated collaborative work with the *New Syria Party* based in North America.

After the partial initial success of that endeavor, he determined that the renaissance should take place in the homeland where events on the grounds would foster the acceptance of new principles. He returned to Syria in 1930 with a clear purpose of initiating a political movement that would undertake the revival of Syria along the principles he was formulating. He thought to study the affairs of the homeland before undertaking any plans, so he settled temporarily in Damascus, as he believed it was the apparent center of patriotic movements. The dominant political force in Damascus was *al-Kutlah al-Wataniyah* (translated as the *National Bloc*) whose leadership was composed of absentee landlords and commercial bourgeoisie. It cajoled and ruled the non-literate urban and rural masses. Saadeh made contact with the members of *al-Kutlah al-Wataniyah* through Jamil Mardam, one of the leaders of the group who was well acquainted with his father.

Overall, however, the French had managed to subdue the populace and the politicians of the Syrian hinterland by the brutal suppression of any sign of insurgency [1] and a policy of arrest, exile, intimidation or bribery. The French High Commissioner wrote in 1934, "*Politics is asleep. Minds have turned to administrative, economic and financial affairs. There is hardly any talk of parliament or the treaty. As a result the nationalist party, not knowing who or what to attack, is becoming weaker and disintegrating*"[2].

Saadeh stayed in Damascus for a year and a half during which he was in personal contact with members of *al-Kutlah*, but finding no way to cooperate or reach an understanding with them he decided to relocate to Beirut. He moved to Beirut in the

---

1. The brutality of the French suppression of the insurgency in 1925 was amply documented in the international press. As an example see Times magazine issues of August 17, 1925, September 21, 1925, October 12, 1925, November 09, 1925, November 23, 1925, November 30, 1925, December 14, 1925

2. Martel to the French Foreign Ministry, April 13, 1934, quoted in Peter A. Shambrook: *French Imperialism in Syria, 1927-1936*. Garnet & Ithaca Press, Reading, 1998.

CLANDESTINE BEGINNINGS (1932-1936)

winter of 1932 and got in touch with the American University to give German language lessons. After intense discussions with a select number of university students who showed affinity for the principles he expounded, he formulated the basic principles for political action and proceeded to build the party towards the end of 1932.

Two main streams of political thought were prevalent in Beirut. The concepts of *Arabism* and *Phoenicianism* were malleable ideologies that lent themselves to multiple interpretations. Various sectarian communities seized upon them as a source of legitimization of their own interests. *Arabism* was used as an umbrella for wide coalition building among Sunni politicians and *Phoenicianism* as a means of creating ethno-national distinctiveness for the Christian Maronites. The communities, however, were divided on these issues and the policies pursued by the Mandate played an influential role in shaping alignments. For the majority of Maronites, Arab nationalism represented the latest incarnation of Muslim hegemony. Members of the other Christian communities did not care to play a subordinate role in a Maronite-dominated state and hence were not eager to embrace *Phoenicianism*.

Saadeh was determined not to allow political and personal expediencies to undermine the national revival plan. When it came to creating a political organization, he was extremely careful and circumspect. The political scene at the time was overrun with traditionalists, city notables, clergy, and cronies of the colonialists. The existing political forms of national militancy were inadequate to carry new ideas. Saadeh reasoned that the nucleus for the movement required a core of youthful, energetic, and educated individuals that would spearhead the growth of a national organized movement. Thus, the founding of the Party was in secret among university students. Saadeh was not founding an elitist group in perpetuity.

After numerous individual discussions, Saadeh gathered a group of five individuals and officially declared the emergence of the political organization. Over the next few weeks, however, he noticed some disquieting behavior on the part of two members of the group. Fearing a re-enactment of the experience in Latin America, he decided to eliminate the risk carefully. The group had no charter yet, therefore Saadeh had no authority to dismiss members. In secret agreement with the other three members, Saadeh convened the whole group, expressed his discouragement of being able to move the political agenda forward, cited the immense obstacles, and announced his intentions of dissolving the organization and postponing the political work indefinitely. A few days later, he contacted the chosen three and the organization was off to a timid start.

There were multiple reasons for adopting a secret format for the SSNP. First, secrecy was necessary to test the seriousness of intent of participants. A clandestine organization offers no immediate gratifications for participants as far as social visibility, prestige, or electoral gains. The mission of the Party was to undertake a broad and radical social transformation of the Syrian nation. Such a task required a degree of commitment and militancy in Party members that was hitherto unaccustomed in a nation where modern political institutions were nonexistent. Furthermore, a long history of subservience to foreign occupation and intellectual and economic stagnation had left a population with no direction, no true self-identity, and no belief in self-worth. To prepare a militant organization capable of leading the struggle for the revival of the Syrian nation, it was essential to take the Party and its membership through a phase of formative calm indoctrination. Second, secrecy was necessary to protect the nascent organization from the dangers of premature confrontations with traditional political forces and the French Mandate before its internal structure had reached a defensive cohesiveness that would ensure its ability to weather the turmoil of open militancy. Since the ideology of the SSNP was opposed naturally and predictably to the concept of a foreign mandate, secrecy was essential to avoid compromising the safety of party

CLANDESTINE BEGINNINGS (1932-1936)

members. Under the mandate law, French authorities had the right to arrest any group of individuals meeting in a number of five or more if it suspected that the meeting had 'belligerent intentions'. It was inevitable that reactionary elements in the Syrian political system would be threatened by the emergence of a disciplined national movement aimed at eliminating the basis of their political power, and at setting principles for the conduct of national policies that supersede sectarian politics. During this formative period, the emphasis of the SSNP was on the active recruitment of youthful and educated elements of the Syrian community in urban and rural areas alike. The spread of the Party was based on personal contact and was initially slow, but soon grew to reach over one thousand members by the time Saadeh was apprehended by the French authorities in 1935.

FIRST GENERAL MEETING

For reasons of secrecy, the SSNP held very few meetings during the clandestine period. A limited administrative central meeting was held in December 1934. The first general meeting was held on June 1, 1935 and attended by 300 party members representing the central and regional administrative staff of the SSNP[3]. The meeting was crucial to consolidate the esprit-de-corps of the organization, imbue it with a sense of its own strength, and ensure alignment on goals and principles. The meeting was held at the villa of Nehmeh Thabit, the head of the Council of Directors (*Majlis al-Umud*). The agenda included a general report on the state of the SSNP summarizing the activities of the directors, poems by Salah Labaki and Yousef al-Dibs, and finally a speech by Saadeh.

The general report[4] gives a unique detailed glimpse of the status of the SSNP after 3 years of clandestine activity. From

---

3   *Ila al-Souriyin al-Qawmiyin al-Ijtima'iyin: Zikra la Tamout* (To the Syrian Social Nationalists: A memorable Day), *Complete Works*, volume 6, pp 85-87.

4   Jean Dayyeh: *Muhakamat Antoun Saadeh* (The Trial of Antoun Saadeh). Fajr an-Nahdah, Beirut, 2002.

THE SYRIAN SOCIAL NATIONALIST PARTY

Saadeh delivering his speech at the first general meeting of the SSNP on June 1, 1935, wearing the official party uniform and behind him the SSNP flag

the report we learn that the SSNP by that time had branched across the entire Syrian coastal area from Haifa to Alexandretta and into the major cities of the hinterland including Damascus and Hama, as well as many villages in the Lebanese mountains. The growth of the Beirut branch was particularly accelerated comprising almost half of the Party Membership. The SSNP had also instituted a youth program and lowered the minimum age of membership from 18 to 16 years. Arrangements had been made to use an existing nominal organization called *Hizb al-Islah al-Jumhuri* (Republican Party of Reform) as a front for SSNP meetings. A regular inspection system was in place with

Clandestine Beginnings (1932-1936)

Saadeh and other SSNP leaders regularly visiting Party branches throughout the country.

During the meeting, Saadeh delivered his first official policy speech in which he laid down the basic political and operational strategy of the SSNP. Besides being a piece of great oratory, the speech was the first major policy address delivered by Saadeh to the members of the SSNP. It is a comprehensive speech that deals with a wide range of topics meant to consolidate in a single document all the policy issues confronting the party: social unity, assessment of local political leaderships, defining a framework for foreign policy and foreign propaganda, implications of the principles of the party to political life and finally presenting a heroic vision of the future imbued with hope and strength.

Like all political organizations, the SSNP needed to create its own iconography and symbols that embody its image and central messages, emblems that will be readily recognizable as representative of the SSNP. Work developed on several fronts covering the party flag,[5] salutes, and party anthem.[6] In addition to these visual symbols and external manifestations, the SSNP adopted other traditions such as the use of Arabic numerals in

---

5   The flag of the SSNP contains three colors: black, white and red. Black represents the background in the center of which there is a white circle, and in its center is a red cyclone with four sides. The black background is divided horizontally by white lines. The colors have symbolic meanings: black symbolizes seriousness and authority, white symbolizes honesty and devotion and red symbolizes strength and courage. Another element in the iconography of the SSNP is the party salute: Tahya Souria (Hail Syria or Long Live Syria). This salute also predated the SSNP and many Syrian writers, at home and abroad, used it in their writings. Adopting it by the SSNP in its written literature as well as in its chants has made the salute symbolic of the party. An example of use among immigrants is reported in an article in the *New York Times*. The *Times* correspondent quotes from an article written by Joseph Khoury, an editor of the Syrian periodical *ash-Shaab* published in New York. The expression tahya Souria (Hail Syria) is unmistakably used. *New York Times*, October 6, 1918.

6   The party anthem lyrics were written by Saadeh in 1937 during his third imprisonment, to a Russian tune, but the music was later composed by Zaki Nassif. An alternate set of lyrics was developed by the poet Said Aql and was set to music but was not adopted and did not gain popularity.

lieu of Hindu numerals. Later SSNP commentators have sought historical argumentations in support of this choice.[7] The rationale for the adoption, however, as expressed in the early SSNP literature was more of a modernistic rather than nationalist fervor.[8]

INFILTRATION BY FRENCH INFORMANTS

New evidence suggests that the infiltration of the SSNP by agents of the Government was more pronounced and earlier than suspected. The French authorities and their Lebanese surrogates were aware of the existence of the party as of November 1934. They appear to have learnt of Saadeh's activities from the President of the American University of Beirut, Bayard Dodge, who had been alerted to the issue by the Dean of the school of Arts and Sciences. The Mayor of Beirut was receiving detailed reports of conversations, meeting minutes, official party forms and documents, and other information in the month leading to the arrest. An informant had forwarded to the Mayor on October 16, 1935, a detailed list of the party leadership

Saadeh and several of his lieutenants were arrested early in the morning of November 16, 1935. He was taken to the headquarters of the *Sureté Générale* where interrogations were initiated immediately.

The arrest was a rigorous test for the will and determination of the party leadership. Within days of the arrest, reports started appearing in the local press accusing the SSNP of relations with foreign governments. The accusations were naturally directed at Italy and Germany. The German Consul rapidly took steps to deny the allegations, and addressed an official complaint to

---

7   One of the earliest enthusiasts for the historical argument was Yussef Muruweh. In a pamphlet entitled *al-Arqam al-Suriyah fi al-Tarikh* (Syrian Numeral in History), published in 1956, he advocated the theory that "Syrian" numerals were derived from a Syriac origin and were based on the number of angles in the depiction of the numeral.

8   See *An-Nahda* issue 52, page 1.

INFILTRATION BY FRENCH INFORMANTS

Saadeh arrested by French Mandate security forces on November 16, 1935

the secretary general of the High Commissioner expressing his displeasure with the persistent stream of accusations proliferating in the local press.[9]

The discovery of the SSNP naturally attracted the interest of foreign consulates.[10] Overall, these consular reports do not reveal any intimate knowledge of the SSNP beyond what could be gathered by any effective consular representative.

---

9 Jean Dayeh: *Saadeh wal-Naziyah* (Saadeh and Nazism). Fajr al-Nahda, Beirut, 1994, pp 49-59.

10 Jean Dayeh: *Saadeh wal-Naziyah* (Saadeh and Nazism), 1994, p 50.

Newspapers in Beirut were particularly vehement in their attacks on the new party. The first was *La Syrie*, the semi-official organ of the Mandate as well as the Francophone *L'Orient*. *Sawt al-Sha'b* (Voice of the People) the communist organ and *al-Bashir*, the mouthpiece of the Jesuits were expectedly opposed. Moreover, when a press release was distributed on December 3 defending the SSNP, *al-Bayraq* (The Flag) decried the "syrianess" of a party with predominant Lebanese membership and voiced its concern for the independence of Lebanon. Similar concerns, but with less vitriol were voiced by *al-Maarad* (The Forum).[11]

Newspapers outside the French Mandate area were sympathetic. In Jerusalem, the newspaper *Palestine* published on Nov 27 an article defending the party signed by a SSNP member, and another Jerusalemite paper *al-Karmel al-Jadid* (The New Karmel) had favorable op-ed pieces on Dec 4 and January 18.[12] The Jewish press as exemplified in the English daily *The Palestine Post* reported on November 18 the discovery of the SSNP and continued to report on the development of the case throughout 1936.

News of the discovery of the SSNP made it to the Foreign Press in the US and France. The *New York Times* declared "United Syria Plot Bared – Union with Palestine and Lebanon Sought – Many Arrested."[13] By January of 1936, news of the SSNP and its program were appearing in French periodicals. The *Cahiers du Bolshevism* reported on the *Parti Populaire Syrien* under its

---

11   Gibran Jureij, *Min al-Ju'bat*, volume 2, pp99-102.

12   *Ibid.*

13   See *New York Times*, November 23, 1935, page 6. "Syrians stone cars; wound 2 French soldiers: Troops Rushed to Halt Riot at Damascus: "The trial of 39 members of the new Syrian National Party was nearing... Included among those who will go on trial is a naturalized United States citizen of Syrian birth, Fouad Moufarej, formerly of New York. The trial will be based on the single charge that the party was organized as a secret society and was not registered according to French law. The authorities, however, are investigating various allegations that the group is supported by Germany, Italy, or Soviet Russia". *Chicago Daily Tribune* (1872-1963), Chicago, IL:Jan 22, 1936, p15.

Bulletin Colonial.[14] The Parisian periodical *L'Oeuvre* voiced its concern for the stability of the Mandate and its program and repeated a litany of accusations of foreign subsidy and alignment with anti-French European powers.[15]

It is remarkable that the discovery of the existence of the SSNP drew the public attention it did considering that the Lebanese political scene was consumed with the presidential electoral campaign pitting Emile Eddeh against his archrival Bishara al-Khoury. The elections were to take place at the beginning of January 1936. In Damascus, triggered by the death on November 21 of the elderly political leader Ibrahim Hananu[16] a general strike was imminent.

On the 20th of November, and likely as a response to the discovery of the SSNP, the French High Commissioner issued a series of decrees strengthening the control of state elements and the powers available to quell any rebellion.

The interrogations of Saadeh and his colleagues lasted six weeks and were conducted, as was usual under the Mandate, under the leadership and supervision of a French examining magistrate assisted by a Lebanese judge and a Lebanese court clerk.

Many of the forty arrested members were soon released on bail pending the trial after intervention from various groups such as the Lebanese Bar Association, particularly since a few of the assrested SSNP members were lawyers. The release afforded Saadeh the opportunity the address the pressing needs of the

---

14 *Cahier du Bolchevism*, 13eme annee, Numero 1-2, January 15, 1936.

15 Gibran Jureij, *Min al-Ju'bat*, volume 2, pp99-102.

16 Ibrahim Hananu was born in Aleppo in 1869 and studied law in Istanbul. He had been a fierce opponent of the French mandate. He was in his sixty-sixth year and had been in poor health because of tuberculosis. He was viewed as a national hero having kept the ranks of the Aleppo National Bloc unified and successfully prevented the Damascus wing of the Bloc from making damaging compromises with the French authorities.

organization that was nearly decapitated by the arrests. He sent decrees from jail carried by the released members of the SSNP appointing an executive committee headed by Salah Labaki.

The investigation was concluded on January 4, 1936, and the detainees were referred to trial under the charge of organizing a secret political party aimed at disrupting political order, jeopardizing the security of the state, and aiming to change the form of government. The detainees were charged with holding secret meetings, collecting money, and forming illegal commercial interests and militias.

A HISTORICAL TRIAL

The trial was initially scheduled for January 16, but was postponed because of the Lebanese presidential elections. A new president, Emile Eddeh, was elected on January 20. The trial started on January 23, 1936. Saadeh, members of the *Majlis al-Umud* (Leadership Council) and other members of the SSNP were to be tried by a joint French-Lebanese tribunal.

Early that morning [17] Saadeh and the only two members who were still under arrest, Nehmeh Thabit, the President of *Majlis al-Umud*, and Zaki Naqash, the *Amid al-Harbiyah* (Minister of Military Affairs), were led to the courthouse. Three judges presided, led by a French judge assisted by another French judge and a Lebanese judge. The attorney general, a Frenchman, represented the state. The defendants and their lawyers represented the intellectual and political elites of the country. Saadeh's lead lawyer Hamid Frangieh, for example, was elected recently to parliament and was well connected in the traditional Christian political establishment.[18]

---

17   *al-Ma'rakah al-Siyasiyah al-Tarikhiyah al-'Ula* (The First Political Historical Battle), *Complete Works*, Beirut, 2001, volume 7, pp 7-22.

18   Hamid Frangieh (1907–1981) received a thoroughly francophone education in French missionary schools. In 1930, he graduated in law from university St. Joseph in Beirut. Besides his career as a lawyer, he became in 1933 one of

A Historical Trial

Saadeh during his first trial in January 1936 by the French Mandate court with two of his lieutenants

The presiding judge started the proceedings by calling the name of the accused: *"Antoine Saadeh!"* Saadeh did not respond nor stand. The judge called again: *"Antoine Saadeh!"* None of the accused responded. Confusion swept through the courtroom and attendees who knew Saadeh were wondering what was transpiring. Saadeh's lawyer looked at him and said: *"The presiding judge is calling you."* Saadeh answered: *"I did not hear the judge call my name."* The presiding judge noted the conversation and asked the defense lawyers to approach the bench. He was told by one of the lawyers: *"The accused is present but did not answer the call because he was not called by his name."* The presiding judge then asked, *"What is his name?"* Whereupon Saadeh informed

---

the cofounders and columnists of the "Le Jour" newspaper. He was elected to parliament repeatedly between 1932 and 1957 before he withdrew from political life due to illness. He was appointed minister several times: Minister of finance in 1938 and 1944, and minister of foreign affairs and education in 1941, 1945, 1947, 1948, 1949, and 1955.

his lawyer to tell the judge that his name was Antoun Saadeh. The judge looked upon the calm demeanor of the young man before him and instructed the court record keeper to correct the name to Antoun Saadeh. Then he called *"Antoun Saadeh."* Saadeh stood up and answered *"Present!"*

The presiding judge then asked Saadeh if he understood French, and on hearing the affirmative proceeded to detail the case against the defendants based on the documents and reports in his file. In summary, the judge contended that the SSNP was working clandestinely for a revolutionary purpose aiming to change the form of government, endangering the safety of the country, preventing members of the state from exercising their civil rights, and fomenting hatred of the French. The revolution was being prepared in earnest as documented by the robust organization of the party and the maps of military installations found in the possession of party members, but that the SSNP lacked the finances to fulfill its purpose, hence the front commercial enterprise that had been recently started for that purpose. The judge then examined the hierarchical structure of the SSNP, commenting that the meticulous order and design of the organization suggest influence of recent similar efforts in Europe. The judge then invited Saadeh to respond instructing the defendants to limit their comments to the legal aspects of the proceedings and not to turn his court into a political circus.

Saadeh was then asked if he would speak in French. Saadeh answered that he wished to speak in Arabic. The judge entreated him to speak in French since he was fluent in the language. Saadeh retorted that in view of the seriousness of the charges and that he was being asked to improvise a verbal response, he needed not to be encumbered by having to speak a foreign tongue. When the judge insisted, Saadeh responded: *"Your honor, I am a Syrian and in Syria, and I lead a liberation movement that aims to make national sovereignty absolute, so I will not accept to be made to speak in my country a language that is not my own!"* It was then agreed that Saadeh would address the court in Arabic and

A Historical Trial

that the court secretary would translate sentence-by-sentence Saadeh's response.

Saadeh then proceeded systematically to address the charges laid against him and his Party. To the first charge of organizing a clandestine political organization, Saadeh admitted his responsibility for the founding of the SSNP. As to the clandestine character of the organization, he declared that it was a temporary measure with no nefarious intent. Next, Saadeh addressed the issue of endangering the integrity of the state. The state in question was the newly formed state of Lebanon. Saadeh, by calling for a broader Syrian unity was "endangering" the integrity of this invented state. His response to the charge was uncompromising:

> "I am accused of endangering the integrity of the state and desecration of the homeland. I find myself compelled to declare based on reason and not emotion that the integrity of the unity of our country and the desecration of the homeland have been achieved in fact in San Remo, Sèvres, and Lausanne, and that the parties responsible for that are not the SSNP."

The prosecution objected that the accused had bypassed the issue of defense to address political issues unrelated to the case and hence irrelevant and unsuited to this forum. The presiding judge sustained the objection of the prosecution and admonished Saadeh to desist from this political track, to which the latter responded:

> "Your honor, and honorable prosecutor general, our case is a political case. We are not here because we are thieves or bandits, but because we are a political social movement! These charges leveled against us are they not political charges so how can I not tackle political issues when I respond to political charges. Furthermore, what I have stated are historical facts for in San Remo our country was

divided and our homeland splintered, and in Sèvres and Lausanne were concocted the remaining blows against our social, economic and political unity. Clarifying these facts is my right and my duty not only in defense of myself but also in defense of the integrity of my homeland and the rights of my nation!"

This served only to further infuriate the prosecution and annoy the presiding judge. After several interventions from his own attorneys, Saadeh agreed to continue saying that he said as much as he needed to say about those issues.

Saadeh then addressed the charge of changing the form of government. He stated that changing the form of government might be necessary for the better interests of the country as the needs of societies change with time. In any case, since the SSNP had not reached a definitive conclusion on this issue, it cannot be faulted for considering the matter. As to the issue of mimicking foreign political organization, Saadeh referred the judge to his speech of June 1, 1935 and other documents that clearly state the independence of SSNP thinking, free of any foreign influence and resistance to foreign propaganda.

As to the abrogation of the civil rights of citizenry, Saadeh explained that the conditions under which the SSNP was founded necessitated the organizational form adopted. Here he and the judge were both making reference to the strict hierarchical discipline that the SSNP adopted.

> "A nation ... in which there is no freedom of expression of political ideas and national doctrines, a nation that has no public forum and where the organization of political parties is forbidden, is a nation living no doubt in unusual circumstances. Unusual circumstances require unusual policies. I founded the SSNP to empower my fellow citizens to exercise their abrogated civil and political rights freely and not to prevent them from exercising these

rights." At this critical juncture, Saadeh digressed to define from his perspective the role of the Mandate. "Our right to sovereignty is recognized officially by international treaties. It is also recognized by the Mandate. Our condition under the Mandate puts a heavy responsibility on our shoulders that I wish to highlight specifically and that is: The Mandate was installed to provide administrative advice and guidance and what that implies is that all other prerogatives are the safeguarded rights of the people under the Mandate whose independence has been recognized. For if the Mandate is to help us, our duty towards the Mandate is to foster the maturity of our national rights and national strength in ways that preserve our unique character. By founding the SSNP, we are shouldering this duty and hence aiding the Mandate power with its mission."

Sentences were delivered on January 28, 1936. Saadeh was sentenced to six months imprisonment and a fine of 25 Syrian pounds. Thabit, Qubersi, Naqash, and Ayubi were each sentenced to one month with suspended sentence and a fine of 25 Syrian pounds. Fifteen other party members received a two weeks suspended sentence.

The terms of imprisonment represented the obligatory minimum under the prevailing laws and reflected the leniency of the court. It is important to consider here the reasons for the leniency. The social standing of the SSNP members under trial (they represented for the most part the local intelligentsia) and the more serious threats faced by the Mandate are the likely reasons behind the clemency.

During this period of imprisonment, momentous events were taking place in the country in particular the question of the two treaties: the Franco-Lebanese and the Franco-Syrian. On instructions from Saadeh, two leading members of the SSNP met in Damascus with the Syrian Delegation heading to Paris for the continuation of negotiations and delivered a memorandum addressing economic aspects of the treaties. Subsequently, another memorandum addressing Syrian unity and the status of Lebanon was delivered to the delegation before its departure on March 22.[19]

Politicians interested in Syrian union, such as Lebanese Sunni political leaders hoping to benefit from the support of Christian representatives, initially embraced the SSNP tentatively. Leading members of the SSNP were invited to participate in the meeting of *Mu'tamar al-Sahel* (Congress of the Coast) held in the house of the noted Sunni politician Salim Ali Salam on March 10, 1936. While the Sunni politicians wanted the predominantly Sunni regions of the *Grand Liban,* (the coastal areas) detached and unified with Syria, the SSNP was calling for full unification of the *Grand Liban* and the hinterland.

VISIBILITY AND WIDESPREAD INVOLVEMENT (1936-1938)

The Mandate authorities had tracked and monitored the growth and progress of the nascent clandestine organization and chose to intervene when the SSNP was reaching a critical mass that could rapidly acquire a political role. It chose to be lenient in its sentencing of its leaders likely underestimating their resolve to continue on their charted path. The Mandate attempted to limit the impact and national role of the SSNP through the subservient local governments that exercised various forms of intimidation, persecution and threats. When these failed, a negotiated temporary political truce would be attempted.

As soon as the initial trial and prison sentences were dispensed with, Saadeh led the Party on a course of intense public involvement in national and social affairs unprecedented in the

---

19 The final composition of the delegation was dominated by National Block leaders. Peter Shambrook: *French Imperialism in Syria, 1927-1936*. Garnet & Ithaca Press, Reading, UK, 1998, p 204.

modern history of Syria. The SSNP and its leader addressed themselves to every aspect of Syrian life: the Zionist settlements in the south (Palestine); the Turkish expansionism in the north (the district of Alexandretta); the economic morass; the persecution of intellectuals (the feminist pioneer May Ziadeh); the incursion of clergy into the political scene; the reactionary parties in the mock national assemblies formed by the Mandate authorities; the rights of workers; the formation of trade unions; deforestation; the artistic directions of poets, painters and writers; the organization of SSNP branches in all the major cities of Syria; and the growth of the intellectual heritage of the Party by the writings of the leader and his young associates.

The Party brought a vibrancy to the national scene and an intellectual impact that were unexpected for its numerical size. The main reasons for this phenomenon are the charismatic leadership of Saadeh and his ability to elicit impassioned commitment and response from his followers. This phase of the history of the SSNP was punctuated by the Mandate authorities repeatedly attempting to repress the growth of the Party by resorting alternatively to repetitive imprisonment of Saadeh, to encouragement of reactionary confessional parties to compete with the SSNP, to suppression of the freedom of the press and attempts at political assassination.

The impact of the SSNP is best illustrated by the flurry of attempts to limit its spread and curb its activities. The clergy and traditional politicians marshalled their press and pamphleteers to undermine the appeal of the Party in particular target groups. The Christian clergy attacked the Party as being anti-religious and anti-Lebanon. The French hastened to encourage the founding of political parties with distinct confessional appeal to compete with the SSNP. Members of the old regime felt understandably threatened by the new movement and the pressure on the Party mounted. The battle was ideological and political. On the former front, the Party felt secure. Its teachings had been expounded in Saadeh's writings in pamphlets and the Party's daily newspaper *an-Nahda* (Renaissance), and bolstered by the publication of Saadeh's pivotal book *The Emergence of Nations* in which he laid the scientific foundations of Syrian Nationalism. On the political front, the Party's resources were meager. Funds were limited and the growing political base was still not large enough to challenge the old order and the Mandate. If the national liberation movement was to definitively confront the Mandate, it needed international support. On this basis, Saadeh embarked on a trip to Europe and the Americas to garner support from Syrian immigrants.

FREEDOM INTERLUDE

Paradoxically, the imprisonment of Saadeh and his lieutenants in November of 1935 gave the SSNP a public platform and national visibility it would have been pressed to achieve had they remained a clandestine group. Gaining visibility is ephemeral. To play a decisive role on the political scene, Saadeh and the SSNP needed to show credible strength. True, leaders of the SSNP had been invited to the Congress of the Littoral, participated in localized public demonstrations, and agitated in the press, but a more definitive show of strength was needed.

Saadeh was released from prison on May 12, 1936.[20] His lieutenants and a troupe of SSNP members met him. That evening several private celebrations took place and on subsequent days a protracted schedule of small meetings unfolded. Saadeh was dissatisfied with this plan and had requested a large gathering as a show of force.[21] Fearful of the repercussions of such a gathering,

---

20 The *Chicago Daily Tribune* reported his release: "*Syrian Nationalist Freed. Beirut. Syria. May 12, (AP). Antoun Saadi, leader of the new Syrian Nationalist party, completed today his prison term imposed in November for organizing a secret party. He has determined to continue his activities in the cause of independence. Within three years, Saadi recruited 10,000 followers, largely from the ranks of young intellectuals, causing concern for French authorities administering France's mandate over Syria*". Chicago Daily Tribune (1872-1963). Chicago, IL: May 13, 1936, p18.

21 In a letter from prison dated March 8, 1936, he tells one of his lieutenants: "*I*

the leadership of the SSNP convinced Saadeh to substitute a drawn out schedule of regional receptions. Saadeh acceded to their request although he chafed at the lost opportunity.[22]

Having dispensed with the long schedule of receptions and meetings with regional groups, Saadeh resumed his administrative leadership of the SSNP by relieving Labaki from his position as deputy leader and directed his attention to the momentous political issues at hand. One pressing activity presented itself: taking a public stand on the issues of the Franco-Syrian and Franco-Lebanese treaties under consideration.

THE FRANCO-SYRIAN TREATIES

In the mid-1930's, the French Mandate was faced with turbulence and resistance from several fronts. Political activists that had reached prominence through feudal standings, economic prominence in the cities, or clergy support were clamoring for more political influence and a form of local autonomy. In Iraq, the British Mandate had been transformed by the Anglo-Iraqi treaty of 1930 into an Alliance between the British government and the government of Iraq. To assuage political activists in Damascus and Beirut, the French government of Leon Blum's Popular Front entered in 1936 into negotiations with the local governments that led to the drafting of two treaties modeled on the Anglo-Iraqi agreement and aimed, in principle, at providing

---

will be released on the 12th of May and on that day I want to see the Party with its branches, flags and discipline for our task is great. Let the members prepare for this with vigilance for the final say in the destiny of Syria should be ours". Dayeh, Jean: *Muhakamat Antoun Saadeh* (The Trial of Antoun Saadeh), Fajr al-Nahda, Beirut, 2002, p202.

22 He seemed conflicted about this development for in correspondence with some lieutenants he puts a brave face on the development: "After my release from prison on May 12, we continued in our quiet policy to be able to persevere in our constructive work. We prohibited the members from mounting any demonstrations and announced a plan for visits whereby each region sends an official delegation. This program lasted for two weeks during which I was unable to do anything except receive delegates". Letter to Assaf Abu Murad. *Complete Works*, volume 9, pp9-10.

local autonomy while maintaining important ties between France and the two Syrian states.

The treaties were eagerly ratified in both Beirut and Damascus parliaments but received no such expedient acceptance in the French parliament. When the government of Blum lost power, the colonialist officers and the French right assured the demise of those treaties. The SSNP opposed the treaties on the premise that they did not establish unequivocal national sovereignty. It viewed the treaties as ploys by the Mandate to maintain a grip on Syrian affairs. Furthermore, the treaties were imposing a forcible mandate with no legal basis, and which was not sanctioned by the Syrians, into an arrangement that did not differ substantially from its precedent, but was endowed with legality having been accepted by the "indigenous population". Whereas Syrian politicians were seeking temporary political gains, the SSNP's strategy was guided by the overriding importance of national rights and absolute sovereignty.

On June15, 1936, Saadeh published what became known as the *Blue Memorandum* (*al-Balagh al-Azraq*). The Blue memorandum stands out as one of the most important political policy statements that Saadeh was to make during this period. For years to come, he would hark back to this document and invoke it as a metric of the veracity of his analysis of the confrontation with the French Mandate and for the failures of the traditional political forces in Syria.

Negotiations were being conducted in Paris and while the SSNP had submitted memoranda to the Syrian delegates, Saadeh felt that the developments in these negotiations were not progressing in a manner favorable to Syrian interests. In the *Blue Memorandum*, Saadeh aimed to expose the nefarious nature of the French position and to call attention to the danger lurking behind the diplomacy:

"The Mandate has been very successful in Lebanon

itself with the election of the extremely separatist Lebanese government by a parliament that is anything but representative of the political and economic interests of the people.

The Lebanese question is an integral part of the Syrian cause and should not be considered separately... All Syrian questions, including the question of Lebanon, should be unified in one general program and one cause. It is reasonable for the cause to advance in stages as long as it retains its unitary character and as long as it is not chained in treaties for unacceptably long periods. ... Opposing unity and insisting on the politics of separatism is a harebrained policy that perpetuates our dire conditions and does nothing to improve our national status either politically or economically.

The Syrian Nationalists, whose party branch in Lebanon was dissolved by the government, are the primary organized force in Syria and I declare in their name that any treaty that does not contain clauses to preserve Syrian national unity will be met by their refusal...

If the edict of the President of the Lebanese Republic has dissolved the branch of the SSNP in Beirut, it did not dissolve the Syrian Nationalists themselves. They continue their work in Lebanon as in all other regions as members of the Lebanese state entitled to express their opinion in all matters pertaining to their destiny and interests..." [23]

Saadeh opposed the ideas of those treaties on the premise that they did not establish unequivocal national sovereignty. He viewed these treaties as ploys by the Mandate to maintain a grip on Syrian affairs. Furthermore, these treaties were transforming an enforced mandate with no legal basis and which was not

---

23 *Complete Works*, volume 2, pp31-36.

sanctioned by the Syrians into an arrangement that did not differ substantially from its precedent, but was endowed with 'legality' having been accepted by the 'indigenous' population. Whereas Syrian politicians were seeking temporary political gains, Saadeh's strategy was guided by the primordial importance of national rights and absolute sovereignty. Saadeh's concerns were fully vindicated by the professed views of the French negotiators.[24]

These treaties would have enshrined and codified the separation of Lebanon from the rest of Syria and carried the potential for further dismemberment of the hinterland. Since these treaties would come under the purview of the *League of Nations*, then the separation would receive legal international status or be condoned by international regulations, a further bolstering of the separatist agenda.

THE SECOND ARREST

Politically clumsy actions by party members sent Saadeh and several comrades back to prison. The event was almost banal, but it provided both the Lebanese and French authorities the pretext to get the SSNP and its leader out of the way. The Lebanese government under the leadership of the devout francophone president Emile Eddeh wanted the status of Lebanon codified by a separate treaty, and a vocal agent for Syrian unity was not to his liking.

Saadeh was arrested within forty days after his release from his first imprisonment. The proximal reason was the assault on the journalist Aref al-Ghorayeb by members of the SSNP.[25] The

---

24 Pierre Vienot in *Politique Etrangère*, Volume 4, issue 2, pp 103-121, 1939.

25 The periodical *al-Masa'* (The Evening) was publishing articles maligning the SSNP and accusing it of being on the payroll of a foreign government. Members of the SSNP in Beirut started stalking Aref al-Ghurayeb, the author of the pejorative articles, and finding an opportunity on June 17, they followed him to his apartment, forced the door and delivered a severe beating.

more important reasons, however, stemmed from the efforts of the Lebanese government of Emile Eddeh to assert its control over the Lebanese political landscape and ensure harmony with the policy of the Mandate. Hence, the official charge was the reconstitution of an illegal political party that had been dissolved by presidential decree the previous March 1936.

During the course of the investigation into the assault on 'Aref al-Gharib, the authorities discovered a copy of an emergency decree dated June 20, 1936 that directed party members to initiate acts of civil disobedience in all the regions of the French Mandate if the government were to resume persecution of the SSNP. This find was the *casus belli* for the issuance of an arrest warrant.[26]

The Lebanese authorities leveled against Saadeh the charges of sedition, illegal organization of a political party, and acting as agents of foreign government. The accusation of a relationship with Italy was leaked to the press, which led the Italian ambassador in Beirut, like his German colleague before him, to visit the High Commissioner's office and lodge a complaint about these allegations. This intervention resulted in further consultations between the High Commissioner's office, the office of the Presidency of the Lebanese republic, and the Attorney General's office which resulted in the latter denying the truth of these allegations.[27]

Saadeh's incarceration was prolonged beyond the requirements of a thorough investigation of an assault incident, and in spite of the total lack of evidence of any relationship with foreign powers. It seemed that a deliberate prolongation of his confinement was being executed, ostensibly to keep him away from the

---

26 For a detailed description of the events see an article by Antoun Saadeh: *Muzakarat al-Hizb al-Souri al-Qawmi al-Ijtima'I ila Usbal al-Umam sanat 1936* (Memorandum of the Syrian Social Nationalist Party to the League of Nations in 1936), in Antoun Saadeh: *Complete Works*, volume 6, pp 555-558.

27 *Complete Works*, volume 4, pp1-7.

political scene while the two treaties were being negotiated and president Eddeh was able to put the Lebanese house in order by engineering a reconciliation between the Maronite Patriarch and the French Mandate. Every bureaucratic maneuver to delay the release was utilized.[28]

MEMORANDUM TO THE LEAGUE OF NATIONS

On August 12, 1936 while Saadeh was still in prison, the SSNP represented by Nehmeh Thabit submitted a detailed memorandum to the League of Nations on the subject of the separation of the Lebanese state from the Syrian hinterland.[29]

The memorandum fits in with the escalation of the SSNP's opposition to the terms being discussed for the Franco-Syrian treaty and the preliminary deliberations of the Franco-Lebanese treaty. We see a continuous thread from the documents presented to the Syrian delegation in March, to the *Blue Memorandum* in June, to the *Memorandum to the League* in August, to articles in the local press. A crucial aspect of the memorandum was its presentation of a political formula for the resolution of the conflict between the outcomes of the Treaties (codified separation of Lebanon from the hinterland) and the unification of Geographic Syria. The compromise formula was federalism of the Syrian States.

In the memorandum, Thabit acknowledges that the best political system for Syria is a unitary state. However, because of clear obstacles a federal system has merits as a *transitional* state. Thabit contends:

---

28 The *Palestine Post* quipped that 6250 pages of evidence had been collected and that the documents weighed 30 kilograms!

29 The petition was filed as being from the "*Syrian National Party regarding the independence and future political and economic welfare of Syria, with supporting documents and statistical data*". The letter carrying the response of the French government arrived at the *League* on November 4, 1937 (CPM1964). The report of the League reviewer M. Palacios was registered on November 18, 1937 (CPM1997).

"Partitioning the country into separate states has nefarious consequences not only in the economic sphere, but also impacts negatively on national and political development... If we assume for the sake of argument that Syria was not at the end of the World War ready to be under one government, there is no reason why a single government was not possible under the Mandate. The creation of independent states in Syria, each tied to the interests of the clergy and feudal lords affects negatively the progress of the country towards manifesting a single nationhood... We assert that Syrian nationhood is an undisputable fact based on the examination of geographic, economic, social, cultural and historic ties. The creation of more than one sovereign state in geographic Syria on the pretext of some social or political ills is not only irrational but also contrary to the national interests of the Syrians. There is a need to establish a system that addresses the social and political challenges that the nation suffers while at the same time allowing the natural progress towards a complete unitary national state. Thus, in view of the erratic conditions created by the Mandate, *we propose the establishment of a federal Syrian government covering all the Syrian lands under the French Mandate* (emphasis added)... A unitary central government is the natural consequence of nationhood. Unfortunately, the Mandate has not fostered such a development. *We therefore submit that a federal system is the best system that allows for the actualization of Syrian nationhood without undue turmoil in some segments of the population that may fear this development under a unitary state* (emphasis added)... The federal system that we propose while limiting administrative powers over the subunits of the federation, promotes the development of a central jurisdiction over matters of broad national interest (e.g. military). This system will allow the desires and needs of subunits to be acknowledged at the local level."

This proposal was aimed at avoiding the emergence of distinct, different and insular communities in Syria (as happened subsequently). It also allowed for the development of a central government strong enough to unify the constituent states in their pursuit of common goals. Coupled with the work of the SSNP at the grass root level, the federalist state [30] would evolve into a unitary state. This proposal engineered a solution to the political problem at hand by accommodating temporarily the political cleavages brought about by confessionals divisions.

Strengthening the Ideological Base

Up to this date, the SSNP did not have a core document expounding its ideology and aim. While the Basic and Reform principles were defined, their implications and meanings required further elaboration. So Saadeh undertook during his imprisonment to prepare an ideological treatise to address this need. This text was to evolve through three editions with various additions and elaborations until its last form in the 1947 fourth edition. The first edition of this exposition of the SSNP ideology was printed in a small booklet of 45 pages.

The text detailed the tenets of the SSNP and addressed topical issues the SSNP was facing at the time such as the opposition by the National Bloc,[31] and the question of the invented national

---

30 The federal status did not escape the attention of foreign journalists. The reporter of the *Chicago Daily Tribune* writes: "*These five states [Lebanon, Alaouites, Druze, Damascus, Aleppo] come under a coordinated mandatory administration, the high commissariat, established at Beirut, capital of Lebanon. There are no passport or custom barriers between the five states, and the arrangement looks like a federal one, not unlike that of America*". Alex Small: *From across the sea. Chicago Daily Tribune* (1872-1963). Chicago, IL: May 24, 1936, p15.

31 "From the moment the SNP appeared on the political scene as the liberator of the rights of the populace and the sovereignty of the nation from the monopoly of the feudal classes that had bargained away our national sovereignty, the reactionary forces hastened to oppose it in the name of the Arab cause. They alleged that with its second basic principle, the SNP aims to antagonize the Arabs and resist the idea of close relations between Arab states. These

identities of Pan-Arabism (and the accusation of being anti-Arab)[32] and Lebanese separatism (and the accusation of being an enemy of the various states in Syria).[33]

The other task that Saadeh undertook while in prison was the development of the structure of the SSNP by the formation of local committees and regional councils, in effect introducing a form of progressive democracy within the centralized structure of the Party. This task completed the architecture of the political organization. It imbued the organization with democratic traditions that foster involvement.

This organizational refinement consisted of the institution of a system of regional elected councils progressing from the smallest unit (*al-Mudiriyah*, town or neighborhood unit) to the full party level. The council of the *Mudiriyah* is a consultative body whose membership needs to be approved by a majority vote. It sends a representative to the *Munaffaziyah* (district level branch) council, which has both advisory and supervisory functions. This district level council reviews and approves the budget of the district and supervises all regional plans not initiated under a central

---

reactionaries and manipulators did not even define for the public the nature of this Arab cause that they claim to represent."

32 "The establishment of an Arab front was and continues to be one of the great aims of the SNP. This idea was on our mind before we founded the SSNP and continues to preoccupy us until this day. The absence of such a statement in the original text of the Aim of the SNP was merely because of the prioritization of the imperative issue of our national renaissance and independence."

33 "The SNP does not focus its efforts on the dismantling of the internal political structures as hoped for by proponents and feared by opponents of such activities. Rather, the SNP focuses on national survival in the arena of nations. The SNP considers that some forms of government in geographic Syria can be considered national when appropriate, but that these forms need to evolve in conformity with national interests and the establishment of the concept of nationhood. All that concerns us in current governments is that their existence does not impede or thwart our major national interests". The issue of existing governments relates directly to the question of federalism discussed above. It was by this time clear to the SNP that any realistic political plan had to take into account the semi-permanence of the existing political entities, the proto-states in geographic Syria."

directive. This council can recommend by two-thirds majority the dismissal of the district executives. The district council elects one of its members to a general congress of the party. The latter is called into session once a year by the leadership. The general congress reviews the party budget, proposes projects or administrative changes and makes general recommendations on party affairs. This congress elects a president and secretary who remain in contact with the executive leadership when the congress is not in session. Membership in this general congress is restricted to one term.

TACTICAL PRICE FOR FREEDOM

Just as his arrest was political, Saadeh's release from prison had to be under a political formula agreeable to the Lebanese government (accepting of the legitimacy of the existing Republic). In a document Saadeh addressed to the members of the SSNP upon his release, he wanted to clarify how operating within the framework of existing "proto-sates" does not contravene the national unity doctrine.

> "Our political stand as pertains current events and political conditions remains as stated in our public statement released on June 15, 1936 [the Blue Memorandum] … The plan we have followed towards our final goal and from which we will not deviate does not ignore facts on the ground when addressing political issues… The facts are that Syria is divided into internationally recognized regions, which create a serious problem in national and international rights that requires political and organizational flexibility to solve…
>
> The requirements of public political activity for the branches of the Syrian National movement in Lebanon, al-Sham, Palestine and Jordan… force us to consider the particular political programs that need to be developed for each branch of the movement to ensure that all branches

work for the same great aim without endangering the safety of the movement.

The safety of the National movement and satisfying the requirements of public political action in Lebanon make it imperative that we formulate a program for the work of the Syrian National movement branch in this region. For this purpose, we will convene a meeting of party leaders in Lebanon to evaluate the conditions and define a plan of action... After completing our plan for Lebanon, we will prepare a program for al-Sham, Palestine and Jordan. We are confident that this approach will create broad opportunities for national action and allow the branches of the Syrian National movement venues of serving the common national cause without ignoring local conditions...

The plan of developing a specific program for every branch of the Syrian National movement will facilitate our work within the confines of the present conditions and prevent the misunderstanding of the movement's cause...

The enemies of the National movement will spare no effort to misinterprete every technical political plan of our movement. We declare that our principles are unchanged and that all political programs for the branches will be based on and consistent with our original principles..." [34]

Ideologically, the SSNP had to face the question: Is a one state necessary for a one nation? While historical processes allowed for the emergence of nations despite the absence of a single unified polity, contemporary nations were in need of political unity in their struggle for emancipation and survival. Nations and states had emerged independently, but is a unified national state required to safeguard the interests of the nation? The promise of

---

34 Saadeh, Antoun: *Complete Works,* volume 2, pp366-367.

the promulgation of state-specific political action programs may reflect adaptability to the facts on the ground. On face value, this is a setback to unification nationalism that strives to render the cultural boundaries of the nation (its social form) and its governance boundaries (its state) congruent. While the SSNP's program did include a re-organization of the political space, it was not restricted to this goal. It aimed at a comprehensive transformation of the social-cultural-political framework of Syria transcending, but not ignoring, unification nationalism.

DIRECT DIALOGUE WITH THE MANDATE

Establishing a dialogue with the Mandate authorities was an obvious task of any political movement. Upon his release from prison in November of 1936, Saadeh asked his lieutenant Abdallah Qubersi to contact the head of the Political Department at the High Commissioner's office and arrange a meeting.[35] At this meeting were present the head of the Political Department Baron Kieffer, Saadeh, and Qubersi. Baron Kieffer was a prominent and influential member of the administration of Comte de Martel, the French High Commissioner. He had been involved in the negotiations with local leaders pursuant to the disturbances in the hinterland earlier in the year.[36] He was also along with Count de Martel and Robert du Caix a member of the French team in the negotiations of the Franco-Syrian treaty.[37]

---

35 The meeting took place after his release from his second imprisonment. *Nida' ila al-Umma as-Souriyat* (A Call to the Syrian Nation), *Complete Works* Volume 3, p 364.

36 On February 3, 1936, Kieffer is quoted in the *Palestine Post*, page 2, in reference to the arrested demonstrators in the disturbances and strike in Damascus *"that he sympathizes with the imprisoned youth, but looks with contempt upon those leaders who exploit the patriotism of the innocent for their own ends"*. On February 21, the *Palestine Post* reported (page 1) that Kieffer met for several hours with several notables from Damascus to discuss the process for the resolution of the strike.

37 Kieffer was in Paris for the negotiations between the Syrian delegates and the French representatives of the *Quai d'Orsay* as reported by the *Palestine Post*, April 12, 1936, page 1. He was again in Paris in mid June, *Palestine Post*, June

Direct Dialogue with the Mandate

Saadeh and Kieffer delved into various political and historical topics, an opportunity for Saadeh to articulate the merits of the national movement and the potential for mutual understanding that would serve the interests of both Syria and France. The French diplomat was cordial, but this cordiality had undertones of subversion.

The Treaties: Riots and Challenges

The Franco-Lebanese treaty orchestrated by President Emile Eddeh was a major setback to unification efforts and must have thwarted the Muslim communities who were demanding the reversal of the annexation of the Muslim districts to Lebanon and their restitution to the Syrian state. For Lebanese separatists, the treaty consecrated the frontiers of the *Grand Liban* of 1920.[38]

Saadeh's release from his second imprisonment coincided with the confessional riots of November 1936 in the wake of the conclusion of the Franco-Lebanese treaty negotiations.

On Sunday, November 15, 1936, the *Hizb al-Wihdah al-Lubnaniah* (Lebanese Union Party)[39] led demonstrations in Beirut in celebration of the signing of the treaty 2 days before.[40] Lebanese Union Party members in their official uniform (*White*

22, 1936, page 1. He also represented the French side in the negotiations for the Franco-Lebanese treaty in October of 1936 where Kieffer was the principle negotiator dealing with the Lebanese president. *The Palestine Post*, October 19, 1936, page 2, and October 29, page 2.

38 Fadia Kiwan: *La perception du Grand Liban chez les Maronites dans la période du Mandat* in Nadim Shehadi, Dana Haffar Mills (editors): *Lebanon: A History of Conflict and Consensus*. I.B. Tauris, London, 1988, pp pp 124-148.

39 The Lebanese Union Party (LUP) was founded by Toufic Awad a nephew of the Maronite Patriarch. Awad was a vehement supporter of the Mandate and Lebanese separatism. Both President Eddeh and the French supported the LUP and even instructed civil servants to encourage people to join the party.

40 The description of the events is summarized from Shafiq Jeha: *Ma'rakat Masir Lubnan fi 'Ahd al-Intidab al-Faransi* (The Battle for Lebanon's Destiny during the French Mandate), Maktabat ras Beirut, Beirut, 1995, volume 2, pp 554-558.

Shirts) marched towards the offices of the Government at the *Petit Serail* on Martyrs' Square. President Eddeh and his government made an appearance on the balcony of his office and he was greeted with applause. This was expected to be the end of the event. Instead, the demonstrators marched through the Muslim areas of the city as an act of defiance against those opposing the treaty. The Muslims responded to this provocation by gathering around the area of the Basta Mosque where fiery speeches by Muslim politicians fueled their anger and sent them on acts of rampage. Christian crowds responded in kind, petty criminals and fanatics on both sides damaged property in the capital, and rioting was unchecked. The French army was called in to contain the riots and disperse the demonstrators. The repercussions incited angry partisans of both sides to plan further activities.

In response to the riots, the SSNP marshaled forces to stem the tide of hatred and violent clashes. Organized teams of SSNP members worked in various parts of the capital and the outlying areas to forestall escalation. Saadeh, Labaki[41] and others wrote editorials strongly censoring all parties to the riots.[42]

The above events hastened the emergence of various sectarian political parties, notably *an-Najjadah* (the Rescuers) on the Muslim side and *al-Kataeb* (the Phalanges) on the Maronite Christian side, both of which date their founding to November 1936.

---

41 Labaki's article reproduced in Gibran Jureij: *Min al-Ju'bah*, volume 3, pp 16-18. It was published in *al-Jumhour*.

42 In his editorial *Dam al-Ghawgha'* (The Blood of the Mob), Saadeh writes: "The slogans Independence of Lebanon and Unification of Syria are weapons drawn not for the independence of Lebanon or the unification of Syria but to serve the nefarious interest of corrupt politicians, interests that are concordant with those of the religious establishments and their internecine activities".

THE QUESTION OF ALEXANDRETTA

Another crisis that faced Syria during this period was the question of the district of Alexandretta. Emboldened by French weakness, the Turkish Republic was claiming rights to the Syrian district of Alexandretta. The government of Damascus, eager to have the treaty with France ratified without delay, and to avoid any conflicts with the Mandate and to insure political gain and ascendency, faltered on the protection of national right and failed to mount any effective resistance to the advancing Turks. Saadeh publicly denounced the government of Damascus defeatist attitude, the complicity of the Mandate, and the approbations by the Egyptian government. Having no military force and no access to arms, he proposed to enroll the entire membership of the SSNP in a national army that would defend the northern borders. He appealed to the *League of Nations*, to the French government, and to the various Syrian governments to prevent the Turkish overtaking of Syrian land. His warnings and calls for action were unheeded and the District of Alexandretta was annexed by Turkey in 1939. To this day, the Party holds commemorations of the Day of the Northern Borders and refuses to forsake that piece of Syrian homeland.

Saadeh's analysis of the unfolding question of Alexandretta correctly identified the expansionist intentions of Turkey and the clever maneuvers of the Turkish government playing on the fears of the French of a Turkish-Italian rapprochement, while at the same time creating divisions by infiltrating the province and inciting riots. He also correctly reads the fledgling resistance of the French in the face of Turkish sabre-rattling. Most importantly, however, he recognizes how the ethnic religious Arab nationalism of the *National Bloc* was alienating the non-Sunni inhabitants of the province and undermining any viable resistance to Turkish maneuvers.

Since the Franco-Turkish agreement of 1921, the Sanjaq[43] of Alexandretta had not received any serious attention from the Turkish government. News of the Franco-Syrian treaty, however, rekindled the interest of the Turkish government.[44] The official reason declared was to avoid having a Turkish population being placed under Arab domination.[45] On October 9, the Turkish government officially requested the French government to elevate the Sanjaq into an independent state, linked to France by a treaty similar to the Franco-Syrian and Franco-Lebanese on the premise of protecting the rights of the Turkish inhabitants of the Sanjaq.

On November 23, The French government offered Turkey a choice: If Turkey did not raise the issue of political allegiance of the Sanjaq to Syria, France would take steps to provide guarantees favorable to the Turkish element in the Sanjaq. If the Turkish government insisted on the independence of the Sanjaq from Syria, then the French would refer the case to the *League*. Turkey chose the second alternative.

Saadeh entered the fray on December 14, 1936. In a memorandum to the League of Nations, he declared that the SSNP would consider *"any act aimed at separating Alexandretta from Syria or limiting Syrian sovereignty over the sanjak as an infringement on the sovereignty of the Syrian nation and a violation of Article 22 of the Charter of the League of Nations."*[46]

In the first week of January 1937, Atatürk rushed with Turkish troops to the Syrian frontier and his supporters staged a riot in Antioch.[47] In response, Saadeh addressed a memorandum to the French High Commissioner putting the human resources of the

---

43 Sanjaq is a Turkish word equivalent to province. In the Ottoman period, it was the administrative unit in much of the Near East.
44 Peter A. Shambrook: *French Imperialism in Syria, 1927-1936*, pp291.
45 *Time* magazine June 13, 1938.
46 Antoun Saadeh: *Complete Works*, volume 2, p 58.
47 *Time* magazine Jan 18, 1937.

The Question of Alexandretta

Turkish troops marching before French militarymen in the region of Alexandretta in 1939. This territory which belonged to Syria was given by France to Turkey in exchange for Turkey not entering the war on the German side.

SSNP in the service of any plan to protect the district. Saadeh was reminding the French of their duty under the terms of the Mandate to defend the Syrian territory under their care. He was also setting the example for the Syrian governments to voice a strong position about the issue.

In January 1937, The League decided that the Sanjaq should remain nominally part of Syria, but should enjoy almost total internal autonomy. The agreement reached made the Sanjaq an autonomous region with its defense handled jointly by the French and Turks. The Turkish government then proceeded to raise the ante and massed troops on the border again in a show of force. The French buckled and gradually gave in to Turkish demands.

Saadeh, in an article on January 29, 1937. *"The granting of the right of the defense of the Sanjaq to Turkey endangers the safety of all of geographic Syria,"* he declared. In response to Ataturk's statement that Turkey will collaborate in any initiative toward pacification of the world, and the Syrian hinterland government of the *National Block* running for safety under the pretext of peaceful relationships, Saadeh writes, *"Nothing is more favorable to peace than the willingness of some nations to perish in the struggle for survival. If the Syrian government is headed by people who cherish peace more than life and who stand mute and inactive in the face of danger, their attitude does not represent the will of the nation."* In his words, the nation was getting *"sick and tired of the sterility and paralysis of its traditional politicians."* [48]

Fearing ongoing defeatism on the part of the *National Bloc*, Saadeh addressed a memorandum to the Syrian government on January 30, 1937 expressing the regret of the SSNP in view of *"the position taken by the Syrian government in the face of Turkish maneuvers... that effectively removed Syrian sovereignty over the Sanjaq."* [49] He asked the Syrian government to take a strong stand with the Mandate by including cautionary provisions in the Franco-Syrian treaty. He declared that the SSNP was willing to support the government in any action, no matter how bold, in the support of national right. The inaction of the *National Bloc*, however, was galling.

The *National Bloc* was more concerned with saving the treaty than saving the province.[50] They hoped that a campaign of *"Arab solidarity"* would be sufficient to calm the internal front while they cajoled the French establishment into moving the ratification of the treaty forward. The ethnic approach by the *National Bloc* was doomed to fail. The majority of Arab-speakers in the Sanjaq were not Sunni Muslims, but rather Orthodox Christians and Alawite. The *National Bloc* may have viewed them as insufficiently Arab or unworthy of sustained assistance.

---

48 Antoun Saadeh: *Complete Works*, Beirut, 2001, volume 2, pp 95-98.

49 *Ibid*, pp 99-100.

50 Philip S. Khoury: *Syria and the French Mandate: the politics of Arab Nationalism, 1920-1945*, Princeton University Press, Princeton, 1987

Northern Outreach

In December 1936, Saadeh undertook a public visit to the region of the Alawites on the northern Syrian coast. This area is unique in having high concentrations of groups traditionally considered as esoteric religions with separatist tendencies.[51] French policy in the district was to encourage Alawite separatism and from 1922 to 1936, the Alawites had their separate state. From the French perspective, the Alawite territory had a vital geopolitical position. It could be used, in conjunction with Greater Lebanon, to create an area of French control over a large segment of the Levantine coast.

The French promoted separatism by mere interest and similarly discarded it by mere interest. In 1936, they agreed to the incorporation of the Alawite territory into the State of Syria, as per the Franco-Syrian treaty. This was retracted in 1939 when the treaty was suspended and the area again became *Territoire Autonome Alaouite!*

The trip started on December 18, 1936. Over a four-day period, the convoy visited Safita, al-Mashta, Marmarita, Tel Kalakh, and Tartous. The agenda of the tour consisted of several public meetings during which speeches by Saadeh, local SSNP members

---

51 Firro looking at the political history of the Alawis in the north and the Druzes in the center offers the following observations: *"although the intellectuals of the two communities formulated the ideological arguments which would facilitate the adoption of nationalism together with Islamism, they were wary of the linkage between Islam in its Sunni form and nationalism. They preferred secular nationalism clearly separated from religion, or a nationalism that looked upon Islamic culture as a nationalist culture, without accepting Islam as the religion of a national state. Such tendencies explain the attraction of the Syrian Nationalist Party founded by a Greek Orthodox, Antun Sa'ada, or of the Ba'th ("renaissance") party, which had been formulated as an ideology of Arab nationalism by an Alawi, Zaki al-Arsuzi, and organized as a political party by a Greek Orthodox, Michel 'Aflaq."* Kais Firro: *The Attitude of the Druzes and Alawis vis-à-vis Islam and Nationalism in Syria and Lebanon*, in *Syncretic Religious Communities in the Near East*, edited by K Kehl-Bodrogi, B Kellner-Heinkele, and A Otter-Beaujean, Brill, Leiden, 1997, pp 95-96.

Saadeh delivering a speech during his tour of the Alaouites region in December 1936

and local dignitaries as were made. Additionally, open-air gatherings with brief speeches by Saadeh in colloquial Arabic took place in the smaller hamlets. Courtesy visits to area notables and chieftains either by Saadeh himself or by delegates he sent for that purpose were inevitable. Finally, Saadeh spent some time in extensive review of administrative and organizational issues with SSNP branch leaders.

In Safita, Saadeh addressed a very large gathering of SSNP members and supporters who braved the rain to listen to his speech. Saadeh took the occasion to clarify important aspects of the SSNP's approach to Syrian unity.[52]

> "The Syrian National Party inaugurated its national endeavor by addressing the greatest need of the Syrian nation, namely the need for a common general foundation that unifies the interests of the Syrian people and is suitable to support the

---

52 Antoun Saadeh: *Complete Works*, volume 2, pp 59-63

edifice of Syrian nationhood and the revival of the Syrian nation. It is an endeavor ignored by political groups that antedated the Syrian National Party and their calls for national unity remained sterile and unheeded... We did not simply assert the need and necessity of national unity, but sought the foundations of national unity in the true needs of the people and the interests of the nation and promulgated basic and reform principles that address these needs and safeguard the interests of the nation...

This land that sustains us is threatened from two directions, from the south and from the north. In Palestine, the Zionist incursion continues to acquire fertile lands that can support thousands of Syrians. In the north, the Turkish danger looms trying to breach our borders and acquire another part of Syrian land necessary to our life and progress...

Thirty thousand Syrian nationalists in Lebanon, and tens of thousands of supporters and sympathizers, consider geographical Syria as their homeland and are ready to mobilize to the border in the case of real danger...

I declare that Alexandretta is a Syrian territory necessary to our life and the advancement of our interests and we are ready to defend it at any cost..."

He did not forget that his listeners were farmers and workers:

"The reactionary forces oppose the Syrian National Party because the Syrian National Party wants to liberate the farmer from servitude and indenture.

The reactionary forces oppose the Syrian National Party because the Syrian National Party demands fair treatment of workers and their rights in decent living.

The reactionary forces oppose the Syrian National Party because the Syrian National Party liberates the citizens from the servitude of blind obedience and the authority of corrupt old institutions." [53]

The notable aspects of this trip are that it took place with minimal interference from the local governments or the French Mandate. Saadeh brought a message of national unification to an area noted for its separatist tendencies. The region was fraught with feudalism, tribalism and sectarian conflicts. It was a microcosm of all the social, economic, political, and religious strife afflicting Syria. It was exactly the test region for the success of the national revival ideology of the SSNP.

Saadeh's visit to the Alawites area, although restricted to the district of Tartous in the southern part, is symbolic of the momentous change that the SSNP effected in this area. Philip Khoury, an expert on Syrian affairs during the French Mandate describes that effect as follows: "There were two other institutions which were to have more lasting impact on the Latakia province and the Alawite community more than the Murshidiyyin. One was the emerging radical nationalist organization known as the al-Hizb al-Qawmi al-Suri or, as the French called it, the Parti Populaire Syrien (PPS) and the other was the military. The PPS, with its strongly secular ideology, appealed first to the Christian Orthodox community of the province, as it did in Lebanon, but it also appealed to Syria's other minorities. The Alawite intelligentsia found the party attractive because it rejected Arabism and religion altogether. It also stressed the values of village life over those of the city where Arab nationalism had its deepest roots... Both the army and the PPS promoted in different ways the process of Alawite integration into Syria..." [54]

---

53 Antoun Saadeh: *Complete Works*, volume 2, p64.
54 Philip S. Khoury: *Syria and the French Mandate: the politics of Arab Nationalism, 1920-1945*, Princeton University Press, Princeton, 1987, p 525.

Lebanese Confrontations

Amatour

Demonstrating the material presence of the SSNP in the various regions of Lebanon was a political necessity after the long hiatus caused by Saadeh's repeated incarcerations and the proclamation by the Lebanese government that the SSNP had been dissolved. After the success of the trip to the Alawite district, Saadeh planned further demonstrations in the Shouf and the Metn districts of Lebanon.

The Shouf region was under powerful feudal control. The feudal system in this region was coterminous with the religious minority – the Druze – who under the leadership of Sitt Nazira Junblatt were aligned with the Mandate. SSNP activities in the district started with an initial meeting of regional SSNP officials with Saadeh in Baaklin. This limited display was favored by the local SSNP leadership and endorsed by the head of the SSNP political bureau Salah Labaki who was averse to any unnecessary clashes with the authorities. The visit also involved meeting local dignitaries. On his way to Baaklin on January 9, 1937, Saadeh's convoy was diverted by the police so that Saadeh would meet the *Qa'immaqam* (district administrator) Nazim Akari. Akari, failing to convince Saadeh to cancel his visit, urged restraint in public display. The modest meeting in Baaklin proceeded without incident. Another larger meeting had been planned for Amatour, in the upper part of the Shouf. Opinion was divided within the SSNP leadership whether to proceed or to delay the Amatour gathering. On the morning of January 11, when large groups of SSNP supporters started converging on Amatour from the surrounding villages, the *Qa'immaqam* summoned the senior SSNP administrator in the area and reiterated his advice for moderation. When the full public meeting started at around 3pm, a police force of around fifty uniformed individuals approached the meeting area. The SSNP organizers cleverly made way for the police commander and his troops to be escorted to the front row and displayed all courtesy and hospitality. The meeting proceeded without any incident and all disbanded in an orderly fashion.

The attempts of the local government to dissuade the SSNP from holding the meeting, and the nominal endeavor at intimidation by sending a police force may be viewed as halfhearted. The local players may have had a more significant role in preventing a confrontation in Amatour (and precipitating a clash in Bickfaya) than typically recognized. The diplomatic overtures of the local SSNP organizers vis-à-vis the civil and police officials greatly helped their case. In creating a historical narrative for the early years of the SSNP, an image of defiance is inspirational.

In his speech at the Amatour meeting, Saadeh did strike a note of defiance:

> "We have gathered as an attacking force not a defensive force. Those that enslave people need to be on the defensive, they need to defend their monopolies and privileges. We are a liberation movement and it is the nature of liberation movements to actively advance and effect change...
>
> Our party is no longer merely a national doctrine and a worthy idea. It has become a political force and a material force." [55]

BICKFAYA

The meetings in Amatour and Bickfaya were primarily symbolic events to assert physically the existence of the political party. The events of February 21, 1937 in Bickfaya, however, were of a different ilk. A successful display of SSNP strength and organization in a notable Christian district would not sit well with a francophone president who wanted to monopolize the Christian voice. The SSNP had gained some political credit

---

55 Antoun Saadeh: *Complete Works*, volume 2, pp71-73.

from the event in Amatour and was therefore emboldened by that success.

The confrontation was not spontaneous, but premeditated and born of the exasperation of the Lebanese government officials who had failed to prevent the gathering in Bickfaya at the grass root level. Early in February, when it became known that the SSNP was planning a public meeting in Bickfaya, the *Qaimmaqam* of al-Matn started calling the local civil servants in Bickfaya and surrounding area and the police departments to gather intelligence on the preparations and date of the event. He was also urging the local civil servants to mount an opposition campaign and to file petitions with the government asking it to prohibit the gathering.

On February 21, just over 300 SSNP members in organized formations and flags assembled in the main square facing *Hôtel Continentale*. Saadeh reviewed their ranks and a few speeches were delivered. The government armed forces (around 250 *Gendarmes*) were in steel helmets, full gear and bayonets fixed to their rifles. They advanced on the arrayed ranks of the SSNP and ordered them to disband. The SSNP members tightened their ranks and prepared to face the *Gendarmes*. The two groups were equal in number and mere physical strength and massed bodies were not going to lead far. An agreement was reached by which the *Gendarmes* would stand back and allow the SSNP ranks to retreat in an orderly manner as per their original program since the display was already completed. The *Qaimmaqam* agreed and the SSNP men retreated in an orderly fashion to various destinations. When fewer than a hundred SSNP members were left, the *Gendarmes* attacked in contravention of the agreement and a fierce hand-to-hand combat ensued. Dozens of SSNP men and *Gendarmes* were injured, some seriously and several SSNP members were arrested.

Saadeh decided to thwart the attempts of the government to apprehend him, and planned a series of civil disobedience events that would, it was hoped, force the government to reconsider its oppressive policies. Saadeh went into hiding and started to prepare public opinion for the forthcoming uprising. On March 1, 1937, he issued a blistering indictment of the proxy Lebanese government describing it in the harshest terms and stating the case for freedom of expression against the tyrannical behavior of the government.

"A veil of tyranny unprecedented in history has descended on Lebanon...

For what is Lebanon and who are we? Are we perchance foreigners? This fatuous boasting of loyalty to Lebanon makes it seem as if Lebanon was the private property of those boasting, or that Lebanon is something separate from the Lebanese people and above this people, or that the domain of some and not others, or the domain of only those in government...

We are members of the Lebanese state and have the full right to express our opinion in its affairs and its destiny... The government is not the state; this principle was buried with Louix XIV and lies in peace in his grave...

The government that prevents citizens from free deliberation on the affairs of their state and prohibits them from expressing their civil and political rights is a government that has overstepped its limits and violated the principles on which it stands. It has rebelled on the will of the people who alone has the right to decide its own destiny and that of its government. A government of this kind is a rogue government and I declare it a rogue government...

The government of Lebanon has become a bureau of inquisition..." [56]

---

56   *Ibid.*, pp105-109.

After the clashes in Bickfaya, Saadeh stayed at a secure safe place in Beirut from which he made secret visits to various regions. Saadeh moved his hideaway from Beirut to Aley. Sensing that his cover may have been jeopardized, Saadeh decided to move on to Damascus. His departure, however, was conveyed to the government by an informer and he was apprehended before he could reach the border. The Lebanese government arrested 300 SSNP members during this new wave of persecution.

It is clear from the above that the activities of the SSNP during this phase were continuously plagued by the ability of government informants to gain access to critical posts in the SSNP and to sensitive information.

Saadeh's third imprisonment (from March 10 until May 15) was shorter than his previous stints in prison. This was a punitive type of incarceration by a government uncomfortable with the visibility of the SSNP and the resilience of its leader.

A TENUOUS TRUCE

Saadeh was released from prison for the third time on May 15, 1937 and his release was a culmination of a political process. He did undergo a trial, unlike his release from his second imprisonment. In this second trial, the presiding judge was Lebanese and the proceedings did not gather the interest of the media like the first trial. Receiving a verdict of not guilty was a political necessity for the settlement process negotiated between Saadeh and the government of President Eddeh.[57] The case he made to Eddeh's government was that the SSNP was working for national unity, and that the SSNP did not aim to destroy the Lebanese state.

The "understanding" between him and the authorities was acknowledged in a letter he addressed to the examining

---

57   Jureij, Gibran: *Min al-Ju'bah*, volume 3, p 222.

magistrate George Murad dated May 12, 1937.[58] In the letter, Saadeh asserts the categorical opposition of the SSNP to foreign propaganda and its efforts to combat it by every available means. He states that the SSNP had hoped that the Mandate would facilitate the task of a national reform movement, as it is the task of the Mandate to assure that countries under its jurisdiction rapidly acquire the skills and undergo the reforms necessary for national self-governance. As regards France, he states that the SSNP favors a strong friendly relationship with France to serve the Syrian national interest.

A few days after the release of Saadeh from prison and on the specific request of Khayr al-Din al-Ahdab, the Lebanese Prime Minister, Saadeh paid a visit to an aide of the French High Commissioner. Meyrier was the *Secrétaire Générale* in the Haut-Commissariat. He was frequently an acting High Commissioner when de Martel was absent.[59]

Saadeh extended these gestures of political good will to the French. On July 14, 1937, Bastille Day, he went to the commemorative reception traditionally held at the residence of the High Commissioner in the *Palais des Pins*. As Saadeh went through the line of the reception, the High Commissioner, noting with surprise the presence of Saadeh, said to him jovially *"Zaim means leader, n'est ce pas, so where do you want to lead us?"* To which Saadeh retorted, *"To what is best for both of our countries."* [60]

THE QUESTION OF PALESTINE

Saadeh had been dissatisfied with the course of events in Palestine, but had been unable to voice his views in the midst

---

58 *Saadeh to George Murad, May 12, 1938*, in Antoun Saadeh: *Complete Works*, volume 9, pp 25-28.

59 Jureij, Gibran: *Min al-Ju'bah*, volume 3, pp706-709.

60 *Ibid*, pp281-282.

of the various confrontations and obstacles. The publication of the report by the Peel commission in July of 1937 gave him the platform to articulate formally the position of the SSNP vis-à-vis the Palestinian question.

The Royal Commission was established by the British Government in the wake of the 1936 revolt in Palestine. It was chaired by Earl Peel, former Secretary of State for India. It heard testimonies from November 1936 to February 1937, predominantly by Zionists and their supporters as many of the Palestinian political and religious figures boycotted the Commission. The Commission's report finalized on June 22 and published on July 7, 1937, recommended the termination of the British Mandate and the establishment of two independent states, a Jewish and an Arab one, in the territory of the Mandate Palestine (defined as land west of the Jordan River). An enclave, to include Jerusalem, Bethlehem, Nazareth, the Sea of Galilee, and a corridor from Jerusalem to the Mediterranean would remain under British Mandate to ensure protection of the Holy Places (indefinitely).[61] The proposal was not original and revisited ideas presented previously. It signified that Britain had dismissed the strategic importance of Palestine. The retention of the Holy Places was a manifestation of pure racist imperialism. The British did not believe the *"natives"* capable of preserving the Sacred Places. Only a European power could guarantee this *"sacred trust of civilization."*[62] The most dangerous part of the Commission's report, however, was that it introduced and favored the idea of population transfer to render the two states ethnically homogenous. It sanctioned, promoted, and detailed the mechanisms for ethnic cleansing. *"The existence of these minorities clearly constitutes the most serious hindrance to the smooth and successful operation of partition... If the settlement is to be clean and final, this question of the minorities must be boldly faced and firmly dealt with."* The Commission used the

---

61 See report in J.N. Moore (ed.), *The Arab-Israeli Conflict, volume III: Documents*, Princeton University Press, Princeton, NJ, 1974, p150.

62 Meron Benvenisti, Maxine Kaufman Nunn: *City of Stone: The Hidden History of Jerusalem*, University of California Press, Berkley, CA, 1996, p209.

The 1948 Palestinian exodus, also known as the Nakba, occurred when more than 750,000 Palestinian Arabs were forced to leave their homes in Palestine.

example of the Greco-Turkish *"population exchange"* during which 1.3 million Greeks and 400,000 Turks were compulsorily transferred in the 1920s. In the present case, 1250 Jews would be removed from the putative Arab state and 225,000 Palestinians removed from the territory proposed for the Jewish state. The transfer recommendations delighted Jewish leaders. Ben Gurion wrote,

> "The compulsory transfer of the Arabs from the valleys of the proposed Jewish state could give us something which we never had, even when we stood on our own during the days of the First and Second Temples… We are being given an opportunity that we never dared to dream of in our wildest imaginings. This is more than a state, government and sovereignty – this is national consolidation in an independent homeland." [63]

---

63 Benny Morris: *The Birth of the Palestinian Refugee Problem Revisited*, Cambridge University Press, Cambridge, 2003, pp 47-48.

Saadeh directed his reply to the *League of Nations*.[64] In this memorandum, he offered a reasoned systematic framework for the rejection of the recommendations of the Peel Commission and laid the foundations for formal argumentation in international law. He affirmed the following principles that will remain the framework for the SSNP's position on the question of Palestine.

1. The Jews have not historical rights in Palestine.

2. The claim to a 'Promised Land' is a non-issue in international law. It is a particularistic view of religion.

3. The Balfour Declaration is a political commitment that has no legal power in international law and contradicts Article 22 of the League of Nations charter.

4. There are no benefits imminent or delayed for the Syrians in a partition plan.

5. Any partition plan carries critical and major benefits for the Jews and leads to the formation of an exclusively Jewish state. He considers the issue of population transfer as "forceful dispossession of land that will turn the Syrians into scattered refugees". He was fully aware of the benefits to the Jews that Ben Gurion welcomed: "It allows the Jews to call their state a national home in the broadest sense of the term... and makes the constituency of the state exclusively Jewish."

LEBANESE POLITICS

Saadeh's release from prison was at the cost of offering nominal support of the Eddeh-Ahdab government. With the approach of the Lebanese parliamentary elections, contacts between the SSNP and the various political groups interested in gaining ground in

---

64 Antoun Saadeh: Memorandum of the SSNP to the League of Nations in Response to the Report of the Royal Commission Regarding the Partition of Southern Syria, July 14, 1937", in *Complete Works*, volume 2, pp 133-137.

the new legislative caused concern in government circles. The Lebanese government representative in the negotiations with the SSNP leadership kept insisting that the SSNP should declare publicly its support of the candidates aligned with the government. He threatened that any failure to do so in the shortest delay would lead to a resumption of pressure on the SSNP. Saadeh countered that the government had not done anything concrete to prove that it did not harbor hostile intentions towards the SSNP and had not facilitated its work. He refused to declare the public support of the SSNP until the government fulfilled certain promises, among them presumably was the permit to publish a daily newspaper. In addition, Saadeh requested dropping of charges in pending lawsuits and assurances that persecutions would not resume after the elections were done. He wanted the understanding with the government sealed in a face-to-face meeting between him and President Eddeh.[65] The government, which was in an acute confrontation with the opposition, finally agreed to the terms and the meeting took place. Additionally, the permit for *an-Nahda* was issued. Saadeh then declared his support for the candidates on the government loyalists' slate.

The publication of *an-Nahda* was one of the important fringe benefits of the truce between the SSNP and the Eddeh government. The press with its power to alter public opinion was a key tool in the realization of the political-social program of the SSNP. With the publication of *an-Nahda*, the SSNP had a forum to explain its views about the Lebanese state:

> "We do not demand arbitrary political union sought after by politicians for non-nationalist purposes camouflaged under the banner of nationalism (reference to the unification calls by Muslim leaders of the littoral). We work for national union. Political union depends on the will of the nation. We work constructively within the Lebanese framework for the prosperity and advancement of the Lebanese people.

---

65 Saadeh to Jureidini, October 2, 1937. *Rasa'el Hubb*, pp23.

This work does not imply that we ceased to consider geographic Syria as constituting a socio-economic unity. Once the existence of Lebanon had been acknowledged, it became the realm of all Lebanese, us included. It is the duty of all Lebanese to exercise their civil rights. We are among those Lebanese exercising their civil rights for the betterment of the Lebanese people."[66]

The truce with the Lebanese government was manifest in the measured tones with which *an-Nahda* tackled the governmental crisis in Lebanon. The SSNP also attempted reaching a *modus vivendi* with the Mandate. Noting the retrenchment of French influence in the face of British expansionism in the Levant, Saadeh suggests:

"The latent intellectual and cultural power in the area of the French mandate is the greatest of its kind in the Near East. Freeing this power will open for it and for French influence new horizons in the Near East... An alignment between the interests of Syria and France would guarantee success."[67]

An-Nahda championed a variety of issues related to civil and political rights. It took the banner of women's suffrage and declared its support to give women equal rights not only in the political sphere (the right to vote), but also in the civil sphere by calling for a change in laws governing individual rights still linked to gender-biased religious law.

Lebanese Political Parties

On November 17, 1937, three weeks after the end of the parliamentary elections, the Lebanese government officially disbanded three paramilitary organizations: the *Qumsan al-Bayda'* (The White Shirts, the paramilitary organ of the

---

66 *an-Nahda*, issue 1, October 14, 1937.
67 *an-Nahda*, Issue 1, p1.

Lebanese Union Party, a Maronite organization), *al-Kataeb* (The Phalanges, a Maronite organization) and *an-Najjada* (The Rescuers, a Muslim Sunni organization). On November 20, the Lebanese police raided the offices of these organizations, confiscated their content and sealed them. The Maronite organizations, notably the *Kataeb*, called for a demonstration that took place on Sunday November 21, the one-year anniversary of the founding of the *Kataeb*. The mass rally deteriorated into an armed clash particularly after a French soldier was killed.

The Lebanese paramilitary organizations arose because of the anxiety of their respective groups' vis-à-vis the emergence of the SSNP and the widespread support attracted by its ideology and organization. Later historians would come to interpret the rise of these paramilitary organizations through the prisms of European models of fascism. The truth is much simpler and more direct from contemporary narratives. True some of the founders of these organizations did travel to Europe and observe paramilitary organizations in Germany and Czech Republic (like Pierre Gemayel from the Kataeb and Husayn Sij'an from the Najjadah). Various parties in the Near East adopted colored shirts like their European counterparts (The Blue Shirts and Green Shirts in Egypt, The White Shirts in Beirut and Aleppo, the Steel Shirts in Damascus, the Khaki Shirts in Iraq). These local groups, however, arose in response to local conditions and needs and displayed none of the formalism of their European models.

The first Christian reaction to the SSNP was the Party of Lebanese Unity (LUP). Its leader declared in 1937, *"the LUP was founded to resist the SSNP which was attracting a large number of youth even in the pure Lebanese areas."* The LUP was blatantly an exclusively Maronite party as reflected in its membership, symbolism and ecclesiastical support.[68]

---

68 Saadeh: *Ared Sari' lil-Ahzab as-Siyasiyah al-Munhallat fi al-Jumhuriyah al-Lubnaniyah* (A Rapid Survey of the Disbanded Political Parties in the Lebanese Republic – Part I), *Complete Works*, volume 2, pp 322-326.

In typical sectarian counterbalance to the LUP, the Muslim Consultative Council emerged, but it was not a grass root organization and was supplanted by the Muslim *Najjadah*. These groups aroused and exacerbated sectarian tensions.

On November 21, 1936, the *al-Kataeb* was formed. The group soon split over the conflict between President Eddeh and his archrival Bechara al-Khoury. The *Kataeb* gradually shifted away from President Eddeh, which elicited his wrath, and hence the disbanding order.

The leaders of the future *Najjadah* were originally leaders of the Muslim Scouts. When this latter group gained enough membership to represent a potential political force, the mandate issued instructions prohibiting anyone over 20 from joining and the group was barred from holding mass rallies without government authorization. To bypass these injunctions, particularly after the events of November 1936 to which these leaders were party, the *Najjadah* was formed presumably for graduate scouts who had reached age 20, but in reality as a Muslim paramilitary group. Like its Christian counterparts, "it became a sectarian political organization… and all three organizations endangered national interests and national unity and were a factor in the strengthening of destructive sectarian passions." [69]

Dealing with the National Bloc

The attacks by the *National Bloc* on the SSNP appeared soon after the discovery of the existence of the SSNP and while *National Bloc* politicians remained very ignorant of the SSNP's ideology and organization.[70] From the very beginning, the

---

69 Saadeh: *Ared Sari' lil-Ahzab as-Siyasiyah al-Munhallat fi al-Jumhuriyah al-Lubnaniyah* (Part 1), *Complete Works*, volume 2, pp 322-326.

70 In private, however, National Bloc leaders were not unified on their policy vis-à-vis the SSNP. In a letter from Paris in March 1936, Jamil Mardam advocates to his colleague in the National Bloc Fakhry Baroudi initiating contacts with the

National Bloc used rumor and sectarianism to combat the spread of the SSNP. However inaccurate and biased these claims may seem today, they were not without effect as recurrent defections (publicized by the *National Bloc*) from the SSNP testify. So successful was the political strategy that it thwarted for a while the penetration of the SSNP into significant areas of the hinterland. The characterization of Saadeh as a Christian leader and Syrian nationalism as a sophisticated ploy to divert the masses from the true path of Islamic Arabism and as a cover for Phoenicianism had undeniable force among the unenlightened masses. In a pamphlet titled "Arabism our eternal nationhood" published in early 1936, National Bloc authors state: "The leaders of the SSNP did not call for this Syrian nationalism but for a hidden sectarian allegiance. They feared assimilation as a minority in Arab nationalism so they called for a Lebanese or Syrian nationality to safeguard their sectarian existence".[71] The attacks continued throughout 1936 and were characterized by vehement denouncements of the SSNP and elaboration on its relations with foreign powers. *ash-Sha'ab* newspaper in Damascus on June 30, 1936 declared:

> "The SSNP has exhaled its last breath in Syria and defections from its ranks are continuing. It is fair to say that its existence in Syria has become but a historical anecdote. Our newspaper in Damascus has undertaken to unmask this party and expose the truth that underlies its actions and the secret elements that manipulate it that many of its members were unaware of. We have in our war on this party targeted two aims: to prevent the embroilment of our Syrian youth in the service of a foreign country and to prevent the proliferation of political parties in Syria so that it remains unified in Arab nationalism. It would have been

---

SSNP and supporting its activities in "coastal areas" (a euphemism for Lebanon and the Alawite region) and expressing doubt about any foreign connections with the SSNP. Letter from Jamil Mardam to Fakhri Baroudi dated March 27, 1936 published in *Souria al-Jadidah*, July 15, 1939.

71 Quoted in Saadeh: *Complete Works*, volume 2, p28-30.

better for the leaders of this party to have restricted their efforts in Lebanon alone".[72]

The most flagrant case of confrontation occurred in Hama in June of 1936. *National Bloc* leaders and Muslim clerics forcibly required SSNP members to withdraw from the party and to pledge on the Holy Quran that they would not resume any activity on behalf of the SSNP. Saadeh's visit to the region of Hama and Homs in the summer of 1937 did not succeed in reviving organizational efforts in the city in the face of aggressive sectarian resistance.

The leaders of the *National Bloc* and other hinterland notables looked upon the political groups on the littoral as subsidiary. Even the Muslim leaders of Beirut, Tripoli and Saida chafed at the hubris of the Damascus notables. That Saadeh was a Christian and advocating Syrian and not Pan-Arab nationalism must have rankled their ire. This was further inflamed by Saadeh's attitude to deal with the hinterland politicians as equals.[73]

Saadeh, however, decided to attempt to cooperate with the *National Bloc*. From his jail cell in early 1936, he issued instructions to his lieutenant to open negotiations with the *Bloc*. Salah Labaki and Ma'moun Ayyas traveled to Damascus and met with the Delegation preparing to head to Paris for the Treaty negotiations. A memorandum was later sent to the delegation urging it to safeguard the possibility of a future political union between Lebanon and the hinterland.

Saadeh met Jamil Mardam in the summer of 1937 when the latter was in Sawfar for a meeting between the Syrian and Lebanese governments. The meeting took place at the *Grand Hotel* and lasted for two hours. At the conclusion of the meeting, Mardam

---

72 Quoted in Jean Dayeh: *Saadeh wan-Naziyah*, page 31.
73 *Saadeh to Vice President of the National Bloc*, June 15, 1936. *Complete Works*, Volume 9, p11.

expressed great appreciation for the SSNP and its leader and agreed to a follow up meeting that took place in the fall of 1937. At this meeting, Saadeh raised the issue of Alexandretta and the grave national consequences of the loss of the district. He proposed to the Syrian Prime Minister a plan by which the *National Bloc*, if it so chose, could remain uninvolved yet allow the SSNP to mount a vigorous campaign to safeguard the national interest in Alexandretta. Mardam thinking more in terms of local politics than national consequences demurred and suggested that he found the removal of Syrian sovereignty over Alexandretta not as grave a consequence as Saadeh stated. On the contrary, he saw the development creating serious problems for Turkey because of the non-Turkish elements in the district. Mardam was approaching the issue in ethnic terms. Saadeh was appalled by the irresponsible position of his interlocutor. This grave realization coupled with the continuing opposition of the *National Bloc* to obstruct any SSNP activity in the hinterland convinced Saadeh of the futility of any attempt at collaboration. It was clear that the SSNP and the *National Bloc* had incompatible positions and were likely to be on a collision course.[74]

After the failure of the SSNP initiative with the *National Bloc*, Saadeh had no longer any reason to refrain from open criticism. With the publication of *an-Nahdah*, Saadeh and the SSNP had now a forum to voice their views on events and policies in the hinterland. The *National Bloc* government did not remain silent and arrests of SSNP members recurred between September 1937 and January 1938. Petitions to the Mandate and the *League of Nations* decrying the oppressive tactics of the *National Bloc* government had little effect. The SSNP had delivered two memoranda to the hinterland government objecting to acts of violence against the SSNP by *National Bloc* operatives and the collusion of police forces in these attacks on May 11, 1937 and October 23, 1937, to no avail.

---

74 *Tafakuk al-Kutlah an-Niha'I wa I'tizal Mardam* (The Final Collapse of the National Bloc and the Resignation of Mardam), in *Complete Works*, volume 3, pp350-353.

In addition to critiques on the pages of *an-Nahda*, Saadeh extended his critique of the *National Bloc* to other venues. In an open letter to the Syrian diaspora in January 1938, he offers the following characterization:

> "It pains me to announce to you that all political "actions" that were taking place prior to the emergence of the Syrian National Party were the work of private political corporations working for their private gain and influence. They were unconcerned with the creation of institutions vital for the life of the nation, and lacked any real appreciation of the concept of true nationhood and ideas of national reform... In these corporations, some worked for personal glory, others pursued nefarious personal interests, and most were remnants of the old feudal class, proficient in narrow local politics and very inept on the national level... The "nationalists" in the hinterland called for a single party, the national Bloc, that while not devoid of national sentiment, was not a party with national, social and economic principles, but a group of individuals with influence who pursued limited political goals. The result of their work was the Franco-Syrian treaty, the loss of Alexandretta, and the jeopardization of the upper Jezira." [75]

As the attacks of the *National Bloc* continued and the policies of the hinterland's government towards the SSNP became more and more confrontational and its rhetoric more strident, Saadeh increased the tenor of the critiques on the pages of *an-Nahda*. In February 1938 when the *National Bloc* government initiated a series of arrests involving opposition figures, Saadeh wrote:

> "There is no doubt that the erratic policies of the National Bloc that we have been critiquing on the pages of an-Nahda are sterile from the national perspective. The treaty gained by the Bloc is still suspended between heaven and earth,

---

75 *Complete Works*, volume 2 pp362-365.

but the nation lost the fertile district of Alexandretta and has been shackled by a string of foreign entitlements. Apparently, this great national disaster is nothing in the eyes of the Bloc compared to the gain of the treaty... The leader of the Bloc declares that critique of the government is treasonous... Accusing critics with treason is taking tyranny to new levels." [76]

A new plan by the hinterland government in March 1938 to issue a new currency separate from the one used in Lebanon was further fodder for Saadeh's attack on the *National Bloc*.

"The reversal of the politics of the Bloc from unionist to separatist is astounding and only compounds the Bloc's failure to safeguard the integrity of the Syrian homeland and the national interests of the Syrian nation. The cost of the feeble treaty was exorbitant: to wit the loss of Alexandretta, the disarray in al-Jazira, the re-activation of separatism in the Syrian provinces, the new law for minorities, the customs obstacles between Lebanon and Syria, and now the peculiar idea of a new currency... The concept of economic unity is absent from the political lexicon of the Bloc." [77]

Saadeh chronicles the continuing tyrannical rule in the hinterland:

"The arrest of the leaders of the opposition is not a proof of the strength of the government as much as a testimony to the seriousness of the internal strife. Oppression is resorted to by government when their policies fail... The Bloc has no aspirations beyond the transmutation of the Mandate into a treaty and the monopolization of power in the hinterland and it has fulfilled these aspirations... Their

---

76 *I'tiqalat Dimashq* (The Arrests in Damascus). *Complete Works*, Volume 3, pp172-174.
77 *Naqed jadeed* (A New Currency). *Ibid.*, pp205-206.

aim now is to do all they can to safeguard these gains... The nation is facing a daunting and dire international situation and risks to disintegrate at the slightest attack, yet the Bloc continues with its ethnically divisive policies and aggravates national weaknesses."[78]

Modern historians have generally characterized the politicians of the hinterland in concordance with Saadeh's views. Philip Khoury the foremost expert on the National Bloc wrote: "French control in Syria, contrary to French design, made of nationalism the chief political instrument of a large segment of the Syrian political elite, members of absentee landowning and bureaucratic classes in Damascus and in other Syrian towns. Nationalist slogans – "unity" and "independence" – were used as a crude, lowest common denominator appeal to rally the Syrian masses behind the traditional elite. Although the ideological tool to muster support was new, and the words and content truly different from before, the short-run political goal of the Syrian elite was as old as the hills: the monopolistic control of local political power".[79]

Saadeh's attack on the *National Bloc* culminated in a series of six articles titled: *Huquq al-Ummah bayn al-Kitlah al-Wataniyah wa al-Ajanib* (National Rights between the National Bloc and Foreigners) that appeared in the first two weeks of May 1938. The thrust of these articles is summed up by the following quote:

"No nation has been cursed with a poor political representation destroying its morale and squandering its national struggle the way Syria has been cursed by having the feudal national Bloc represent its national interests... Expecting anything besides erratic efforts from the national Bloc is like discussing philosophy, cosmology

---

78 *Siyasat al-Batch fi ash-Sham* (Tyranny in the hinterland). *Ibid.*, pp217-219.
79 Philip S. Khoury: *Factionalism among Syrian nationalists during the French Mandate*. Int. J. Middle East Stud 13:441-469, 1981.

and economics with the tribes of Zimbabwe, or the Niam-Niam... The world has not seen more juvenile politicians than the leaders of the National Bloc..."

ALLIANCE WITH THE OPPOSITION IN THE HINTERLAND

Among the politicians of the hinterland, Abd al-Rahman Shahbandar (1879-1940) was one of the few with whom the SSNP would find some concordance on views and approaches. Shahbandar's nationalist history uniquely qualified him for rapprochement with the SSNP. Shahbandar was a graduate of the medical school of the Syrian Protestant College (which subsequently became AUB) and connected to the Damascus notables class through marriage (his wife was from the Azm family). After the defeat of the Ottomans, he was a very active advocate of Syrian independence and nationalism. In May 1919 during the Feisal period, he established in Damascus *Hizb al-Ittihad al-Souri* (Party of Syrian Unity) whose slogan was "Syria for the Syrians!" The party advocated complete and absolute independence of Syria within its natural boundaries uniquely similar to those advocated by the SSNP. It also championed these demands with the King-Crane Commission. Shahbandar occupied the post of Foreign Minister in the Feisal government alongside Yusef al-Azma the War Minister and the hero of Maysaloun. He and Azma represented the anti-French nationalist line.[80] After the defeat of the Feisal government, Shahbandar organized the Iron Hand Society in 1921 that agitated against the French and participated in the 1925-1926 revolt.[81] In his exile in Egypt, he was active in the Syria-Palestine Congress, a group that young Saadeh had praised in the 1920s.

During the clandestine period, Saadeh had asked one of his lieutenants, Ma'moun Ayyas, to correspond with Shahbandar

---

80 Eliezer Tauber: *The Formation of Modern Syria and Iraq*, Translated by J.A. Reif, Routledge, London, 1995, pp56-57.

81 Commins, David Dean: *Historical Dictionary of Syria*, Scarecrow Press, 2004, pp. 142, 236-37.

then in Egypt and gauge his views on several issues. That correspondence has survived in the files of the Lebanese judge Hasan Qabalan. Saadeh expressed the hopes that motivated this correspondence on the pages of *an-Nahda* in November of 1937:

> "When Dr. Shahbandar was still in exile in Egypt, the national generation in Syria had high expectations founded on his writings in the major Egyptian newspapers [82] in which he expressed opinions that distinguished him from his peers in Syrian politics. Among these views was his support for social reform, his appreciation of the imperative of Syrian nationhood and his separation between national principles and sectarian fanatism... On his return, a faithful nation celebrated his advent... Soon after his arrival in Damascus and his clash with the government, he became the center of interest of the opposition and was expected to announce a reform program as a basis for this opposition." [83]

Newspapers in Damascus loyal to Shahbandar defended the SSNP against governmental abuses and opened their pages to articles by SSNP members and sympathizers.

Shahbandar, however, was to disappoint these expectations by resorting to manipulative political tactics not much different from other traditional politicians, and by appearing to adhere to religious Arabism. By March of 1938, Saadeh's disillusionment in Shahbandar was manifest in his writings.[84]

Saadeh met secretly with Shahbandar on the latter's request and a mutual understanding appeared to be in the making.[85] Inexplicably, however, Dr. Shahbandar neglected internal political interests and left Syria to Europe and then Egypt on

---

82 The articles Antoun is referring to were published in *al-Muqattam* in 1934.
83 *Complete Works*, volume 2, pp269-270 and volume 3, p173.
84 *Complete Works*, volume 3, pp238-240.
85 *Complete Works*, volume 11, p128.

the pretext of pressing involvement in foreign affairs! While Shahbandar gave several indications in public and in private of his appreciation, admiration and endorsement of the SSNP and its principles, these did not translate into any meaningful alliance.[86] Additional contacts between the SSNP and Shahbandar were continued but the apparent rapprochement did not bear any fruits. Shahabandar's call for *"the Arabic empire, Arab unity, Land of the Quran"* led Saadeh to conclude that his goal was clearly the *"manipulation of the masses for political gain."* [87]

THE CASE OF MAY ZIADEH

No modern Syrian thinker stands higher in Saadeh's esteem than the feminist author May Ziadeh. She figures prominently among the luminaries that Saadeh considers as forerunners of the national revival movement. A few years after the events to be related presently, on receiving news of her death he wrote,

> "There has never been in Syria in the last centuries a great woman thinker like May Ziadeh. Among all the literati that I have met or read, I have found but a small number who match her in education, culture and literary talent. May was a blessing to an aggrieved nation and was therefore a lost blessing. May's original homeland was the monster that sank its claws in her soul and body and almost devoured her in al-Asfourieh and Rubeiz hospital. Besides the joy I feel of dedicating myself to the cause of my nation, few are the things that bring me happiness like the feeling I experienced with the success of the campaign I undertook to save May from the shameful conditions in the claws of the monster." [88]

---

86   *Complete Works*, volume 3, pp315-316.

87   *Complete Works*, volume 5, pp257-258.

88   *Ayam May al-Akhira* (The Last Days of May), *Complete Works* volume 4, pp 320-332.

The Case of May Ziadeh

Feminist author May Ziadeh at her writing desk.

May's tragic course started with the insidious onset and progression of her depression following a series of personal losses. Thinking she might find solace with her Lebanese relatives, she agreed to accompany a cousin of hers Dr. Joseph Ziadeh to Beirut where she arrived on March 4, 1936. Little did she know that Dr. Ziadeh and his family were to exercise towards her a form of exploitative aggression motivated by greed. Within two weeks after her arrival in Beirut, Dr. Ziadeh engineered several psychiatric consultations ultimately resulting in her forceful incarceration against her will in the *Asfouriyeh* mental hospital [89] on May 16, 1936 with a diagnosis of involutional melancholia (an older name for major depression).

---

89 The mental hospital was built in 1898 by Theophilus Waldmeier on a hilly suburb of Beirut known as *al-Asfourieh*. In the 19th century, there was no modern asylum for the mentally ill in the whole of the Middle East. Waldmeier set out for Europe and America, spending two years in pursuit of financial backing and information on the latest methods of treating the mentally ill. In 1898, he returned to Lebanon and purchased 34 acres of land on a hillside overlooking the city of Beirut. The Hospital at Asfouriyeh was officially closed on 10 April 1982.

Saadeh first heard of May's plight in mid-January 1938 when he was approached by an acquaintance who related to him her case. Saadeh considered the case to represent a violation of May's human and civil rights. As an advocate of the sanctity of both, he could not remain uninvolved. His admiration and respect for May were additional incentives.

Saadeh went to visit May the next morning. His description of the encounter suggests that an intellectual affinity gradually developed between the two thinkers. He noted that May "*showed a great spiritual readiness to embrace great ideas and address issues of philosophical and scientific thinking. May was a thinker of great culture and intellectual ability seldom encountered among the Syrian literati that preceded the Social-Nationalist Revival.*"

Immediately after this visit, Saadeh wrote an editorial on the first page of *an-Nahdah* that appeared on the morning of January 19. The article was an open letter to the Attorney General of Lebanon and the office of the French High Commissioner alerting them to the injustice being committed on their watch. This was a brilliant maneuver for it addressed the legal aspects of May's incarceration and called into question the rights of the Consul of Egypt to intervene outside Egyptian jurisdiction. The political implications were significant for were the Attorney General and the High Commissioner's office to remain silent, they would be abdicating their responsibilities of juridical sovereignty and allowing an injustice to be perpetrated at their doorstep. The article electrified the SSNP constituency and women members of the SSNP starting organizing for a potential public demonstration in support of May. Saadeh exerted unrelenting pressure. On January 20, he visited his friend judge Qabalan who facilitated his access to the office of the Attorney General. Fearing that the Lebanese judiciary may hesitate intervening in a case with political association and intervention of a foreign power, Egypt, Saadeh called the office of the political secretary of the High Commissioner, Baron Kiefer, and asked for a face-to-face meeting for that same day which was immediately granted. Saadeh met with Kiefer and detailed for him May's case, the disturbing interference of the Egyptian Consul, and the deep interest of the SSNP and its leader in the welfare of May. On January 21, the Attorney General visited May in her hospital and was deeply moved by her story. He subsequently met with Dr. Ziadeh and news reached Saadeh that complications were arising. He called Nassif and informed him that if May was not released within 48 hours, he would forcefully liberate her. Saadeh renewed his contacts with the Attorney General's office and the High Commissioner's office. The next day, January 22, the Attorney General ordered May to be released to the hospital of the American University and appointed a commission of physicians to examine her including a high-ranking French physician courtesy of the High Commissioner's intervention.

May was released from the University Hospital on February 14 on her own recognizance to live in a house rented and furnished for her by supporters. Within days, however, a Maronite priest of the Ziadeh family filed a lawsuit in the Lebanese courts requesting May's re-incarceration on the grounds of mental incapacity. People claiming to be May's relatives also attempted to force their way into her home. Saadeh ordered the SSNP branch in Beirut to post permanent guards on the house. These guards were instrumental in aborting and preventing subsequent attempts at invading May's privacy and potentially endangering her.

To vindicate May in the eyes of the public, and to strengthen her legal case against her relatives, May's lawyers arranged for her to deliver a lecture at the American University of Beirut under the auspices of *al-Ourwah al-Wuthqa*. Guards from the SSNP accompanied May to the University campus. Saadeh attended May's lecture in West Hall on March 22 and *an-Nahda* publicized the lecture and praised it in a review.

May's legal problems took a protracted course in Lebanon and later in Egypt before she regained access to her assets and belongings. The details of this course need not occupy us here and the interested reader can pursue them in the cited sources. What needs to be addressed now is an evaluation of Saadeh's intervention. How critical was his intervention in securing May's release and safeguarding her freedom? Historians of the events have tended to maximize the role of the literati. Amin al-Rihani who for example wrote a book about his role in the affair. Rihani, however, had poor relations with the Lebanese government and the French and no political standing, his literary fame notwithstanding. While political leaders of great import such as Fares al-Khoury were intimately involved in the case, their involvement was mainly in the protracted legal proceedings in Lebanon and Egypt that followed her release from hospital. The interventions of other political leaders were mainly perfunctory and after the fact (e.g. Emir Abdallah of Jordan, and a few Syrian politicians). Saadeh's role was critical. His intervention was *the single most significant development that secured her release.* Indeed, in less than a week after he became aware of the case, May was on her way to freedom! It is regrettable that historians of the case have either totally ignored his role or underplayed its significance.

Saadeh visited May one last time before he left Lebanon later that spring. He was accompanied by Fakhri Maaluf and Charles Malik. By that time, May was surrounded by a coterie of literati and others all striving to make her happy and to keep her busy. Saadeh was sorry for her fate and the absence of considered and calm care that he thought the writer needed and deserved.

Confronting a Religious Bastion

The confrontation between the SSNP and the leadership of the Maronite church was initiated by the latter. Soon after the discovery of the SSNP, a pamphlet labeling the SSNP as the *"enemy of religion and country"* was published with the blessing of Patriarch Arida.[90]

---

90 Pamphlet is reproduced in Salim Mujais: *Saadeh wa al-Ikliruss al-Marouni*

The author of the pamphlet, Louis Khalil, a priest and close confidant of Patriarch Arida, is clearly addressing a Maronite Christian community when he asks, "Do the principles of the SSNP conform to the laws of God and the teachings of the Church?" After defining his medieval context, he goes further to relate the implications of the SSNP First Reform Principle (Separation of religion and state). "The clear meaning is that the state should separate itself from religion in an absolute sense neglecting our obligations and duties to Almighty God. It will not be founded on belief in God and will not respect His Laws. More precisely, it will be a state without religion Ignoring God in its constitution, legislation and the execution of its affairs as if God did not exist. This is the true meaning of the separation of state and religion, a grave matter for it is a major insult to Almighty God". After more of the same obscurantist drivel, Father Louis Khalil concludes that the SSNP satisfies all the conditions that would bring excommunication on any members of the Catholic Church (Maronites included) who would join its ranks. The modern reader may scoff at the anachronistic language and the medieval concepts in the pamphlet, but in 1936 Lebanon, this was a serious obstacle to confront.

It should not surprise us, therefore, that the Patriarch would take a swipe at the SSNP in his annual homily. The homily of the patriarch was an opportunity for Saadeh not only to defend his party, but also to undermine the legitimacy of political involvement by the clergy. Indeed, Saadeh's rebuttal and the Patriarch's speech were published by the SSNP in a pamphlet distributed widely in Syria and the immigrant communities.

Saadeh's rebuttal was three pronged: first, he offered an unflattering characterization of Patriarch Arida; second, he ridiculed the role of the patriarchy; and third, he showed the incompetence of the Patriarch in the handling of the specific political and civic issues tackled in the homily.

(Saadeh and the Maronite Ecclesiasts), Beirut, 1993.

The Patriarch gave Saadeh the excuse to rebut him by inserting the following paragraphs in his homily:

> "It is regrettable that a group of Lebanese have enrolled in political parties under foreign influence such as the Syrian Nationalist Party and the Communist Party, working against Lebanese independence, and believing in principles nefarious to religion, country and morality. It is the duty of the government to resist these parties working to undermine Lebanese independence and spreading evil principles under the guise of seeking public good.
>
> It saddens us to see the government ignoring the Communist party while it disbands and resists Lebanese organizations... We do thank the government, however, for its actions against the Syrian Nationalist Party...
>
> The primary duties of the government are the protection of the citizenry and their livelihood from internal and external dangers... and the prohibition of societies and parties that threaten the existence of Lebanon and spread corruption and discord in the population such as the Communist Party and the Syrian Nationalist Party and their ilk."

Rebutting the Patriarch had great symbolic significance and Saadeh and the SSNP used this rebuttal to foster acceptance of their secularist agenda. The Patriarch delivered his speech on Dec 6, 1937. It was published in *an-Nahda* on December 8 and on the 9th *an-Nahda* announced the forthcoming rebuttal, and did that recurrently until the first part of the rebuttal appeared on December 21st and continued over four consecutive issues. The periodical then issued the whole rebuttal as a special supplement and it was later issued as a pamphlet with the speech of the Patriarch.

Saadeh offers an anthropological view of the involvement of

religious authorities in civic and political affairs:[91]

"The tackling of social, economic and political affairs by religious authorities today is akin to their handling of physical and mental illnesses in days gone by. Priests claimed a hidden power accepted because of the prevalent ignorance of those backward times. As the advancements in medical sciences have made it impossible for the priest-sorcerer to replace the expert physician, the advancements in social and political sciences have equally made it impossible for an archbishop or a patriarch to supplant a social scientist, a political expert or an economics specialist. Just as the interference of a priest in the care of a patient leads to the ruin of the work of the physician, the interference of men of the cloth in the handling of economic, social and political issues will lead to the disruption of the work of experts in these economic, social and political issues."

He then extends this anthropological approach to the Patriarchal See:

"The Patriarchal See has ancient traditions dating to the periods of the stone age or the early bronze age, certainly prior to the iron age or the industrial age, prior to the age of knowledge, science and specialization, traditions dating back to the age of complete ignorance and utter fear. In these ancient traditions, the Patriarchal See had a primary interest in managing the affairs of the religious group under its care. Religious groups had special issues, unique demands, and a semblance of political unity. Their political representation was religious and their religious representation political. Because religious groups constituted political entities, religious representatives acquired political power. This allowed the Patriarchal See to acquire grave influence that

---

91   al-Rad ala Khitab al-Batrayrek al-Marouni (Rebuttal of the Speech of the Maronite Patriarch), *Complete Works*, volume 2, pp 339-361.

it continues to wield in our political and national affairs, and is primarily responsible for creating our current situation… The intervention of the Patriarchal See after the War in the name of the Maronites from a religious perspective led to the creation of the Lebanese question… The backwardness of social and political thought in the constituency underlies the gravity of the political positions of the Patriarchal See and explains the permanence of the political influence of religious authorities to this day on our national and political causes."

Of the Patriarch himself, Saadeh had this to say:

"Patriarch Arida had a laudable stand on the issue of social unity between Lebanon and the hinterland and appeared to be aligned with the position of the national renaissance. He also had a firm stand on the issue of the tobacco monopoly, but it was unsuccessful because it was too late… he also had some nefarious attitudes such as his support of Jewish attempts to infiltrate Lebanon which drove Archbishop Mubarak to tell him: 'We elected you a Patriarch of the Maronites not a Patriarch of the Jews'… On a personal level, the Patriarch has no clear balanced direction or a particular political doctrine. His political actions are erratic outbursts precipitated by passing events, directed by personal influence of close associates, and based frequently on primitive elementary views and immature understanding of the issues at hand… The Patriarch's approach to the crisis in government in Lebanon is based on the same rule as his intervention in the affair of the tobacco monopoly: seeing disasters after they strike and errors after they occur."

Having established an 'anthropological characterization' of the religious authorities and their views and determined their inadequacy from a modernist approach, Saadeh then proceeds to interrogate each of the issues raised by the Patriarch to illustrate in specific details the veracity of his characterization. He proceeds to identify contradictions and inconsistencies in the speech. What interests us here, however, are not the failings of the Patriarch, but what views Saadeh presents that reflect elements of his political philosophy. One of the issues he tackles in detail is that of civil rights. In response to the Patriarch's statement *"Man is free to believe what he wishes but does not have the right to force others to adhere to his beliefs,"* Saadeh points out the contradiction between this statement and the Patriarch's call for the suppression of the SSNP by the government. He does take, however, this one-step further:

"The issue is not as simple as it may seem because it relates to our political system. We should examine it not in the simplistic realm of the absolute but in the context of our society and the basic rights that safeguard it, namely civil rights enjoyed by members of the sociopolitical system. In a democratic system such as the one allegedly operative in this small country, there are sacred rights that afford every citizen of the Lebanese state the freedom of belief, expression and association, the freedom to hold and express views about the government and its forms. This freedom of exchange of ideas is required for the advancement of society. If elected officials were to abrogate these sacred rights, they would be labeled tyrants trampling the very rights that led to their election. The latter is precisely what his Holiness wishes and supports when he states 'The government is free to suppress political creeds... and all that is harmful to the people.' This is a dangerous statement for it releases rulers from any restrictions and allows for the establishment of tyrannical rule... From where would an ordinary government elected within a defined system to serve the interests of the people gain the divine wisdom to determine which political ideologies it should oppose and suppress and which ideologies it should support and encourage?... To release the hand of a government elected for a finite term returns us to the slavery of the dark ages."

Saadeh had raised this issue of civil rights before during his first trial, and again after the confrontations with the Lebanese government in February of 1937 that led to his second imprisonment, and he would continue to raise it throughout his life.[92]

The message of this rebuttal is clear: the perpetuation of the interference of religious authorities in the political and national affairs of Syria is incompatible with national unity, the integrity of the state, and the equality of citizens under a common law. Secularism is a prerequisite for modernity and anti-secular formulations are obscurantist and anachronistic.

THE FIRST OF MARCH 1938

The tradition of public celebrations of Saadeh's birthday was formally inaugurated in 1938. The First of March 1938 celebrations were to become the prototype of such meetings for many years to come. A special issue of *an-Nahda* and meetings in many cities were to become the norm for such celebrations.

The Lebanese government was wary of such meetings, and freedom of assembly was not a principle the local governments or the French Mandate cared to honor. On Monday February 28, the Minister of Interior summoned Saadeh to his office to discuss the scope of the planned celebrations. Saadeh assured the minister that no street demonstrations would take place and that the plan called for a series of receptions of delegations coming to congratulate their leader on his 34th birthday.

The plans for the meeting in Beirut involved receptions and speeches at the house of SSNP leadership member Nehmeh Thabit, the location of the June 1, 1935 meeting. Receptions were held in the morning starting at 10am, but the meeting venue was changed

---
92 *Complete Works*, volume 3, pp408-412; volume 8, pp318-320.

The First of March 1938

because of impending rain to a location in Burj Abi Haydar where the full meeting and speeches were delivered. Around three thousand individuals attended the afternoon meeting in Beirut.

Saadeh arrived at the meeting venue at 4pm and his speech lasted two hours. The text of the speech had been printed in a pamphlet of 29 pages and distributed to the branches of the SSNP so it could be read concurrently with the meeting in Beirut. In his speech, Saadeh offered a panoramic view of political events in Syrian politics since the First World War to provide context for his review of the early history of the SSNP. The narrative of this history has become a classic and adopted by most authors. Saadeh did not offer this narrative to be merely documentary, but to be evocative of future expectations.

Saadeh's speech of March 1st, 1938 was to become a landmark document. In this speech, Saadeh endeavored to provide an interpretation of the recent history of Syria and its national movement and to crystallize their narratives for coming generations. "The sounds of our chains continue to resonate in our ears and will continue to resonate in the ears of future generations so that our grandchildren will understand and appreciate the meaning of the life of the nation and how much it will cost of our lives we who then would be grandfathers." While briefly anticipatory of things to come, the speech is mainly informative and interpretive of things past. "After all these trials and tribulations, it behooves us to cast an examining look at our past, our present and our future and determine exactly where we are in reference to our goal and our world."

The speech can be divided into two broad parts addressing two distinct narratives: the first is the narrative of the contemporary political history of Syria and the second the narrative of the recent history of the SSNP. Saadeh introduces the first narrative with an encapsulation of the historical eras that led to modern time in Syria. This encapsulation gives us a glimpse of his understanding of the evolution of Syrian history:

"No nation has succumbed to as momentous and as prolonged grave historical developments with long lasting effects as befell our great nation. Barely had Syria re-affirmed its character during the Roman Empire [including its Byzantine phase] that it encountered the Arab Conquest that required it to change its language. It then succumbed to the Mongol invasion that ravaged the land and ruined Damascus to be followed by the oppressive Turkish conquest. This sequence of events to which also belong the Crusades have interrupted the cultural direction of Syria and made its destiny subject to the interactions of these factors powers and their struggle for supremacy. This engendered social and economic chaos and caused havoc in the civilization of this beautiful land. The convergences of invading hordes from the south, north and west threatened the survival of the Syrian character responsible for the great cultural revolutions that dotted the Mediterranean with its cities and carried forth to its shores the arts of Syrian civilization…"

Saadeh chronicles the political events of more recent times in detail. He specifies that the independence seeking activities that arose during the later decades of the Ottoman period were directed principally at ending Turkish rule and contained no clear direction on establishing solid foundations for national revival and progress. He is putting the so-called *"Great Arab Revolt"* and all associated movements in perspective. This directly leads him to tackling the "Arab Cause" and its religious associations.

"This idea was known under the influence of religious factors as the Arab Cause and it gathered under its banner political activists from Syria, Egypt and later Arabia when it sought a religious symbol to rally around. These activists thought that religious power, the power of descendence from the Prophet and religious zealotry, as a sure path to success… Some imagined the Arab Cause as a reactionary movement to establish an Arab empire and a return to the unfortunate age of Haroun al-Rashid… Others conceived the Arab Cause as a return to religious approaches with a Caliphate or Imamate. Some built an ethnic framework around the Arab Cause while others assumed it a true national cause eliminating in the process the various nations of the Arab world and replacing them with an imagined single nation. Others still considered the Arab Cause as a question of an alliance between Arab nations and were thereby closest to reality."

The narrative of the Lebanese Cause also lays bare its sectarian nature.

"The Arab Cause was not the only manifestation of conflation of national issues with religious issues prior to the advent of the SSNP. The Lebanese Cause was another such manifestation. The origins of this cause go back to the bloody sectarian events of 1860, the fighting that took place between the Druzes and the Christians and ended with the intervention of the Great Powers that had interest in weakening Ottoman control and spreading their influence in these parts. A special system was created for Mount Lebanon to ensure the security of the Christians who represented the majority of its inhabitants… The perpetuation of this system for half a century… engendered in the largest Christian sect that benefited from the system an eagerness to perpetuate the status quo and to create the Lebanese Cause. The collusion of this will to preserve the status quo with foreign political interests led to the creation of the *Grand Liban* and subsequently the institution of the Lebanese Republic. The latter is a political entity finding its reason to exist in the sectarian strife of the last century."

The narratives of the Arab Cause and the Lebanese Cause included in this speech were to become constant ideological foundations. Future restatements in numerous writings by Saadeh and his colleagues in the next decade would enlarge on the detail but remained faithful to the framework delineated therein. Saadeh chides the protagonists of the Arab Cause and the Lebanese Cause for their hypocrisy in thinking that they could dissimulate from each other the flagrant sectarian basis of either of their causes. The closing section of the speech is likely the one that the enemies of the SSNP listened to most attentively:

> "Now that we have vanquished these early difficulties and established our institutions, we see a clear path and have complete faith in our victory... The old political school must be eliminated and be replaced by the national political school capable of achieving reform."

The events of 1st March, 1938 were a wake-up call to the Mandate and local governments that the truce with the SSNP was no longer tenable. Why would the Mandate and its proxy the Lebanese government seek to re-initiate their persecution of Saadeh and the SSNP? In the spring of 1938, the SSNP accelerated its efforts to provide basic military training to its membership and to create a cadre of trained officers as a backbone for a provisional army. The SSNP undertook this step despite its meager resources and was determined to execute this plan in 1938 no matter the hardship and sacrifices.[93]

News of these developments reached the mandate and the Lebanese proxy government via an informer. The Mandate would have seen the crowds in Beirut on March 1, 1938, the incursion of SSNP members into the government offices in Damascus on the same day, and learned through its informers of the plans for the general meeting of 72 party branches from the hinterland, all evidence of the mounting strength of the SSNP.

To foil the spies of the French mandate, the day of his departure appeared the most ordinary one. Saadeh visited the Maaluf household in Beirut, as he was accustomed to do, and even

---

93 *Complete Works*, volume 4, p55.

participated in a simple card game. A restricted number of SSNP leaders came to see him there. He then *"took leave in his usual day to day manner"* and headed immediately out of Lebanon.[94] The day before his departure, the Attorney general of Lebanon had issued a subpoena requiring Saadeh to be present at a meeting to look into a case brought against him by Gabriel Munassa, a failed candidate in the parliamentary elections. The government would have used the pretense of fact finding in the case to expand the search into the existence of the SSNP and level additional charges accordingly.

SEEKING INTERNATIONAL SUPPORT

TRANS-JORDAN

Evidence of the SSNP's presence in Trans-Jordan surfaced March of 1938 in an editorial on the pages of *an-Nahda* whose authorship was previously attributed to Saadeh. Trans-Jordan had always been considered by the SSNP as a part of the Syrian homeland. The editorialist of *an-Nahda* wrote *"In this state invented to satisfy British colonial interests, administrative and governmental forms evolved seemingly as an independent state, but in reality totally subservient to British influence, under the jurisdiction of the British Commissioner in Jerusalem, and controlled in all its branches by British functionaries directly responsible to the Government of Palestine."* After surveying the implications of the 1927 treaty, the editorialist describes the situation east of the Jordan, *"an area isolated from the modern world, deep in the grip of social backwardness, intellectual decay and crushing feudalism."* He finally declares that the SSNP is actively pursuing an active role in the political and social life of the region. By the time of Saadeh's visit, the SSNP had established a small branch in the Emirate.

---

94 Kamal Maalouf Abou-Chaar: *Memoirs of Grandma Kamal: Unique Personal Experiences and Encounters.* World Book Publishing, Beirut, 1999, p 94.

Saadeh stayed in Amman with Nayef Qa'war.[95] Visits with Nayef's family and acquaintances meant that secrecy could not be maintained. Nayef had suggested visiting Emir Abdallah with the hope of reaching a political understanding with him that may facilitate SSNP activity in the Emirate. Due preparations for such a meeting were not possible as events were precipitated by the spreading public awareness of Saadeh's presence in Trans-Jordan. On a visit to *as-Salt* on June 18, a close associate of the Emir knew of Saadeh's presence in the city and came to welcome him. Al-Shanqiti[96] offered to approach the Emir's son who was to visit him that afternoon with a request for an interview with the Emir, an offer that could not be refused. However, when al-Shanqiti called the Emir's office, the information about Saadeh's presence in Trans-Jordan without the knowledge of the security forces raised the ire of the Emir who thereupon reprimanded his police commanders.

Saadeh returned to Amman on that Friday afternoon and on Saturday, June 18 went to visit the Emir at the assigned time. Present were the Chief Minister of Trans-Jordan (Ibrahim Hashim[97]) and the Chief of Police. After the customary polite introductions, the Emir told Saadeh that he did not favor the organization of political parties in his domain and that he had heard that such was Saadeh's purpose in Trans-Jordan. Saadeh offered a non-committal diplomatic answer and took his leave.

After the interview, the Emir and his associates conferred and clearly reached a decision that Saadeh was *persona non grata*

---

95 The narrative of Antoun's stay in Trans-Jordan is derived principally from a letter Antoun wrote to Fakhri Maaluf on June 25, 1938 upon his arrival to Cyprus. *Complete Works, volume 9*, pp32-33.

96 Maan Abu Nowar: *The Jordanian-Israeli War, 1948-1951: A History of the Hashemite Kingdom of Jordan.* Garnet and Ithaca Press, 2002, pp 67. Joseph Andoni Massad: *Colonial Effects: The Making of National Identity in Jordan.* Columbia University Press, NY, 2001, p 91.

97 Saadeh does not identify the Chief Minister's name in his letter, but Hashim was the Chief Minister from 1933 to September 1938. Mary C. Wilson: *King Abdullah, Britain and the Making of Jordan*, p 217.

in the Emirate. A mechanism, however, had to be found to effect his extradition. On Monday evening, two days after the interview, a corporal and a uniformed police officer appeared at Saadeh's place of residence and asked to inspect his papers hoping to find a pretext for his arrest and deportation. Finding his papers in order, the officers impressed on him the need to leave the country the soonest as his presence was causing undue anxiety in government circles. On Tuesday, June 21, Saadeh left Trans-Jordan heading to Tiberias where he visited with the Sayegh family and then continued to Haifa.

The failure of the interview needs to be viewed in the context of the political struggles of the time. Emir Abdallah had been firmly pursuing a policy of strict control of all political activity in his realm and it is understandable that a political dissident from Lebanon would be considered undesirable.

Palestine

From there Saadeh continued to Haifa where he arrived with only three Syrian pounds in his pocket. He had paid the driver five Syrian pounds and referred him to Nayef Qawar for the balance of the trip fare. His visit coincided with dramatic measures by the British in an attempt to stem the tide of infiltration of supporters of the Palestinians from Lebanon and Syria manifested by a barbed wire enclosure [98] called "*Tegart's Wall*" after Sir Charles Tegart, adviser to the Palestine Government on the suppression of terrorism! [99]

---

98 The *New York Times* called it "*the biggest barbed wire fence in the world*". See article "*The Problem of Palestine*", *New York Times*, August 24, 1938, page 20.

99 See the article "Tegart's Wall" in *Time* magazine, Monday June 20, 1938: "*Britain's most ingenious solution for handling terrorism in Palestine was revealed in Geneva last week to the League of Nations Permanent Mandates Commission ... Following a suggestion of mail-fisted Sir Charles Tegart, now adviser to the Palestine Government on the suppression of terrorism, a barbed wire barrier to keep out terrorists is being strung along the entire Palestine frontier at a cost of $450,000. This includes a nine-foot barbed wire fence between Palestine and French-mandated Lebanon and Syria, which border*

In Haifa, Saadeh needed to get in contact with the SSNP branch, but he had no addresses or phone numbers. Fortuitously, he encountered a young British woman whom he had met that past winter when she came to Lebanon to ski. She got him in contact with the SSNP members in the city. The requirements of secrecy precluded the notification of SSNP members in Haifa of the imminent arrival of their leader. It is peculiar, however, that Saadeh did not have their contact information suggesting that his departure from Lebanon was as precipitous as the events suggest. Saadeh stayed for only one night and the following day in Haifa, met with the SSNP membership and reviewed their activities and progress. He sent a coded cable to Beirut informing his colleagues of his arrival at Haifa. Funds for his onward travel were secured through the sales of copies of *Nushu' al-Umam* he carried with him. On Wednesday evening, June 22, he boarded the ship *Tristino* headed for Larnaca, Cyprus.

Cyprus

After landing in Larnaca, Saadeh took a bus to Platres, a mountain town on the southern slopes of the Troodos range in the center of the island. The village is situated in a heavily forested area with pine and cedar trees. The remoteness was suitable for remaining undetected.

Saadeh enjoyed the natural beauty of the area. He planned to stay for 4 to 6 weeks in the area recovering his strength and energies before proceeding on the trip to visit the Syrian diaspora.[100] For a man who needed to recover his strength after years of intense struggle and hardship, Saadeh seemed unable to let go. Over the first month of his stay on the island, he wrote over 30 letters. A third of these letters were to Fakhri Maaluf who at the time held

---

> Palestine on the north and northeast. A lot of Palestine's tougher Arabs come from those two mandates. The fence will be completed in August, announced Sir John. Almost as he spoke, a band of Arab terrorists swooped down on a section of the fence, dubbed Tegart's Wall, ripped it up and carted it across the frontier into Lebanon".

100 Letter to Fakhri Maaluf, June 25, 1938. *Complete Works*, volume 9, pp. 32-34.

the post of President of the High Council, in effect the leader of the SSNP after Saadeh's departure. This was a time for reflection on many events and developments, and Saadeh proceeded to share his thoughts with his closest lieutenant.

Saadeh was certain of the nefarious intent of the Lebanese government and the French Mandate towards him, particularly as the strength of the SSNP became apparent, and they got wind of the military preparations underway. There were irreconcilable differences between the national liberation movement and the colonialists and their cronies.[101] Most of Saadeh's co-workers believed that the threat was real and arrests imminent. Abdallah Qubersi, however, belittled the early signs of the threat such as the closing of *an-Nahda*. His contacts in the Department of Justice led him to believe that these developments were the result of misunderstandings that could be easily resolved. All that was required was for Saadeh and Thabit to visit the examining magistrate for a deposition. He clearly did not see the trap. Saadeh was appalled by Qubersi's naïve assessment and the danger he was exposing him and other SSNP members to by his nonchalance. In addition to sharing this assessment with Fakhri, he wrote a severe reprimand letter to Qubersi chiding him for his cavalier handling of a matter of grave consequences.[102] He told him that his misplaced confidence in the judicial system portrayed a level of unprecedented political ignorance about the subservience of the system to the political forces in government. He reminds him *"the national movement that I [Saadeh] lead is the only real threat to colonial policy and all local political elements in collusions with the colonialists."* He warns Qubersi that if the development in the case of Gabriel Munassa leads to his extradition from the British area of control into the hands of the French, that he will hold him responsible. *"If I am captured, you will be my Judas!"*

---

101 Letter to Fakhri Maaluf, July 2, 1938. *Complete Works*, volume 9, pp. 40-45.
102 Letter to Abdallah Qubersi, July1, 1938. *Ibid.*, pp. 38-39.

Saadeh's departure from Syria had been precipitous and under great secrecy. Preparations for the trip to the Syrian diaspora could not be undertaken or announced until after he left Syria. Within a week after his arrival in Cyprus, he started in earnest the planning for the larger trip. He wrote to Fakhri Maaluf:

> "The communications department has to issue a press release to the overseas branches of the SSNP and the Syrian press announcing the trip and preparing for the campaign I will undertake. The Office of Overseas Branches has to send instructions to the leaders of the various regions to prepare."[103]

From Cyprus, Saadeh had planned to go to Egypt and from there to the Gold Coast (present day Ghana, but at the time a British colony) and onward to the Americas. The trip was to start in mid-August 1938.[104] He hoped to reach North America before a delegation of the *Bloc* headed there and then visit South America.[105]

Throughout his stay in Cyprus, Saadeh's letters to his lieutenants in Syria stressed the need to continue with the military training program. He proposed specific individuals for the tasks,[106] and called for the organization of commando units under great secrecy.[107] He informed Fakhri of his discussion with Qawar in Transjordan as to the feasibility of arms purchases there and seems to have been seconded in his plans by the great enthusiasm of Nehmeh Thabit for the 'military option.'[108]

---

103 Letter to Fakhri Maaluf, June 28, 1938. *Ibid.*, pp 35-37.
104 Letter to Fakhri Maaluf, July 12, 1938, *Ibid.*, pp. 55-58.
105 Letter to Fakhri Maaluf, June 28, 1938. *Ibid*, pp. 35-37.
106 Letters to Fakhri Maaluf, July 2, 9 and 12, 1938, *Ibid.*, pp. 40-58.
107 Letter to William Saba, July 2, 1938, *Ibid*, pp 46-47.
108 Letter to Fakhri Maaluf, July 9, 1938, *Ibid*, p. 48-54.

ITALY

Saadeh's original plan was to proceed from Cyprus to the Americas, first to the United States, and then to Central and South America to visit the Syrian communities and establish a system of political and financial support for the SSNP operations in the homeland. The discovery of his whereabouts by the French Mandate and the risk of extradition from Cyprus necessitated a rapid departure from Cyprus prior to the completion of his original travel plans. It is likely that he used the time to explore the potential of establishing political relations with European powers that could be more favorable to the Syrian cause than the French and British. There is a gap in the documentation of his whereabouts of one month between his last letter to Fakhri Maaluf from Cyprus (July 23) and the letter to him from Rome (August 22). What we learn from subsequent documentation is that he arrived in Rome, and had made contact with Italian authorities who had been very courteous towards him and the SSNP. The Italian authorities had afforded him a secure means of communication with the SSNP in the homeland via their diplomatic courier system, and had offered to host members of the SSNP in Italian universities to pursue graduate degrees in fields of their choice. These developments suggest a nascent degree of cooperation. It is unclear, however, why there was no further development of the relationship. The Italian authorities already had their collaborators among Syrian groups, notably Christian separatists in Lebanon and advocates of Pan-Arabism in the person of Shakib Arslan. They may have found these groups more amenable to their purposes. Saadeh stayed in Italy until mid-October 1938 and from there traveled to Germany.

GERMANY

A branch of the SSNP formed in Berlin in 1937 among Syrian students studying in the German capital. The leader of the branch was Masoon Abideen who had originally studied at Konigsberg and then moved to Berlin to complete his studies towards a doctorate. Abideen was very active among Syrians students in

Antoun Saadeh greeted by members of the SNP branch in Berlin and Syrian students studying in the German capital. 1938.

Germany, contributed articles to *an-Nahda* in Beirut, and appears to have established contacts with German authorities obtaining a license to publish a periodical in Arabic dedicated to the issues of the SSNP.[109] After some initial difficulties, Saadeh was able to establish contact with the SSNP branch and planned a trip to Germany to visit his Party members and explore the political position of the German government vis-à-vis Syria. Like their Italian counterparts, German authorities treated Saadeh with great courtesy for his travel to Germany and during his stay. The members of the SSNP met Saadeh at the Berlin train station in organized formations with the SSNP salute. The German fiancée of Abideen presented Saadeh with a bouquet of flowers and the group escorted Saadeh to the *Kaiserhof* hotel where Saadeh spent his stay in Berlin and where he held various meetings with SSNP members and Arab students.[110]

---

109 The periodical named *al-Rasa'el* (Letters) was still in publication in 1941. Letter to William Bahliss, April 8, 1941. *Complete Works*, volume 10, pp.66-67.

110 Fawzi Razeeq: *Kayf ta'araftu ela Saadeh* (How I met Saadeh), first published in *al-Rasa'el*, a publication by the SSNP branch in Berlin and republished in *Souria al-Jadida* April 26, 1941.

He evidently met with German officials concerned with the affairs of the Middle East, and delivered a lecture at Humboldt University about the political vision of the SSNP and its strategy for Syria.[111] There is no available documentation about the nature of these early contacts with the German government. The German government appears to have been reluctant at this point in time to overtly undertake any activity that may appear belligerent towards French or British colonial dominions.[112] Further, what we learn from subsequent correspondence between Saadeh and the SSNP delegation tasked with re-establishing contacts with the German authorities in 1941, was that Saadeh was disappointed that the German government had given preference to its relations with advocates of Pan-Arabism and Pan-Islamism like Shakib Arslan and the Mufti of Palestine Amin Husseini over an alliance with the SSNP.[113]

Saadeh's visit to Germany was naturally a fodder for his opponents' criticism. A year after the visit, in October 1939, the *Arab Agency* based in Damascus claimed that Saadeh had traveled to Berlin with two associates (Rushdy Maaluf and Shafiq Samara) to direct the Arabic broadcast of Berlin radio. Further, the *Arab Agency* claimed that on behest of the German government, Saadeh was collaborating with Daoud Mujais in Berlin to publish an Arabic newspaper in the German capital.[114] Daoud Mujais was a public supporter of the SSNP in Mexico where he resided at the time of the claim,[115] and by then Saadeh had been in South America for close to a year.

---

111 *Complete Works*, volume 3, pp 455.

112 Francis Nicosia: *The Third Reich and the Palestine question*, I.B. Tauris & Co., London, 1985, pp170-171.

113 Letter to William Bahliss, August 6, 1941. *Complete Works*, volume 10, p.126; and September 24, 1941, *ibid.*, pp.168-172.

114 Reported in *Souria al-Jadidah* October 21, 1939.

115 Daoud Mujais was a social reformer and political activist. He was a distant relative of Saadeh and active in Syria before World War I and in Chile and Mexico after.

Exile and Repression (1938-1947)

After completing his visit in Germany, Saadeh returned to Italy and sailed from the port of Genoa to South America. Earlier in the century, the Syrians in South America had shown a commitment to the Syrian cause, particularly when nationalist thinkers like Saadeh's father Dr. Khalil Saadeh were in their midst. Saadeh would later describe his stay in South America as the most odious prison sentence he had ever experienced, but such were not the indications when he embarked on his voyage. He left Syria as the leader of the foremost organized political movement, an embodiment of Syria's salvation and future. His trip was to secure the implements, financial and political, for the national liberation movement. He carried with him a legacy of struggle, a vision of lofty ideals, and the foundations of a new school of thought. He was bringing to his fellow Syrians in the diaspora the opportunity to join the ranks of a transformative political-social-cultural movement that would restore their dignity and hope.

Dr. Khalil Saadeh had died in 1934 and the flames of Syrian nationalism and militancy had weakened. The propaganda of the Mandate and separatist and confessional causes awakened old hostilities and contradictions. The Mandate authorities had contrived with separatists to defame the cause of the SSNP and to raise suspicions in South American states against the activity of Saadeh.

On arrival in Brazil at the end of November 1938, Saadeh rapidly initiated public activities to support the cause of his party and to bring information about the Syrian National movement into the mainstream of public opinion through interviews with Brazilian newspapers. The Syrian community in Brazil knew Saadeh because of his prior residence there and by his reputation. He had lived in Brazil for ten years from 1920 until 1930 and had participated in the cultural life, not only of the Syrian community but the broader Brazilian community as well. Saadeh wasted no time in embarking on a very active and dynamic range of activities in the Syrian community.

With the advent of 1939, Saadeh saw the opportunity to publish a weekly newspaper in São Paulo. The first issue of *Souria al-Jadida* (The New Syria) appeared on March 11, 1939 and the journal was one of the enduring achievements of Saadeh's visit to Brazil. Saadeh used this vehicle to convey to the Syrians in the diaspora and back home in Syria the history of the struggle of the SSNP and its approach to international and national events. The newspaper was the sole public forum and mouthpiece of the SSNP at that time given the draconian suppression of freedom of speech in Syria by the French. Saadeh's efforts in São Paulo progressed well and many elements in the Syrian community were showing favorable responses to the principles that laid the foundation of a strong union in the Syrian nation and eliminated all causes of sectarian discord and socio-economic injustices. On Saadeh's 35th birthday, a banquet was held in his honor during which he continued the tradition of using the occasion to expand on the teachings and program of the SSNP.

The publication of *Souria al-Jadida* was a clear indicator of the success of Saadeh in making inroads into the political life of the Syrian community in Brazil. It also signified that the SSNP had now acquired a platform of considerable reach since the closure by the Mandate authorities of *an-Nahda* the year before. Saadeh's success must have alarmed the enemies of the SSNP and galvanized them into plotting a counter campaign centered on slander and innuendos. Taking advantage of the Brazilian laws prohibiting political activities on behalf of foreign powers, Lebanese separatist elements in the community, in collusion with French diplomatic representatives, advanced to the Brazilian authorities accusations that Saadeh and his companions were agents of European Nazi and Fascist regimes. On March 23,

EXILE AND REPRESSION (1938-1947)

1939, the *Delegacia de Order Politica e Social* issued a warrant for the arrest of Saadeh and his two closest aides. During his incarceration, Saadeh was kept mostly incommunicado and treated poorly.[1] Saadeh was subjected to a detailed interrogation and one can surmise that it must have involved queries about the nature of his organization and any associations with foreign powers.

It is clear from subsequent developments that he succeeded in demonstrating to the Brazilian authorities the independence of his activity from any allegiance or cooperation with foreign powers. He was released on April 30, 1939, five weeks after his arrest. The Brazilian authorities, however, still had to deal with the French request for extradition. To avoid an uncomfortable diplomatic squabble, the Brazilian authorities invited Saadeh to leave the country by the date of the expiration of his original entry permit, two weeks after his release.

Saadeh left Brazil on May 14, and headed to Argentina.[2] The short interval after the release suggests that leaving Brazil may have been a condition of his release. His exoneration, however, was critical as it meant that his colleagues in Brazil would not run afoul of the Brazilian authorities and that their organizational activities as well as their publications could continue unmolested. The arrest, however, had long lasting disruptive effects and a dampening effect on the enthusiasm of the community. In Brazil, SSNP members remained fearful of the authorities, a condition that significantly hampered organizational efforts.[3] The original plan of Saadeh's trip to the Syrian diaspora was to visit the Syrian communities in South America, and then continue to Mexico and subsequently to the United States. Various factors, however, intervened to prolong

---

1   Letter to Ibrahim Tannous July 22, 1939, *Complete Works*, Volume 9, pp. 105-108.

2   Letter to Rachid Chakkour, May 29, 1939, *Complete Works*, Volume 9, page 88.

3   Letter to George Bunduqi, January 17, 1940, *ibid.*, page 222.

his stay in Argentina until the definitive refusal of the French Consulate to renew his travel papers sealed his fate and confined him to the Argentine Republic for the duration of the Second World War and beyond.

In his hurried departure from Brazil, Saadeh had left both the organization of SSNP's activities and the editorial staffing of *Souria al-Jadida* unfinished. His organizational efforts had been thwarted by his protracted incarceration. On arriving in Argentina, he was faced with the dual task of establishing a base of activity in Argentina and simultaneously attending to the needs of the nascent organization in Brazil.

In Argentina, Saadeh was to find a more nuanced political environment and the host country proved more tolerant of his activities. By October 1939, enough groundwork had been laid for Saadeh to appoint a central administrative committee for the SSNP branch in Argentina.[4] The absence of capable aides meant that Saadeh had to undertake the entire burden of grass root activities necessary for the establishment of SSNP branches throughout the Argentine Republic traveling over long distances by rail to centers of Syrian settlements.

The start of hostilities with Germany gave France the pretext to tighten its grip on the colonies and to expand its persecution of the SSNP.[5] During his stay in Tucumán, Saadeh received news of renewed French prosecution of the SSNP in Syria on the pretext of association with enemy powers. The French Mandate authorities had issued a press release in their campaign against the SSNP, declaring that the SSNP and its members were being prosecuted because of their association with a foreign government, proof of which suposedly lay in the fact that Antoun Saadeh was in Berlin directing propaganda via the Arab section of Berlin

---

4   *Sadar an Maktab al-Zaim*, page 244-246.

5   *Souria al-Jadida*, Issue 40, November 25, 1939, *I'tiqal arkan Qawmiyeen* (Arrest of Nationalist Leaders), *Jihadan wa qiyadatan* (Two struggles and two leaderships), *Complete Works*, Volume 3, 432-33, 434-438.

Radio and was allegedly helped in his efforts by Daoud Mujais. However, neither Saadeh nor Daoud Mujais were in Berlin at the time, as Saadeh was in Argentina and Daoud Mujais was residing in Mexico. This fabricated news item did have political and legal implications as it was being introduced as evidence into the judiciary proceedings against SSNP members.[6] Saadeh hastened back to Buenos Aires to secure refuting documents. He appeared to have obtained a *"Certificat de vie"* ("Proof of Life" certificate) from the French embassy in Buenos Aires, on November 29, 1939 which he forwarded to Beirut.[7]

While engaged in the myriad meetings and activities, Saadeh did not lose sight of his onward travel plans to the rest of the Americas. In January 1940, he informed the SSNP branch in Mexico that his trip would definitely take place in May and that the Mexican branch could start making the necessary arrangements for his visit.[8] The prolonged stay in Argentina to cement the gains made for the SSNP and its cause, however, meant that his travel documents issued by the authorities in Beirut needed to be renewed by the French diplomatic missions that handled all such transactions for Syrians abroad. The French Ambassador, by now alerted to the interest and attitude of the Mandate authorities in Beirut towards Saadeh and the SSNP, wrote to them seeking guidance on how to handle the request.[9] The reply received from Beirut and relayed by the Foreign Office on March 2, 1940 is telling: "Antoun Saadeh,

---

6 The receipt of correspondence relaying the news suggests that until this date Saadeh had maintained regular contacts with the SSNP leadership in Syria. Letter to George Bunduqi, November 28, 1939, *Complete Works*, Volume 9, page 199.

7 Jean Dayeh, *Tajribat Fakhry Maaluf*, Dar Nelson, Beirut, 2004, page 269.

8 Letter to Assaf Abi Murad, January 18, 1940, *Complete Works*, Volume 9, page 223.

9 Peyrouton wrote in a cable to the High Commissioner in Beirut: "I have received a request for a Lebanese passport for all destinations for Mr. Khaled Abdul Wahed, of Tripoli, Lebanon, secretary of Antoun Saadeh, leader of the Parti Populaire Syrien... Can I respond favorably to the request? It would be of interest to understand the status of the applicant in addition to that of Antoun Saadeh". AMAE-N, Ambassade à Buenos Aires, Cable from the French Embassy Buenos Aires to the High Commission in Beirut, February 22, 1940. File Antoun Saadeh.

Saadeh at a meeting of the SSNP branch in Buenos Aires, Argentina, circa 1940.

leader of the *Parti Populaire Syrien* is accused by the Military Court of sedition and plotting against the internal and external security of the states under the French Mandate... The renewal of his passport would facilitate the intrigues undertaken by him abroad. It would be therefore appropriate to refuse the renewal." The decision was equivalent to a court order of exile.[10]

With the advent of 1940, Saadeh may have been buoyed by the SSNP's public successes in Argentina, although a robust organization was yet to emerge and the conditions of the activities in Brazil were a constant source of disappointment. The best manifestation of the success of the SSNP was the banquet held in honor of Saadeh's birthday on March 1. In May 1940, he undertook another tour of the northern Argentine provinces to promote the cause of the SSNP and invigorate its nascent organization.

The initial successes of Saadeh in Tucumán in November 1939 and in Santiago in May 1940 were solely due to his personal

---

10 Letter to Ibrahim Tannous, May 27, 1940. *Complete Works*, Volume 9, page 268-272.

efforts, but the absence of a team to shepherd these successes, nurture discipline and deeper understanding of the cause and the means to serve it, meant that these units remained weak. Saadeh had to reorganize the directorate of the Tucumán branch repeatedly after its inception in November 1939. He reorganized the directorate in May 1941 because of its "administrative paralysis,"[11] in June 1942,[12] and again in December 1943.[13] The directorate of Santiago was reorganized for the same reason in June 1942,[14] this pattern of paralysis could also be observed in other units.

The immediate communication needs of the SSNP in Argentina in the face of recurrent attacks led Saadeh to put into effect an original plan of publishing a newspaper in Argentina, a plan he had delayed to preserve the role of *Souria al-Jadida*. The first issue of *az-Zawba'a* (Cyclone) appeared on August 1, 1940. After a weak start, the periodical gained a robust structure and a high quality content even though its physical form suffered from the idiosyncrasies of the printing presses in Argentina.

Saadeh attempted a diplomatic overture with the French in a letter he addressed to the French ambassador dated October 1, 1940, stating the position of the SSNP and its willingness to start a dialogue with the French. The French, in the words of their High Commissioner in Beirut, asked for the unconditional surrender of a foe against whom he had been waging a vicious asymmetrical war since the start of hostilities in Europe. They were unnerved by the resilience of this foe that did not desist from its struggle and capitulate. They had accused the SSNP of being an agent of foreign interests, namely those of Germany, alleging that Saadeh was in Berlin, while French diplomatic pouches conveyed news of his activities in Brazil and Argentina, and

---

11 *Sadar an Maktab al-Zaim*, page 278.
12 *Ibid.*, page 284.
13 *Ibid.*, page 300.
14 *Ibid.*, page 282.

the French-controlled local courts had in their files a "certificat de vie" issued to him by the French embassy in Buenos Aires! They also accused the SSNP of receiving foreign money (an often repeated claim never substantiated in prior arrests and prosecutions) while the confiscated financial records of the Party showed meager resources. Furthermore, the French accused the SSNP of being recalcitrant and unresponsive to French offers of dialogue while they themselves violated their promise of safe conduct and arrested those SSNP representatives who presented themselves for negotiation.

The advent of 1941 carried momentous developments in Syria in the wake of the French military defeat, the establishment of the Vichy government and the implications of such on the balance of power in the Near East between British and French forces. Saadeh subjected the claims and counterclaims of Axis and Allied propaganda to thorough analysis and criticism on the pages of *az-Zawba'a*. The pronouncements of Foreign Affairs ministers and various colonial potentates were luring the Syrians into a familiar trap. Saadeh was particularly critical of Syrian politicians who became mouthpieces for foreign interests. Just as he ridiculed the proxy-ruling elites in Damascus and Beirut for their sycophantic expressions of allegiance and solidarity to the cause of France at the onset of the war, he now criticized the political elites that were clamoring in support of the Axis cause. A particular target was Shakib Arslan who emerged as the major spokesperson for the pro-Axis trend. The activities of Shakib Arslan and the adherents of his Pan-Islamism/Pan-Arabism movement were sowing discord and division within the Syrian community, and his advocated positions of wholesale reliance on foreign powers were contrary to the national interests of Syria.[15]

---

15 When in 1941 Germany issued its communiqué in support of "Arab peoples", Arslan quickly endorsed it. Saadeh warned against such wholesale endorsement that may have been motivated by service to German interests rather than Syria's national cause. *Takrar al-Aghlat al-Madiyat* (Repeating Old Mistakes), *Complete Works*, Volume 4, pp. 143-45.

Shakib Arslan and his cousin Amin[16] were the driving force behind the Arab Congress[17] that convened in Argentina in 1941 which was confusing Syria's international position, and Shakib Arslan's praise of sycophants like Rachid Khouri[18] was giving fodder to their malignant influences in the community. Discrediting Arslan and exposing his servitude to foreign interests[19] and his sectarian worldview were necessary in the battle to defeat internal enemies of the Syrian cause. In his writings about Arslan, Saadeh charted the varied and complicated career of the man who was dubbed the "Prince of Eloquence" (*Amir al-Bayan*) for his prodigious literary productivity.[20]

Contacts between Saadeh and the SSNP in Syria had been curtailed and ultimately severed by persecution and censorship. What little information that was gleaned from general news items was meager but suggested that the SSNP remained defiant in the face of the unremitting onslaught of French colonial oppression.

---

16 In his writings about the Arslan cousins, Saadeh avoided using their traditional titles of Emir as he had done with other notables with titles. He considered this practice as a direct consequence of the reform principles of the SSNP and its call for the abolition of feudalism in all its forms and derivatives including pseudo-aristocratic titles. *Inhiyar Dawlat al-Alqab: Nazra fi al-Aristocratiya as-Souria* (The Collapse of the Titles' Sate: A View of Syrian Aristocracy), *Complete Works*, Volume 6, pp. 15-19.

17 *Li'bat al-Mu'tamar al-Araby* (The Ploy of the Arab Congress), *Complete Works*, Volume 4, pp. 172-76.

18 Shakib Arslan was a self-promoter who ladled public accolades to sycophants who would return the favor. Such for example was his attitude towards Rashid Khoury, the mercurial religion hopper, who was praised by Arslan for his adoption of Islam (Khoury's return to Christianity (albeit of the Arius kind) is conveniently ignored). *Rasula al-Mahazel*, *Complete Works*, Volume 4, pp. 184-87.

19 Saadeh labelled Shakib Arslan as "the agent of German propaganda in the Arab World". *Souria wal-Iradat al-Ajnabiyah* (Syria and Foreign Schemes), *Complete Works*, Volume 5, pp. 218-21.

20 Arslan kept his name in print between the world wars by producing a journalistic and literary corpus of formidable proportions: he wrote 20 books and 2000 articles. Raja Adal, "Constructing Transnational Islam: The East-West network of Shakib Arslan" in *Intellectuals in the Modern Islamic World*, edited by Stephane Dudoignon, Komatsu Hisao and Kosugi Yasushi, Routledge, London, 2006, pp. 176-210.

Saadeh continued his grassroots efforts to reach as wide an audience for the SSNP platform among the Syrians in Argentina as his energies and health allowed. In April 1941, we find him traveling to Pergamino. Saadeh delivered a lecture on "Critical Factors in the Syrian Quest for a New Era."[21] In May 1941, he traveled to Tucumán in north-west Argentina to attend to deteriorating conditions in the SSNP branch.[22]

His efforts to expand the footprint of the SSNP in the Americas consumed all of his time. Saadeh particularly targeted the Syrian community in Chile as it was financially and politically dynamic. The Chilean community was well positioned to support the SSNP both financially and politically.[23] A social guide of the community published in 1941 by the Palestinian Club reflects a population in the main cities of Chile with many prosperous notables.[24] The success however was modest and fleeting.

One of the most interesting and pivotal series of articles to appear during Saadeh's years of exile is titled *as-Sira' al-Fikri fi al-Adab as-Suri* (Conceptual Controversies in Syrian Literature) which first appeared on the pages of *az-Zawba'a* in 1942 and was published soon after in book form. The importance of this series and its lasting effect on intellectual and literary currents in

---

21 *Complete Works*, Volume 4, page 208

22 Letter to Juliette, May 10, 1941, *Rasa'el ila Dia'*, page 78. Letter to Juliette, May 15, 1941, *ibid.*, page 79.

23 *Associacion Commercial Sirio-Palestina: Las Industrias de las Collectivades de Habla Arabe en Chile*, Santiago, Chile, 1937. The national fervor of the community also manifested itself in periodicals such as *al-Watan* published by Daoud Mujais between 1920 and 1928. Mercedes del Amo: *La Literatura de los Periodicos Arabes de Chile*. MEAH, Seccion Arabe-Islam 55:3-35, 2006.

24 The Business guide estimated that there were over 10,000 Syrians in Chile. Like most Syrian communities in the Americas, they worked predominantly in commercial activities with emphasis on trade, industry and small enterprises. The community also had a sizeable body of professionals particularly in healthcare with around 75 professional physicians and pharmacists. *Guia Social de la Colonia Arabe en Chile (Siria – Palestina – Libanesa)*, recopilacion y direccion Ahmad Hassan Matar, obra Auspiciada por el Club Palestino, Imprenta Ahues Hnos, Santiago, Chile, 1941.

modern Arabic literature cannot be overemphasized. The style of the book is of an elegant philosophical purity and the concepts it presents are of great originality and import.[25]

The growth of the branches of the SSNP in Argentina was one of those effervescent events that follow the application of a *force majeure* to a previously dormant community, namely Saadeh's presence. As the description of his trips within the Argentinean Republic demonstrate, his presence, talks and example reverberated within the Syrian communities and enthusiastic elements joined the party. There was, however, a shortage of capable individuals who could be relied upon to harness the enthusiasm and lead the party branches. This deficit of leaders at the grass root level within the Syrian communities was to lead to nefarious consequences: members brought into the SSNP branches their squabbles, conflicts, and preconceived notions as to what the SSNP was or ought to do, without local leaders to indoctrinate them in the new system. This chaos meant that the resources of the members and the community could not be marshaled for the cause. Further, the conflicts were to dissipate the momentum created by Saadeh's work and sap his energies and patience.

It is against this framework that we need to understand Saadeh's repeated postponement of his trip to North America until that time when it became impossible to undertake. He perceived that the Argentinean SSNP was still a weak sapling that would not survive his departure. Saadeh had undertaken a Herculean task: the organization of the Syrian diaspora globally to support a national endeavor at home. The conditions of the SSNP and the imperatives of the ongoing global struggle (World War II) forced him to undertake it alone. The intervention of the war

---

25 The eight articles appeared biweekly in the issues of *az-Zawba'a* starting on August 15, 1942 and ending on December 1, 1942. In the preface to the first edition, Saadeh indicates that he had made some minor corrections to the text. Further edits were made to the second edition published after his return to Syria in 1947.

made the undertaking even more daunting. Any success in the diaspora would be impossible to translate to the homeland under the conditions of universal warfare. The conflict had severed any potential venues for such a translation. Even the simple exchange of information, let alone the provision of financial support, was rendered impossible by the extension of the war to the Near East and North Africa. Such conditions were bound to generate feelings of futility in a diaspora that was not vibrant with national sentiment to begin with. This explains Saadeh's repeated and persistent efforts of highlighting on the pages of *Souria al-Jadida* and *az-Zawba'a* the achievements of the SSNP in Syria, even digging for glimpses of its activities in the confused and meager reports of wire agencies more pre-occupied with the movements of colossal armies than the occasional demonstration or pamphlet by a clandestine persecuted political group. Saadeh maintained a valiant effort through 1940 and 1942 and his success is reflected in the regularity of the publications of *Souria al-Jadida* and *az-Zawba'a* and the meetings of the party and the founding of cultural institutions.

By 1943, however, the toll of the global conflict was sapping any residual enthusiasm in the community and defections and abandonment became frequent. This was further compounded by recurrent rumors about the disquiet of Argentinean authorities vis-à-vis foreign political activities, rumors that were largely untrue, but nevertheless effective in scaring the faint-hearted. Questions about the relevance of any political work in the diaspora under the conditions of the local conflict and the prevalent conditions of the Syrian diaspora communities became more frequent even among leading members of the SSNP. The inspiration of a grand national undertaking was threatened by the mundane and weighed by a sense of incapacity and futility. Saadeh must have felt like a lone warrior in the arena hobbled rather than succored by his aides. The language of his letters became terse and harsh. The actions and statements of his lieutenants exasperated him. His reputed tolerance and patience frayed. Not only did he see that he could not render aid and support to his organization at home, let alone change the course of political events, but even his personal dignity is assailed from within without the SSNP. The SSNP opponents however had readily grasped the central role Saadeh played in the SSNP. They likely reasoned that he was the critical pillar upon which rested the existence and success of the organization and therefore they focused their attacks on him personally.

Constrained to remain in Argentina with no means of financial subsistence, Saadeh was forced to go into small trade. His goals were to provide for his family, to safeguard the dignity of his office as leader of the SSNP, and to support the activities of the SSNP, notably the publication of *az-Zawba'a* and the diffusion of SSNP ideology among Syrian immigrants. This avenue left him open to treachery by individuals that attempted, and sometimes succeeded, to defraud him of the fruits of his labor. Saadeh was facing financial ruin, the dignity of his office was the target of the basest calumny, and his precious energies diverted from serving the national cause. Ironically, these calamitous developments were not the consequence of interventions by any of the numerous foes and enemies of the SSNP, but rather by SSNP members, some of whom had professed devotion for many years, and were trusted and valued by both Saadeh and his wife. Despite his preoccupation with commercial ventures, Saadeh continued his devoted work for the cause of the SSNP. In this murky environment, Saadeh had to supervise the publications of two Party newspapers, attend to the operations of the SSNP branches in Argentina, Brazil, Chili, Mexico, the USA and western Africa. Throughout 1944, he managed to provide material for and supervise *az-Zawba'a*. True, he did not pursue in these issues any in depth philosophical subjects as he had done in the preceding years, and the majority of his articles were topical. Nevertheless, his writing continued to reflect his incisive intellect and he continued to expound on the tenets of SSNP ideology and worldview.

Renewed Repression in the Homeland

Saadeh's departure from Syria coincided with developing international conditions that led the Mandate to revise its policy of containment towards the SSNP via local governments, to a more brutal policy of broad and sweeping interventions. The policy of containment had its successes in disrupting the planned spread, organization, and growth of the SSNP. The international political horizon, however, foretold of a major conflagration, and the Mandates, French and British alike, needed a more secure control of the Eastern Mediterranean. National liberation movements could not be tolerated to operate at any level. The SSNP would experience this change in colonial policy directly, particularly at the level of its leadership. Many of its most experienced leaders and organizers would be apprehended and incarcerated for prolonged periods of time. Hundreds would be incarcerated in concentration camps. Devoted but inexperienced replacements would emerge. Nevertheless, the disruptive actions of the Mandate would exhaust the human resources of the SSNP, force a lack of centralized organized authority, result in disharmonious regional initiatives, and a widespread lull in militancy.

Immediately after Saadeh's departure from Beirut in June of 1938, the Mandate authority's forces raided the offices of the SSNP[26] and suspended the publication of *an-Nahda*.[27] A campaign of targeted arrests continued throughout the summer of 1938.[28] Despite this atmosphere of intimidation and repression, the SSNP continued to operate and held a general meeting of the heads of its administrative units in September of 1938.[29] The actions of the Mandate forced the Party into its clandestine mode of operations to protect its constituency, but it continued its defiant stance by issuing public statements, staging

---

26 Jureij, Gibran: *Min al-Ju'bat* (From my Files), Volume 4, Beirut, 1993, p.225.

27 *Ibid.*, p.226.

28 *Ibid.*, pp. 250-262.

29 *Ibid.*, p.278.

Exile and Repression (1938-1947)

ad hoc public demonstrations, and publicly commemorating its traditional occasions such as the first of March 1939.[30]

The French had greatly increased their military presence in the eastern Mediterranean in anticipation of the repercussions of the impending conflict in Europe. American Embassy dispatches, which monitored French military strength, clearly demonstrate the dramatic increases in the French military presence by 1940, even when compared with their troops in place during the 1925 uprisings. In 1925, the French had 20,000 troops in Syria supplemented by 6,500 Syrian soldiers under the control of French officers.[31] The French troops themselves were largely colonial consisting of Moroccan, Algerian and Senegalese soldiers with French officers. By early 1940, the number of troops exceeded 100,000 and was still largely composed of colonials.[32] This change in military strength made it effectively unlikely that the SSNP would have been able alone to dislodge the French. The numbers of French troops decreased after the armistice with Germany, following the defeat and the establishment of the Vichy government in France, but the residual strength of 64,000 French troops still in Syria by December of 1940 was a formidable barrier.

Following the outbreak of the Second World War, the French authorities proclaimed martial law, and banned the SSNP on October 7, 1939 and unleashed a campaign of persecution against its membership.[33] Hundreds of SSNP members were arrested and held in detention camps without trial. The French claimed that the SSNP was collaborating with France's enemies and as proof claimed that Saadeh was in Berlin. Saadeh who was by then in

---

30 *Ibid.*, p. 435.
31 Dispatch from US Embassy in Constantinople to the Office Chief of Staff, Military Intelligence Division, January 2, 1925.
32 Military Attaché Report, Military Intelligence Division, War Department General Staff, Ankara, December 31, 1940.
33 Jureij, Gibran: *Min al-Ju'bat*, Volume 4, p.519.

Argentina obtained proof of his whereabouts from the French embassy in Buenos Aires and he dispatched this to the SSNP in Lebanon which debunked the French claim.[34] In the midst of this campaign, the French resorted to subterfuge to track and arrest members of the SSNP leadership. Claiming interest in negotiating with the SSNP, the French authorities promised immunity for representatives that the SSNP might send to negotiate. However, when Nehmeh Thabit presented himself at the appointed place, he was unceremoniously arrested.[35] The remaining members of the leadership relocated their headquarters to the rural region of al-Kura in the north of Lebanon taking advantage of remote cabins and caves in the area.[36]

The misfortunes of war did not alter the attitude of the French imperialists vis-à-vis movements of national liberation. As the persecution continued after the armistice between France and Germany in June of 1940, the SSNP maintained its acts of defiance and resistance issuing public statements and distributing pamphlets on a regular basis in the latter half of 1940.[37] It also continued in the practice of impromptu public speeches at any opportunity in various areas particularly in the urban centers of Beirut, Damascus and Aleppo.[38] In August of 1940, the military French court issued sentences of imprisonment and exile against a large number of SSNP leaders tried in absentia. The sentences ranged from 10 to 20 years of imprisonment followed by equal periods of exile to be served consecutively!

French efforts at apprehending SSNP leaders were successful and replacement leaders were arrested sometimes within days of assuming office, particularly following any conspicuous acts of defiance. When the lead executive of the SSNP issued a

---

34 *Ibid.*, p.558.
35 *Ibid.*, p.524.
36 *Ibid.*, p.545.
37 *Ibid.*, p.661.
38 *Ibid.*, p.667.

EXILE AND REPRESSION (1938-1947)

communique exposing the efforts of France to ship the Lebanese gold reserve to France, he was arrested within 2 days![39] Because of the impossibility of maintaining a full cadre of leaders, the SSNP experimented with administrative solutions reducing the number of functions and empowering single individuals with broad executive privileges.[40] The hinterland branches were equally disrupted by the repression but continued to operate exploring new alliances with opposition groups in their areas, particularly the party of Dr. Shahbandar who had been recently assassinated.[41] In response to the difficult conditions, decentralization of authority began to take root.[42]

As the imminent confrontation between Vichy forces and the British in Palestine and Iraq approached, concern over the fate of the political prisoners galvanized their families to lobby for their release. The effort was led by Nehmeh Thabit's sister Claudia, herself an active member of the SSNP. Several political notables and clergy approached General Dentz interceding on behalf of political prisoners interned in Southern Lebanon at the concentration camp of Mieh wa Mieh and the fortress of Rashaya, in the direct path of any invading force from Palestine. Dentz was facing serious shortages in military equipment and personnel. He was also having serious problems with defections, not only by French officers and soldiers defecting to the de Gaulle camp, but also from paramilitary forces made up mostly of contingents of ethnic minorities (Circassians, Druzes etc.). Indeed, the defections of Circassian paramilitaries prior to the British assault on June 8, and Druze paramilitaries during the fighting contributed significantly to the rapid deterioration of the Vichy front south of Damascus, and accelerated the advance of British forces towards the Syrian capital.

---

39   Ibid., p.716.
40   Jureij, Gibran: *Min al-Ju'bat* (From my Files), Volume 5, Beirut, in press, p.14.
41   Ibid., p.15.
42   Ibid., p.59.

Faced with the intercession of the Lebanese notables and clergy, Dentz found a suitable solution to his problem that would simultaneously provide him with paramilitary forces and trim the ranks of nationalist opposition. He requested as a term of the release of the political prisoners that the SSNP marshal its forces to support the Vichy war effort. An SSNP representative met with French officers to coordinate activities and receive arms and instructions. The reluctance of French officers to dispense weapons to a group only recently considered an enemy of France, and the policy of the French to equip paramilitary forces with obsolete weapons and limited ammunitions, may have saved the SSNP from certain disaster. Paramilitary battalions were expected to bear the brunt of the attacks of the Allies and were positioned immediately north of the border with Palestine.[43] Vichy forces were sacrificing paramilitary troops to protect the withdrawal of their regular forces, and indeed the paramilitary forces lost over 70 per cent of their combatants. A similar fate would have awaited the SSNP!

SSNP prisoners were released on June 11, 1941, two days after the start of hostilities.[44] The reprieve was temporary. As soon as the Free French were in control, they re-initiated the repression and most of the released were back in prison by August of 1941![45] The extensive nature of this new wave of arrests with over a hundred SSNP officials in prison at the Mieh-wa-Mieh concentration camp south of Beirut alone, with numerous others in the prisons of Beirut, Tripoli, Beit-eddine and Rashaya, seems to have dampened any apparent militant activities for most of 1942.

While in captivity, the SSNP leadership submitted multiple memoranda to the British initially asking for the release of lower

---

43 N.E. Bou-Nacklie, "The 1941 Invasion of Syria and Lebanon: The Role of the Local Paramilitary". *Middle Eastern Studies*, Volume 30, No. 3, July 1994, pp. 512-29.

44 Jureij, Gibran: *Min al-Ju'bat*, Volume 5, p.61.

45 *Ibid.*, p.160.

rank detainees to lessen the burden of the war on their families, and arguing for the cessation of persecution of the SSNP which had been proven to have no ties to any forces hostile to the Allies, but to no avail. The British, of course, held the upper hand militarily despite the efforts of Catroux and de Gaulle to retain Vichy troops and functionaries, without success. Many of the troops elected to be repatriated.

The Free French had promised the independence of Lebanon and Syria and a negotiated end to the Mandate. The Spears mission would hold them to that promise.[46] British Major-General Sir Edward Spears, who had been a great supporter of the Free French movement, clearly deciphered French intentions to delay the negotiations and maintain the Mandate unchanged until the war was over and the British had left northern Syria. He proceeded to undermine French policy and embolden local politicians both in Beirut and in Damascus. One of his maneuvers was to press the French to hold parliamentary elections. It was not until January 1943 that France agreed to reinstitute nominal constitutional privileges in the so-called independent states in return for control of a liberated Madagascar.[47]

Despite the protracted years of persecution, the SSNP retained a sufficiently important political base in certain areas of Lebanon to exercise a crucial role in swaying the results of the Lebanese parliamentary elections away from the pro-French camp of Emile Eddeh. This converged with the mounting influence of General Spears that not only led to the election of a new president and formation of a new cabinet, but also encouragement of that cabinet to wrestle more independence from the French. The support of the SSNP for the faction of Bichara Khoury in the election did not translate into any immediate concrete gains. The Party leaders remained in prisons under the direct control of the

---

46 Aviel Roshwald: "The Spears Mission in the Levant: 1941-1944", *The Historical Journal*, Vol. 29, No. 4 (Dec., 1986), pp. 897-919.

47 *Journal officiel de la France libre*, February 23, 1943.

French military. The support did establish, however, a political bond that would be strengthened by future events.

The defeat of the French supported candidates in the August 28 elections gave Spears a further tool to use in his quest to unseat the French. He encouraged and induced the Lebanese government of Bichara Khoury to have parliament amend the constitution eliminating all clauses that allowed the Mandate its legal fig leaf. Heleu, the French Commissioner, who had advised against such a move, was incensed and ordered the arrest of the Council of ministers and the president of the republic.[48] Some of the Lebanese leaders succeeded in evading arrest and escaped to the Shouf area where the SSNP had a strong base that undertook to provide armed protection and repulse incursions by the French military at the cost of their lives. In addition, the arrested Lebanese leaders were taken to jails filled with SSNP members who provided them with encouragement, moral support and critical information through their established networks. This strengthened the determination of the Lebanese officials to resist French intimidation. Their steadfastness, the failure of military raids to snuff out centers of rebellion, and most crucially overwhelming British pressure and a stern ultimatum, led the French to capitulate.

The SSNP had supported the anti-French faction electorally, undertook to confront French troops, and supported imprisoned Lebanese government officials. It would finally reap the rewards of its actions. The resolution of the Lebanese crisis brought about the release of all SSNP political prisoners. This release was not only a manifestation of the gratitude of the ruling faction for services rendered, but also a realization that an alliance with

---

48 Catroux made explicit statements that the Lebanese were not to blame for the events and that the whole affair was orchestrated by foreign elements! La Syrie et le Liban entreront-il dans la guerre? *Journal des Debats*, December 2, 1943. Numerous editorials in the French press asserted the belief that the heavy-handed British involvement was to blame. For Vichy editorialists see *Journal des Debats,* November and December, 1943.

the SSNP may prove beneficial in the end. Pro-French groups remained powerful and the French tenacious and determined to reinstitute the Mandate or some form of control as soon as British influence could be neutralized.

POLITICAL ACCOMMODATIONS

The alliance between the Lebanese political faction of Bichara Khouri, Riad Solh, Camil Chamoun, and the SSNP leadership of Thabit, grew over time. Evidence of this can be seen in the legalization of the status of the SSNP as a legitimate political party, which allowed it to operate freely within Lebanon in the spring of 1944. Senior government officials were frequent participants at SSNP rallies and were celebrated in SSNP demonstrations. Happy with the reprieve from constant persecution, the SSNP leadership of Thabit made substantial accommodating gestures towards Lebanese political leaders likely lured by the promise of participating in government in some important capacity. Recognizing that the "Syrianism" of the Party was not compatible with the aims of its alliance partners, the SSNP leadership resorted to a decentralization of the SSNP organization and chose to operate in Lebanon under the generic name of the "National Party." This was coupled with various initiatives consistent with this new persona such an abridged printing of the Party Principles consisting of only the reform principles, prohibition of the Party salute (Hail Syria), a redesign of the Party flag to exclude the now iconic Zawba'a, and the marginalization of non-aligned SSNP leaders.

The new political conditions offered the SSNP the opportunity to rebuild its ranks and rejuvenate its energy. A dynamic revival of its militant spirit was possible. However, the new political strategy, born of its Lebanese alliance, thwarted this opportunity. The Party was now advancing only its reform platform and calling for the strengthening of the Lebanese state. It still dabbled in Syrian affairs issuing memoranda supporting pacification of ethnic unrest in the hinterland, opposing Jewish settlements in Palestine, and condemning the "Greater Syria" project of King Abdullah of Jordan. These activities, however, were not threatening to its allies and the leadership continued to focus its energies on the Lebanese political arena. The decentralization scheme offered SSNP dissidents outside Lebanon an opportunity to secede and a group of SSNP leaders in Damascus rebelled against the Thabit leadership. While the latter was pursuing firmly a Lebanon first agenda, it had no intention of allowing the growth of opposing factions within the ranks of the SSNP even outside Lebanon. It used the pretext of breach of Party discipline to censor the dissidents and relieve them of their positions. In correspondence with Saadeh, Thabit would characterize them as rebellious individuals seeking personal advancement.

The National Party grew numerically in Lebanon, opened regional offices and cultural clubs, held rallies, public lectures, and celebrations, founded a publishing house, and issued a daily newspaper aptly named *Sada an-Nahda* (Echo of the Renaissance). Indoctrination efforts were diluted and toned down. Saadeh would later describe this phase as the "militancy of afternoon tea parties."

Another development of equally far reaching consequences was the emergence within the leading body of the SSNP of intellectuals who had a less than solid understanding of the Party philosophy and basic ideological tenets. Having acceded to sensitive leadership positions through individual brilliance and literary ability, they started to expound within the framework of the Party a doctrine derived particularly from the works of Kierkegaard and the Russian philosopher Nicholas Berdyaev. These developments did not come to Saadeh's attention until after the end of the war when contact with the Party in Syria was reestablished.

Re-Establishing Contact

Throughout the war, direct communications between Saadeh and the SSNP in Syria were interrupted. He tried to piece together a coherent narrative of the fate of his Party from snippets appearing in both the Syrian and foreign press. The information was meager and fragmentary, but Saadeh staunchly defended his comrades in the face of attacks in the press, adducing the motives for their actions from the principles of the SSNP and policy precedents prior to the war.[49] *al-Huda*, for example, claimed recurrently that the SSNP leaders were released from prison in June 1941 by the Vichy French because they were aligned with Germany and Italy. Saadeh refuted the allegation by pointing out, correctly, that Vichy had kept the SSNP cadres incarcerated throughout the period of its control and did not release them until a few days before its defeat at the hands of the British army, despite the presence of the German commission in Beirut.

It was not until early 1946 that Saadeh had any contact with the SSNP leadership in Syria when he received, via the Gold Coast Directorate in Africa, a letter sent to his brother's address in Brazil. He wrote back to Nehmeh Thabit in January asking him to establish regular contact urgently.[50] The SSNP leadership in Beirut deputized Ghassan Tueini who was traveling to Boston to pursue studies in political sciences to contact Saadeh and to brief him on the conditions of the SSNP and Syrian affairs in general.[51]

Immediately after receiving Tueini's first letter in February of 1946, Saadeh replied to him welcoming the contact and giving

---

49 Letter to Amin Al Ashqar December 20, 1945; Letter to Rafiq al-Halabi December 25, 1945. *Complete Works*, Volume 10, pp. 508-10, 514-17, respectively.

50 Letter to Nehmeh Thabit, January 19, 1946, *ibid.*, page 5.

51 Letter to Ghassan Tueini February 21, 1946, *ibid.*, pp. 25.

him general instructions to facilitate his mission.⁵² Saadeh directed Tueini to start his report from the time of the verdicts of the French Military Tribunal, suggesting that direct contacts with the SSNP may have been operational until that time. He asked him to focus on the following items:

1. The Syrian Nationalist idea, its acceptance and diffusion in all the regions of Natural Syria since 1938;

2. The general political conditions in the country since the British occupation of Northern Syria;

3. The "National Party," the reasons for its appearance in Lebanon in its current form and the guarantees for its ongoing activities and how the other branches of the Party react to its appearance;

4. The internal conditions of the Party from the administrative and morale perspectives;

5. The positions of the British, Russians, the French and domestic parties vis-à-vis the Party;

6. The declared international political position of the Party;

7. The return of Saadeh [to Syria]: the timing, venue (secretly, publicly or forcefully), and the likely positions of foreign powers, local governments, and domestic political groups in the various regions of Syria.

After examining the general report sent by Tueini, Saadeh observed a clear deviation from the balance he had established between political realism and adherence to a principled national strategy. Tueini had suggested that it was time for the Party to shift its emphasis from ideological to political matters, since ideological emphasis had led to a fossilization of political thinking. Tueini expressed what appeared to Saadeh an erroneous revisionist version of the foundational phase

---

52 Letter to Ghassan Tueini, February 21, 1946. *Complete Works*, Volume 11, pp. 25-31.

of SSNP history, particularly since a number of new leaders and party intellectuals were expressing views consonant with Tueini's report, aimed at establishing a new direction for the SSNP. According to Tueini, the earlier stance of the SSNP of focusing primarily and excessively on the idea of the nation and its elaboration had resulted in "academic rigidity," and the Party needed greater political flexibility. To remedy this state, the Party undertook a new approach based on its reform principles, giving precedence to political action over ideological debate. This flexibility enabled direct participation in political life in various Syrian states.

Saadeh took exception to this interpretation and proceeded to educate Tueini on the early history of the SSNP and the rationale for its policies and earlier positions. He warned Tueini that a proper study of the history and traditions of the SSNP was necessary to avoid experimentation by new leaders not versed in the policies and standards of the Party. Without a proper understanding of the Party's history, there was a risk of 'perpetual inventions' that wasted resources and led to deviations from the unity of thought and action that was a hallmark of the SSNP. Saadeh acknowledged that the entry of the Party into the political field and obtaining a permit to operate publically as a Lebanese party, and the establishment of semi-decentralized administrations in the rest of the Syrian regions, would result in problems that invited careful consideration. Saadeh recognized that the years of hardship and administrative disintegration of the Party because of incessant wars had led to some hasty measures.[53]

---

53 *Ibid.*.

The "National Party"

Saadeh's awareness of the deviations in the SSNP policies was based on multiple sources. Indeed, Assad Ashqar had written to Saadeh from Egypt explaining the rationale that motivated the changes.[54] With the re-establishment of contacts with the SSNP leadership in Syria, Saadeh started receiving correspondence from Party leaders that was discordant with the declared position of the "National Party." Maaruf Saab in a letter dated July 13, 1946, described to Saadeh what he perceived were deviations in ideology and policy, and worrying aspects related to the administration of the Party.

Saadeh was careful in his public pronouncements to frame some of the observed changes within the context of continuity of policy until he could fully assess the magnitude and intent of these changes.[55] He wanted to avoid any public display of perceived disagreements with the declared policies of the SSNP leadership in Syria. Despite his reservations, Saadeh spared no effort to support the SSNP in Syria and to promote a tightening of the bonds between the diaspora branches and the center in Syria. In preparation for issuing a new periodical in Beirut, the SSNP initiated a subscription campaign to raise funds. Saadeh encouraged branches to contribute money to SSNP headquarters in a special campaign separate from their regular membership dues. He directed branches to establish direct connections with the expatriates' office in Beirut and follow the directives they received from that office.[56]

In the course of his preparations for the voyage home, Saadeh addressed two communiqués to his constituency in Syria. The first was on the occasion of the public gathering on September 1,

---

54   Letter to Nehmeh Thabit, September 5, 1946. *ibid.*, pp. 216-29.

55   *az-Zawba'a*, issue 85, page 1: *Khitab Ra'is al-Majlis al-A'la* (Speech of the president of the High Council). *Complete Works*, Volume 7, pp. 141-43.

56   Letter to Yacoub Nassif, April 7, 1946, *ibid.*, pp. 55-6.

The "National Party"

1946, called for by the "National Party" under the rubric "Day of Reform." The second was in January 1947. The missives leave no doubt about Saadeh's views about the prevalent political situation in the homeland.

On September 1, 1946, the SSNP held one of its general public meetings in Dhour el-Shweir under the heading "Day of Reform." The first of September in Lebanon was traditionally celebrated as Lebanese Independence Day under the French Mandate since it was on that date that General Gouraud had declared the formation of *"Le Grand Liban."* In his letter to the assembled SSNP members, Saadeh congratulated them on their steadfastness and struggle and contrasted their work with that of other political parties.[57] Evoking the date of the meeting, Saadeh condemned the date of September 1 as commemorative of the fake or imaginary independence declared by Gouraud and hailed by sycophants and reactionary sectarian groups. He asserted that Gouraud had not only separated Lebanon from the hinterland but given it little true independence. While acknowledging that the present state was "the first tangible result of our faith in our cause and our patience in adversity", he stressed, "this reform is not the last reform we want, and this independence is not all the independence we desire."

In January 1947, he addressed a second letter to the SSNP constituency that was reflective of his position vis-à-vis the governments of the Syrian states and foreign powers.[58] The letter carried themes that would become causes of contention

---

57 Saadeh's letter was read at the time of the gathering by Fayez Sayegh and was published the next day in *Sada an-Nahda*, Issue 132, September 2, 1946. *Tahiyat az-Zaim mina al-Mahjar lil-Muhtashidin fi Yawm al-Islah* (Greetings from the Leader to the Assembled on Reform Day), *Complete Works*, Volume 7, pp. 171-73.

58 This second letter was not made public at the time by the SSNP leadership in Syria fearing that it might alarm the Lebanese government. Saadeh ordered it published after his return in the SSNP internal Bulletin in June of 1947. *Risalat mina az-Zaim ila al-Qawmiyin* (Letter from the Leader to the Nationalists), *ibid.*, pp. 178-83.

within and without the SSNP. His aim was to illustrate again how the elements of true sovereignty and independence were obtained only within the ranks and ideology of the SSNP rather than through the accidents of international politics. "I say this to make it clear that the sectarian and feudal arrangements that have replaced occupation and the mandate in the north are not the result of the struggle of Syrian nationalists nor are they acceptable to them." It was therefore critical for Saadeh to assert the position of the SSNP and to counter the subversive influence of the political narrative advanced by the new political entities and acquiesced in by the SSNP leadership in Syria.

Return Preparations and Challenges

In April 1946, Saadeh received the first letter from Thabit directly. He expressed to his lieutenant his joy at the resumption of direct contact, and his appreciation of the conditions that may have led the SSNP leadership to adopt alterations in the outward manifestations of the Party.[59] He approved the effort to obtain a license from the Lebanese government to operate publically as a necessity to establish stability and to allow the Party to undertake public initiatives to increase its influence. He expressed reservations about pronouncements related to the ultimate goal of the Party appearing in speeches and articles by Party leaders, but suggested postponing tackling the subject until his return to Syria. He gave Thabit a summary of what had transpired in his life. He then broached the issue of his return to Syria, and whether he needed to accelerate liquidating his financial assets.[60]

By May 1946, Saadeh received news that the SSNP leadership had filed a request with the Lebanese government to issue him a passport.[61] He was informed later there were likely to be

---

59 Such as the change in the flag, the new name of the Party, the elimination of the forms of salute, and the separate printing of the reform principles.

60 Letter to Nehmeh Thabit, April 20, 1946, *Complete Works*, Volume 11, pp. 83-87.

61 Letter to Naaman Daw, May 29, 1946, *ibid.*, pp. 105-6.

delays due to the resignation of the Cabinet and the political instability in the country.[62] In the absence of an official Lebanese diplomatic mission in Argentina, Saadeh approached the French Embassy to explore alternatives.[63] The ambassador received him very amicably on June 10, 1946, and promised to facilitate his obtaining travel documents after contacting the relevant Lebanese officials.[64] The procedure required that a telegram be sent by the French to Beirut with the requisite information; it would then be necessary to await the Lebanese officials indicating their consent or refusal by return telegram. Despite repeated letters informing the headquarters in Beirut of the delays by the Lebanese government officials, no progress was achieved. Saadeh asked SSNP members in Brazil to contact the Lebanese diplomatic mission in Brazil on his behalf and discuss with them the matter of issuing him a passport. The Lebanese ambassador Yussef Sawda flagrantly opposed this even though Thabit had assured Saadeh that there was no opposition from the central Lebanese government.[65] The discordance between Thabit's assertions and Sawda's position, however, suggest either that the Lebanese government was deceiving Thabit, or that there were factions within the government working at counter purposes. It was clear that the Lebanese government and its representatives in Brazil were denying Saadeh his citizenship rights in contravention of Lebanese law and international law.

By August of 1946 having not received any communication from the SSNP, he wrote to SSNP members in various parts of the world urging that they contact the SSNP headquarters to alert them to the breakdown in communication.[66] On August

---

62 Letter to Jibran Jreij, June 20, 1946, *ibid.*, pp. 109-10.

63 Note to the Ambassador, French Embassy files. Also, letter to Buenos Aires SSNP director, Aug 16, 1946, *Complete Works*, Volume 11, pp. 172-74.

64 Letter to Ghassan Tueini, Nov 11, 1946, *ibid.*, pp. 263-66.

65 Letter to Ghassan Tueini, November 11, 1946, *ibid.*, pp. 263-66.

66 Letter to Boulos Massaad in Cairo, August 2, 1946, *ibid.*, pp. 141-2; Letter to Mohammad Shamnaq in Homs, August 9, 1946, *ibid.*, pp. 160-61; and Letter to Ghassan Tueini, August 4, 1946, *ibid.*, pp. 143-59.

February 1947, Saadeh bids farewell to friends as he departs Brazil for Syria

16, he finally received a letter from Thabit explaining that the delay was partly due to "political matters" and in the letter urged Saadeh to continue preparation for his return. Saadeh promptly started writing to various SSNP branches in Argentina, Brazil and Africa asking them to assume certain responsibilities to facilitate his return projected for October-November 1946.[67] On September 5, he confided in Thabit that he felt there had been an inordinate delay in resuming contact with him, as there were communication channels that could have been used, particularly via the African Gold Coast branch that may have led to his return in early 1946. While Saadeh was circumspect with Thabit, he was receiving letters from SSNP members expressing concern

---

67　On September 1, he writes four letters to the following individuals: Letter to Buenos Aires SSNP director, August 16, 1946, *ibid.*, pp. 172-74; Letter to Najib Israwi in Brazil, September 1, 1946, *ibid.*, pp. 191-5; Letter to William Bahliss, September 1, 1946, *ibid.*, pp. 196-7; Letter to Rafiq Halabi in Gold Coast Africa, September 1, 1946, *ibid.*, pp. 198-202.

and dismay at the policies declared by the SSNP headquarters.[68]

Saadeh managed to sell his store[69] by October 15, and moved to Buenos Aires in November 1946.[70] It is ironic that the French who were largely responsible for the long sequestration of Saadeh in Argentina would be the instrument of his release from this captivity. The French did accommodate him by issuing him a *laissez-passer* on January 8, 1947 allowing him to travel to Brazil. In Sao Paulo, and with the aid of the SSNP branch, he managed to wrestle from the Lebanese consulate travel documents which would allow him to return to the homeland.

CAIRO INTERLUDE

Saadeh left Sao Paulo on February 13, 1947 heading to Rio de Janeiro where he stayed until the 15th of the month. He reached Portugal on February 16, and finally arrived in Cairo on the morning of February 18.[71]

In Cairo, Saadeh stayed at the pre-eminent Shepherd's Hotel where diplomats, politicians and financial and cultural elite of the city used to conglomerate in earlier times. His presence was conspicuous as he was meeting with Syrian expats, students, and his lieutenants who traveled from Beirut to meet him. Among the people who he met was the occasional newspaper reporter in the pay of the Lebanese government sounding him on his views and intentions. The daily *al-Ahram* duly reported his presence in Cairo and his intent on returning to Syria.

The battle for the leadership of the SSNP started in Cairo when Saadeh met with Nehmeh Thabit and Asad Achqar. Saadeh discovered that the leadership conceived of the 'National Party'

---

68 Letter to Maaruf Saab, September 21, 1946, *ibid.*, pp. 244-5.
69 Letter to Antoun Dahi, September 29, 1946, *ibid.*, pp. 249-50
70 Letter to Buenos Aires SSNP director, October 26, 1946, *ibid.*, pp. 256-60.
71 Letter to Juliette, February 22, 1947. *Rasa'il ila Dia'*, pp. 217-218.

Saadeh in Cairo in February 1947 meeting with Syrian students studying in Egypt.

not as a political accommodation but rather as a full departure from the concept of Syrian nationalism and a unified national cause. Further, based on this framework, they had entered into alliances and arrangements with Lebanese politicians to operate along such lines and consequently join with the government in an alliance in the forthcoming parliamentary elections. Since Saadeh's return and precedent views created uncertainty in the minds of their allies, Thabit and Achqar sought to alleviate those doubts by introducing amendments to the SSNP constitution that would limit Saadeh's authority and allow for continuation of their political strategy since they had virtual monopoly over the organization of the SSNP.

Saadeh Returns From Exile

Saadeh's reception on his arrival in Beirut was spectacular. Never in the history of the city or the region had a political figure received such a display of enthusiasm and loyalty. Saadeh was met by the largest number of welcoming crowds ever assembled in the modern history of Syria. Syrians thronged from various parts of the country to greet their returning leader. It was a display of political power that emboldened his devotees and worried his adversaries. In his speech on his day of arrival, Saadeh addressed two narratives, both different from the prior formulations of the SSNP. The first narrative related to the current status of the Syrian states arising in the wake of the British-French struggle in the Near East. The second narrative addressed the SSNP's vision of the future.[1] As he stepped to the podium and ushered for silence, comrades in attendance were eager to hear his voice. He had been preceded by Fayez Sayegh, the Director of Culture and Propaganda, and a celebrated orator whose speech was particularly impassioned on that day. Saadeh opened his speech by expressing his joy of having returned after 9 years of exile to join his comrades that "represent a nation that has refused to accept the grave of history as its lot in life." He praised his comrades for fifteen years of organized struggle after which "we stand today as a live, free and victorious nation" having overcome the efforts of foreign powers to keep the nation divided between sects and creeds. "Today our flags wave in the sun with no foreign flags beside them, and if our flags stand-alone unhampered and unfettered by foreign flags, it is due to your ideology, your faith, your work and your unified struggle." Then he directly broached the topic of independence that was no doubt on the minds of the Lebanese politicians who had dispatched several informants to record the speech and report back. "We are today in a state of

---

1   Homecoming Speech, *Complete Works*, Volume 7, pp. 204-207.

Saadeh on his arrival in Beirut on March 2, 1947 received by multitudes of SSNP members and supporters.

independence that is not the ultimate goal of what we aim for in life, but is a step of many that this nation undertakes, one of many, and the credit for its achievement is to a large part due to your organized work and struggle."

THE BATTLE FOR FREEDOM

Astounded by the size of the popular reception that they witnessed firsthand, and likely alarmed by the public position announced by Saadeh that confirmed the failure of Thabit and Achqar in their mission, the Lebanese President and Prime Minister moved swiftly to counteract the political momentum Saadeh had garnered. The government issued a subpoena for Saadeh to appear in front of a magistrate to clarify what the government initially called "ambiguous statements," but what government-allied newspapers labelled "treasonous statements." The Lebanese government's intent from the subpoena was clearly nefarious. Saadeh could have been arrested, expelled from the country, or worse. The assault of the government on human rights was unabating. Having famously lost the battle against Saadeh's right to return to his homeland, it was now

SAADEH RETURNS FROM EXILE

Saadeh on his arrival in Beirut on March 2, 1947 surrounded by the leaders of the SSNP. To Saadeh's right is Nehmeh Thabit, president of the High Council of the Party.

waging a battle against his freedom of expression. The pretext that the authorities used to issue the subpoena was that Saadeh in his homecoming speech declared that the existence of the State of Lebanon as null. This was obviously a misinterpretation of the speech. In his speech, Saadeh defined for his welcoming followers the real conditions of Syria, including Lebanon, the real nature of the political arrangements dividing the nation into several independent states, and he reaffirmed the determination of the SSNP to continue its struggle along the same principles on which it was founded.

Saadeh addressed a letter to the director of the *Sureté Générale* denying the false accusations of enmity towards the Lebanese state, and asked the director to convey to his superior's Saadeh's complete respect of the will of the people, affirming that his views towards the Lebanese state remained consistent with prior statements and declarations.[2]

As Saadeh refused to appear before the magistrate, the government changed the subpoena to an arrest warrant and the

---

2   Letter to the director of the Sureté Générale, *Complete Works*, Volume 11, p. 304.

minister of interior declared that Saadeh was wanted dead or alive. By making his alleged unacceptance of the existence of an independent Lebanese state the reason for the arrest warrant, the Lebanese government was aiming to put a wedge between the SSNP and the Lebanese population. Saadeh countered this tactic by addressing several public statements to the Lebanese people clarifying the dedication of the Party to the independence of Lebanon, but never failing to maintain that Lebanon remains a part of the Syrian nation. Furthermore, at the risk of his personal safety, he granted from his hideaway several interviews to journalists (who could easily have been Government informants) to utilize the interest of the public in the dramatic aspects of the affair as an opportunity to expound his political views.[3] Saadeh took his case to the people and on March 6 issued a public statement refuting the claims of his adversaries that he was an enemy of the state of Lebanon.[4]

The Lebanese government initiated a well-orchestrated campaign to subvert his efforts at assuming leadership of his party, initiating required re-organization, and participating effectively in the upcoming parliamentary elections. Various separatist political groups in Lebanon came to the aid of the government such as the Lebanese Phalanges and the francophone press in Beirut. The SSNP counter-campaign on the pages of its newspaper *Sada an-Nahda* garnered some initial success and succeeded in silencing some political foes, but as this counter campaign was gaining strength, the government closed down the paper. Saadeh was energized by the loyalty and enthusiasm of his supporters, but he rapidly noted that the magnitude of the support displayed on the day of his arrival was not manifest in the actual organization of the party. His headquarters in the mountain was secured by armed escort and guards, but this curtailed his freedom of movement and outreach. He could move only with an armed escort.[5]

---

3   He gave interviews to around ten newspapers in a period of two months.
4   First communique to the Lebanese people, *Complete Works*, Volume 7, pp.208-209.
5   Letter to Juliette, March 19, 1947. *Rasa'il ila Dia'*, pp. 219.

SAADEH RETURNS FROM EXILE

Antoun Saadeh with armed guards 1947.

Saadeh continued his rebuttal of the accusations by the government by issuing another public statement addressed to the Lebanese people on March 28, 1947.[6] In this new statement, Saadeh reiterated his position vis-à-vis the existence of the Lebanese state and his adherence to the principle of the will of the people being supreme in deciding the fate of its political forms of government. He then launched an attack against the prevailing conditions in Lebanon detailing the injustices that were pervasive in the Lebanese government and in society at large. His plan to elicit enough public protest to reduce the pressure on the SSNP had very modest success. Thabit and his associates criticized Saadeh for leading them and the Party into this unnecessary enmity with the Lebanese government. They attempted to dissuade Saadeh from the course of action he had undertaken and to convince him to surrender to the authorities. They sabotaged the central administration of the Party by absenteeism, delays, contrariness, contention, and cantankerousness. They spread vicious rumors about Saadeh within the ranks and attempted to undermine his authority and leadership. Simultaneously, they aggrandized their militancy and questioned maliciously Saadeh's wartime struggle.[7]

---

6 Second communique to the Lebanese people, *Complete Works*, Volume 7, pp.217-219.

7 *Nehmeh Thabit, batal al-Khiyanat* (Nehmeh Thabit, the traitor hero), *Complete*

The attempts of the Thabit camp to amend the constitution and reduce Saadeh's control over the affairs of the SSNP continued. Thabit lobbied for support in this scheme with the members of the Higher Council. Careful not to alienate his constituency and cause a major breach in the SSNP, Saadeh called for a meeting of the Higher Council at which he confronted Thabit and addressed the issue. He made the case that a return to the original goal of the SSNP and adherence to its unified national strategy represented the desires of the broader constituency, and that the trust that the constituency had in Saadeh's leadership was not consonant with the request of modifying the constitution. Saadeh's arguments and charisma won the day and Thabit's support in the higher council disintegrated. After the meeting, Saadeh dissolved the Higher Council and the political bureau and appointed a new team.[8]

In April, he moved his headquarters from the Shouf region to his hometown of Dhour Shweir. The erratic living conditions enforced by the government campaign against him and the preoccupation with the Lebanese elections and the ongoing dispute with the Thabit regime, prevented Saadeh from undertaking any effective administrative or political reforms in the Party. Matters of personal security were primordial. The only guardian of his freedom was the armed protection provided by SSNP membership.[9]

In a third communique addressed to the Lebanese people on May 19, the eve of the elections, Saadeh exhorted the Lebanese electorate to support true reform by ensuring SSNP representation in parliament with the SSNP candidates. He reiterated his commitment to the independence and prosperity of Lebanon and repeated that the SSNP principles are the best recourse to solving what ails Lebanon.[10]

Works, Volume 7, pp.298-304.

8   Letter to Rafic Halabi, June 22, 1947, *Complete Works*, Volume 11, pp.308-311.

9   Letter to Juliette, May 17, 1947. *Rasa'il ila Dia'*, pp. 222.

10   Third communique to the Lebanese people, *Complete Works*, Volume 7, pp.254-255.

Parliamentary Elections

The Lebanese parliamentary elections were to take place on May 25, and the Syrian elections on June 8. The SSNP chose initially not to engage directly and observed the unfolding of the chaotic campaigns of the various candidates, focused as they were on personal and religious interests. It declared that it was willing to participate in a coalition for the opposition based on its reform principles. This initiative did not garner any tangible support, so the SSNP decided to put up its own independent candidates.[11] Ten candidates were slated in the five electoral districts of Lebanon. Members of the opposition as well as candidates affiliated with the government who were not selected on the government slates, approached the SSNP with a proposal for a coalition. This was purely a coalition of convenience and for the limited purpose of the election. Nevertheless, the SSNP leadership reasoned that it might open the door for a political compromise with the government since the brother of the president was a leading proponent of such a coalition. Saadeh hoped that such negotiations may pave the way to a resolution of the campaign of intimidation and harassment the SSNP was subject to.[12]

The 1947 election has gone down in history as the most fraudulent election ever held in Lebanon.[13] Intimidation, coercion, stuffing of ballots boxes, and falsification of results were so flagrant that even government ministers came out criticizing the practice. In some jurisdictions, there were more ballots than voters to ensure the election of favored candidates. The losers clamored for an insurrection and acts of disobedience and appealed to the SSNP to join in that effort. The SSNP was uniquely targeted by the fraudulent actions. It chose, however, not to join in with

---

11 *Qawa'id at-Tarshih llniyabat fi al-Hizb al-Qawmi al-Ijtima'i* (Principles of candidacy for elections in the Social Nationalist Party), *Complete Works*, Volume 8, pp.246-251.

12 Letter to Juliette, May 5, 1947. *Rasa'il ila Dia'*, pp. 220-221.

13 'Akl, Jurjī, (editor), *The black book of the Lebanese elections of May 25, 1947*, Phoenicia Press, NY, 1947.

the opposition in an unprincipled insurrection. The efforts of the opposition soon petered out and control of the government remained in the clutches of the oligarchy. On May 30, five days after the election, Saadeh issued a communique characterizing the election as a tragicomedy, detailing the infractions committed, and questioning the validity and legality of the elected parliament. He criticized the general absence of civic responsibility and unprincipled alliances. He chided the citizens of Lebanon for allowing the rampant disregard of civic liberties exercised by the government as it persecuted the SSNP, aimed to arrest its leader, and suspended the operation of its newspaper. He warned, however, against the calls to civil disobedience by the opposition whose corrupt plans and aims were no better than those of the government.[14]

The manufactured success of the ruling oligarchs meant that the resulting government did not need to come to a political agreement with the SSNP, and its campaign against the Party and its leader could continue. Indeed, raids against SSNP strongholds intensified. The campaign aimed at maintaining pressure on Saadeh and disrupting his effective leadership of the Party did curtail his efforts at re-organizing the ranks of the SSNP. If the defiant fugitive garnered any sympathy from the public, it could not be turned into any tangible political momentum.

The "Greater Syria" Scheme

Soon after the end of the elections, Saadeh travelled secretly to Jordan to meet with King Abdallah and his representatives to review a potential alliance and examine the degrees of concordance between the King's "Greater Syria" project and the aim of the SSNP. The King had sent emissaries to meet with Saadeh in his hideout in Lebanon and proposed an alliance.[15]

---

14   Fourth communique to the Lebanese people, *Complete Works*, Volume 7, pp.258-262.
15   Letter to Juliette, June 5, 1947. *Rasa'il ila Dia'*, pp. 223-224.

During Saadeh's absence, the SSNP had publicly opposed the Greater Syria project on political grounds and in accord with its political alliances with Lebanese politicians who were opposed to the scheme. News of the visit leaked to the press, and it does not seem to have led to any concrete plans or understanding as neither the SSNP nor the King manifested any actions or declarations that would suggest otherwise. Accusations that the SSNP was allied with King Abdallah would be raised by opponents of both and they represent no more than partisan rhetoric. Indeed, during the SNPs direst hour in July 1949, Jordan did not come to its aid nor did it provide any succor even nominally.

THE BATTLE FOR LEADERSHIP

In the weeks following the elections, the confrontation between Saadeh and the Thabit camp reached a crisis level. Saadeh had been patient with his old comrades choosing to dialogue with them rather than ostracize them. However, as they saw his tightening grip over the Party and their political plans in tatters, they moved from latent opposition to frank insubordination and public confrontation. In early July, Saadeh suspended Thabit, Ayyas, and Achqar from all responsibilities and activities within the party. The suspended members, save Achqar, declared their resignation and the formation of a new Lebanese party which they invited their supporters to join. Thabit issued a public statement criticizing Saadeh and blaming him of endangering the future of the SSNP and of Lebanon. Thabit's attempt was ineffective and his new party was an abortive attempt by a desperate man. Achqar on further reflection realigned with Saadeh and declared his allegiance publicly.[16]

With the defeat of Thabit and his group, the government had lost a lever of pressure on Saadeh and the SSNP. Thabit and his group had monopolized the central leadership of the SSNP and had held most of the sensitive posts in its hierarchy. Thabit had

---
16 *Khitab az-Zaim fi Deek al-Mehdi* (Speech by the Leader at Deek al-Mehdi). *Complete Works*, Volume 7, pp.399-401.

been in effective control of the SSNP as he combined his role as president of the Higher Council (which is the legislative branch of the SSNP hierarchy), with membership in the executive council and presidency of the political bureau, in effect monopolizing all relevant positions within the Party. The Thabit administration had neglected, wittingly or unwittingly, to develop a next generation of leaders and qualified Party administrators. Further, they had excluded dissenters from positions of power and alienated them to the point of defection from the organization. This dearth of experienced party cadres hampered and delayed much of Saadeh's plans and burdened him with unnecessary chores.

The government's campaign against the SSNP and its leader was entering its seventh month and had resulted in a stalemate. Neither side had enough political or military power to win the standoff. Over many months, Saadeh waged a counter attack against the Government, its policies of repression and oppression, its falsification of elections, its economic and political favoritism and the unbridled growth of government sponsored capitalist power. Gaining some support among senior members of the judiciary by arguing for the constitutional right of freedom of expression and assertion of non-belligerence towards the Lebanese state, Saadeh pushed for a political compromise. The initiative was finally successful and the warrant for Saadeh's arrest was withdrawn after the formality of a personal visit to the Attorney General on October 9, 1947.[17]

PALESTINE IN PERIL

With the "Lebanon first" policy of the Thabit administration and the disruptive confrontation with the Lebanese government that pre-occupied its ranks, the SSNP was not prepared to materially engage in the battle for Palestine. Nevertheless, the imminent and present danger of a catastrophe in southern Syria impelled

---

17 *Risalat az-Zaim ila al-Qawmiyyin al-Ijtima'iyyin Bimunasabat Intisar jhad al-Hizb* (Letter from the Leader to the Social Nationalists on the occasion of the victory of the Party in its struggle), *Complete Works*, Volume 7, pp.335-336.

it to actions despite its chronic shortage of resources and need of breathing room to rebuild its organization. Witnessing the disarray in the actions of various Palestinian and Syrian groups in combating Zionist advances, the SSNP could not afford to remain silent. Taking advantage of the tenuous truce with the Lebanese government, the SSNP called for a massive rally in Beirut on the anniversary of the Balfour declaration on November 2, 1947. This was critically important on the national front to mobilize internal forces, and equally important on the international front as significant decisions at the United Nations were due later that month.

SSNP branches throughout Syria were invited to this demonstration and convoys from as far away as Aleppo headed to Beirut. The plan, however, unnerved the Lebanese government that always feared that such a massing of SSNP supporters could be used to challenge its authority and even overthrow it. It informed the SSNP that it had instituted a ban on public gatherings and demonstrations and the Balfour day demonstration would not be allowed to proceed.

The government claimed that the Arab Council in Palestine had requested that efforts be directed at raising financial support for its own fighters in lieu of public demonstrations. The SSNP countered that the Arab Council was not a representative body and did not have monopoly over Palestinian issues, nor did it have qualifications to be the sole authority on all initiatives for the Palestinian cause. The Lebanese government was using the Arab Council as an excuse that suited its purpose of crippling any political activity by the SSNP. The accommodation reached barely a month before meant a cessation of overt military activity against the SSNP, but did not mean an end to efforts of intimidations and subversion. The threat of the use of force to disperse any gathering and the risk of being drawn into renewed confrontation with the Lebanese government and the further drain on time and resources led the SSNP to cancel the planned demonstration. In lieu of the demonstration, Saadeh issued a

The Syrian Social Nationalist Party

750,000 Palestinians were expelled and made refugees by Zionist paramilitaries, and subsequently Israeli forces 1947–49.

long communique in which he provided a comprehensive review of the evolution of the Palestinian question since World War I, detailed the disarray in the activities of the Syrian states and politicians, and stressed the need for organized cooperation and a unified Syrian national effort.[18] He called on Syrians from various states to come together in a unified national effort. The call was not heeded and the disarray continued. The consequence was that within a month the United Nations voted for the partition of Palestine on November 30, 1947.

The SSNP attempted with all its means to prevent the loss of Palestine. Its efforts were often resisted more by local governments than by Zionist forces. The traditional political and religious leadership in southern Syria refused to allow the SSNP access to arms, and repeatedly refused offers by the SSNP to enroll its members in the military forces fighting Zionist groups. Despite their meager resources, SSNP members fought against the Jewish forces in Haifa, Acre, Galilee, and the environs of

---

18 *Risalat az-Zaim fi Sadad Wadi' Filastin wa Mawqif al-Hizb al-Qawmi al-Ijtima'i* (Communique of the Leader on the Status of Palestine and the view of the SSNP), *Complete Works*, Volume 7, pp.356-368.

Jerusalem and suffered many casualties. They also participated in military operations along the Lebanese and Syrian fronts. The lack of arms and ammunition was compounded by the refusal of the Arab Supreme Command to supply SSNP members and units with arms from their depots for purely political reasons. SSNP units throughout Syria marshalled what resources they had to help shelter, feed, and care for the waves of refugees evicted from Palestine in one of the largest operations of ethnic cleansing of the 20th century. Saadeh placed the responsibility of the Palestinian tragedy squarely on the heads of the reactionary politicians who controlled the Syrian governments, resources, and institutions for their incompetence, bickering, internecine fighting, and refusal to join in a unified Syrian effort to serve the national cause.[19]

Following the loss of Palestine, the SSNP spared no effort in alerting the Syrians to the dangers of Zionist settlements. It recognized that the establishment of the Jewish State in 1948 was only the beginning of a policy of expansionism that endangered the entire Syrian homeland. The Party also resisted and censored all attempts at normalization of relations with the Jewish State or political alliances between sectarian Lebanese separatist groups and the Jewish state.[20]

Rebuilding the SSNP

The ideological fabric of the Party had been weakened by neglect of the study of its principles and philosophy, and foreign concepts were growing in its midst. The literature of the SSNP was without direction and prominent intellectuals in leadership positions were popularizing concepts in party publications divergent from the philosophy of Social Nationalism.

---

19   *Balagh min Maktab az-Zaim fi Sadad Filastin* (Communique from the office of the Leader regarding Palestine), *Complete Works*, volume 8, pp. 235-236.

20   *Tasrih al-Mutran Mubarak* (The pronouncements of archbishop Mubarak), *ibid.*, pp. 182-183.

The neglect of ideological formation of Party cadres required a broad ideological education program that Saadeh undertook in the series of weekly lectures delivered in the Cultural Forum of the SSNP between January 7 and April 4, 1948. The Cultural Forum had been founded in the 1930s, and in some preliminary discussions with college students Saadeh had promised to revive it. While the original cultural forum was a restricted activity usually involving mostly SSNP intellectuals, the series of weekly lectures was opened to the public and garnered a wide interest in Beirut. Intellectuals from various political streams attended the lectures. While only 75 people attended the first lecture, by the third lecture the number routinely exceeded 500 attendees. Saadeh assigned trustee George Abdel Massih who had mastered an Arabic shorthand method to take notes and an edited transcript of the first five lectures was published in Saadeh's lifetime. The transcripts of the subsequent lectures appeared posthumously. For several decades, the transcripts of these lectures became the standard text for the popularization of the ideology of the SSNP and are one of the most influential ideological factors in the survival and growth of the Party. Generations of SSNP members learned the ideology of their Party from this book. These didactic lectures are a tour de force in their eloquence and erudition. They represent a detailed study of the basic and reform principles of the SSNP, and the philosophy of Social Nationalism contained therein.

Saadeh gave great attention to the formation of Party intellectuals. He conducted a series of closed seminars and workshops with select groups of SSNP writers, poets, and intellectuals dealing with various philosophical concepts and views varying from esthetics to ethics. These were held in the context of the Cultural Forum on Saturdays in parallel with his public lectures delivered on Sundays. The SSNP issued a special publication *al-Nizam al-Jadid* (The New Order) dedicated to publishing studies dealing with the philosophical tenets of Social Nationalism, the history and heritage of Syria, and the poetry and literature of the Syrian renaissance.

Rebuilding the SSNP

Outreach Activities

Reviving the organizational structure of the SSNP was a more difficult task mostly because of the lack of resources and trained manpower. The years of decentralization of the administration of the Party had led to a weakening of the structure of the SSNP and a good deal of its members had either joined other groups, retired from political work, or sat idle awaiting direction. Saadeh undertook a tour of the branches of the SSNP in the various parts of Syria. In the early part of 1948, Saadeh visited several areas in the Lebanon including Freykeh (January), Tripoli and Qalamoun (January), Jal-el-Dib (February), Burj al-Barajeneh (February), and Aley (March). He also undertook a short trip to Damascus in March. The need to expand the popular base of the SSNP and consequently its political power, drove Saadeh to undertake two major grass-root outreach initiatives in the latter part of 1948. While expanding the popular base of the Party was the responsibility of the various departments of the SSNP, Saadeh's personal endeavors had always had a multiplier effect. His charisma and appeal always drew large crowds to SSNP gatherings. The tours allowed Saadeh to evaluate the status of his organization, gauge the trends in the popular sector, and meet local politicians, notables, and powerbrokers.

The tour in Lebanon was achieved through short trips to various locations including the Kura district in the north (September 19), the Shouf district (September 30 and October 3), and the Jezzine district in the south (October 10). The tour in the hinterland was prolonged and spanned the entire month of November 1948. Saadeh began his trip in Damascus on November 3rd. Saadeh stayed in the Syrian capital through November 12th. Between the 14th and 16th of the month he was in Homs, in Hama on the 17th, and then he headed to Aleppo where he stayed from the 19th to the 26th of November. His Aleppo stay was interrupted by a return trip to Hama on November 24th for a lecture. From Aleppo, Saadeh headed to the coast and between November 26th and December 5th visited the cities of Latakia, Tarsus, Banias and Safita. This was reminiscent of his visit in 1936 with its memorable displays of horsemanship and festivities.

Polemics and Ascendency

Saadeh conceived of the SSNP as a defiant agent of change willing and ready to take on the reactionary bastions in Syria, dismantle their intellectual frameworks, and expose their nefarious influences on Syria's future. The prolonged suspension of the SSNP newspaper *al-Jil al-Jadid* (The New Generation) by the Lebanese government led Saadeh to seek alternate venues to deliver his messages to the people. Tours and speeches played a role, but the written medium of periodicals was a necessary component of the outreach. The publisher of *Kul Shai'* (All News), a young journalist named Mohammed Baalbaki, had engaged Saadeh in a discussion of national issues that ultimately led Baalbaki to join the SSNP. In the interim, Baalbaki welcomed Saadeh's Op-Ed pieces on the front pages of his periodical. Saadeh covered a range of issues on the pages of *Kul Shai'* with a unifying theme of dismantling the theoretical constructs of reactionary groups and their political ideas. The articles appeared on a weekly schedule between mid-January to mid-April 1949 and ceased when *al-Jil al-Jadid* resumed publication. Baalbaki had engaged Saadeh in a discussion of Pan-Arabism to which Baalbaki originally adhered, so it was natural for the opening article to be dedicated to that topic.

Saadeh had maintained throughout his career that an elucidation of national identity was the necessary pre-requisite to sound political activity and that national renaissance should be based on a robust understanding of the elements of nationhood and nationalism. The most prominent topics of these editorials were the issues of national identity and the debunking of religious Pan-Arabism and religious based Lebanese isolationism. Saadeh tackled the bankruptcy of Pan-Arabism and trampled the feeble attempts of its proponents to defend it. He tackled the tenets of Pan-Arabism and its sectarian religious undertones, and its

Rebuilding the SSNP

Saadeh during a tour in the Syrian hinterland reviewing SSNP members.

corrupt usurpation of leadership in Syria and its responsibility for the loss of Palestine.[21] He also confronted the separatist Lebanese movement and its equally sectarian underpinnings stoking the fires of religious discord and past grievances to secure political gains.[22] He countered the claims of the two sectarian trends by illustrating how the aim of the SSNP would secure the formation of a realistic Arab front in lieu of the confused plans of the Pan-Arabists.[23] He also discussed how the SSNP political program was the salvation of the Lebanese[24] from the curse of religious discord.[25] He also tackled the fad of "reform movements"

---

21 *al-Uruba Aflasat* (The Bankruptcy of Pan-Arabism), *Complete Works*, volume 8, pp. 256-258

22 *al-In'izaliyat al-Lubnaniyat Aflasat* (The Bankruptcy of Lebanese isolationism), *ibid*, pp. 259-262.

23 *Intisar al-Qawmiyat as-Syriyat Yuhaqiq al-Jabhat al-Arabiya* (The victory of Syrian nationalism will lead to a strong Arab front), and *Harabna al-Urubah al-Wahmiya lajel al-Urubah al-Waqi'iya* (We fought fictional Pan-Arabism to establish realistic Arabism), *ibid.*, pp. 263-266 and 267-271, respectively

24 *Wa Harabna L'inqaz al-Lubnaniyyin* (We fought to save the Lebanese), *ibid.*, pp. 272-277.

25 *Al-Hizbiyyat ad-Diniyyat La'nat al-Umma* (Religious fanaticism is a national curse), *ibid.*, pp. 305-307.

appearing on the scene, a reference to the emerging sectarian "Progressive Socialist Party" of Kamal Junblatt among the Druzes.[26] To clearly delineate the distinction between the Syrian nationalism of the SSNP and the political schemes of the Iraqi Prime Minister Nuri as-Said and the Jordanian Prince Abdullah, Saadeh expounded on the motives and the machinations behind the two seemingly concordant political schemes.[27]

The SSNP was winning the war of ideas and ideologies, and making inroads into the constituencies of traditional Christian and Muslim politicians and eroding their base of support. This progress was translated in the local elections in Lebanon in 1949 where SSNP candidates made substantial gains.[28]

THE ZAIM COUP

On the night of March 30, 1949, contingents from the Syrian army cordoned off Damascus and blocked all major thoroughfares into and out of the city. Military convoys converged on main government headquarters while smaller forces apprehended leading government officials including the president Shukri al-Quwatly, the prime minister and several ministers and high-ranking officials. The coup encountered no resistance and by sunrise on March 31, 1949, Husni az-Zaim was in control of the capital and nominally the country. Syrians were treated to a spectacle that was to repeat itself numerous times over the next two decades as Zaim inaugurated the trend of government take-over by the armed forces. The token 'Communique no. 1' that would become the prototype for future similar announcements, and the flurry that followed, informed the citizenry of the change in leadership, called for calm, threatened that seditions

---

26 *La'ihat al-A'qaqir la Tasna' Tabiban* (A list of drugs does not a physician make), *ibid.*, pp. 308-312.

27 *Nahnu Suriyun la Helalkhasbiyun* (We are Syrians not Fertile Crescentians), *ibid.*, pp. 278-281.

28 *Intikhabat al-Mukhtarin Darss Baligh* (The Lessons of the recent elections of notaries), *ibid.*, pp.377-378.

or resistance acts would be dealt with harshly, and promised reforms to better the lot of the citizens.

In a fake nod to democracy and the will of the people, Zaim paid a visit to Fares Khoury, the head of the Syrian parliament and invited the representatives to a dialogue aimed at legitimization of the new leadership. When these proved fruitless, Zaim dissolved parliament and promised future elections at an opportune time. Written resignations by the President Quwatly and his Prime Minister were extracted in due course and facsimile copies published in the local press. Wide ranging reform legislations derived from the playbook of various political parties, including the SSNP, were enacted by edicts from the new leader. The Syrian populace was bewildered by the unaccustomed event and traditional notables who relied for their political base on loyalties and affiliations were not equipped to mount any resistance. Further, the mounting discontent with the prior civilian government and the increasingly evident corruption gave way to a euphoria expressed particularly among students and young workers who thronged to the streets, when allowed by the army, to express their support. The adulation of the mob was stirred by agents of the regime and regional functionaries intimidated by the brute power of the army declared their allegiance publicly. It appeared that Zaim was safely enthroned in power. When asked for an impromptu comment at a social gathering on April 3, Saadeh cautiously choose to focus on the ills of the overthrown regime and its suppression of freedom of expression and assembly. He warned his listeners from putting their hopes on capricious events and advised patience until the new regime clearly declares its policies.[29]

On April 13, 1949, the SSNP newspaper offered a cautious but positive assessment of the Zaim coup praising its reform initiatives that it declared consonant with SSNP initiatives and hinted at the role of SSNP elements in their formulation. It also expressed the hope that the new regime would allow

---

29 Letter to Abdallah al-Qubersi, April 3, 1949. *Complete Works*, volume 11, pp. 385.

more opportunity for expansion of the role of the SSNP than its oppressive predecessor regimes.[30]

The refusal of the Lebanese government to recognize the Zaim regime infuriated the latter and precipitated a crisis between the two states. Zaim started courting the opposition forces in Lebanon, among them the SSNP. Zaim's threats of interference in Lebanon alarmed the Lebanese government and increased its scrutiny of the activities of the opposition, as well as its efforts to nurture domestic and pan-Arab support. Egypt was instrumental in attempting to resolve the Zaim-Lebanon conflict through its influence on both parties. Contacts between Zaim and the SSNP also alarmed the Lebanese government and played a role in accelerating the efforts of the Lebanese government against the SSNP.

A Gathering Storm

The ongoing revival of the SSNP, the growing popular discontent with the Lebanese government, electoral fraud, and usurpation of resources, made the rulers of Lebanon more determined to eliminate the SSNP and Saadeh from the Lebanese political scene. This they proceeded to do by harassment and tyranny. SSNP members were dismissed from government offices and pressured out of civil service posts. Party meetings and large gatherings were proscribed on flimsy excuses of maintaining order and tranquility. Party publications were intermittently banned or confiscated (the SSNP newspaper *al-Jil al-Jadid* (The New Generation) was banned for one year starting April 1948), and armed police were frequently sent to forcibly disperse SSNP gatherings. This series of events culminated by the Government instigating the Phalanges party to attack the printing press of the SSNP daily paper on the evening of June 9, 1949, in an attempt to assassinate Saadeh, or at the very least create a pretext for

---

30 *Muqabalat ma' Iza'at al-Hizb al-Qawmi al-Ijtima'I hawl al-Inqilab fi ash-Sham* (Interview with the spokesperson of the SSNP about the Coup d'etat in Damascus), *Complete Works*, volume 8, pp.316-317.

his arrest.[31] The transparency of the plan was betrayed by the Government moving swiftly to issue warrants of arrest for the victims of the incident (SSNP members and Saadeh) and no attempt at disciplining or even reprimanding the aggressor Phalanges. In effect, the Government had declared open war on the SSNP. Its members were arrested and jailed, its publications and offices confiscated, and its leader pursued. The arrests of Party members were so massive that within a few days more than 2500 were either in prison or in detention camps. Saadeh went clandestinely to Damascus to organize and lead the fight against the Lebanese government. He met with Zaim who had his own gripes with the Lebanese government and was promised support.

The Lebanese government was determined in its plan to extirpate the SSNP from the Lebanese political scene. To contain the onslaught, Saadeh sought to open a negotiation channel with the government akin to what transpired during the prior confrontation after his return in 1947. Much had changed, however, and the resolve of the government in the pursuit of its radical goal was bolstered by significant regional and international support. Nevertheless, Saadeh sent a trusted negotiator to contact the office of the Lebanese Prime Minister Riad Solh, the main force behind the government action. At the arranged meeting, the SSNP negotiator was treated to a barrage of accusations by Solh claiming that Saadeh and the SSNP were in collusion with the Zionists to topple the Lebanese government and establish a new regime allied with Israel! These were the same charges that Solh had declared publicly to explain the campaign against the SSNP. Assertions to the contrary only stoked Solh's fake ire. He went on to suggest slyly that if SSNP leaders were to denounce Saadeh's collusion with the Zionists, the campaign against the SSNP would wind down and prisoners would be released.

---

31   *Bayan az-Zaim ila al-Qawmiyyin al-Ijtima'iyyin wa al-Umma as-Suriya* (Communique from the Leader to the Social Nationalists and the Syrian nation), *ibid.*, pp 383-387.

Despite early promises of support, Zaim was growing tepid on the alliance with the SSNP that he had used for his purposes to pressure the Lebanese government. The more reconciliation he achieved with Solh, the less his enthusiasm for the SSNP. By late June, it was clear that relations with Zaim had soured [32] and the SSNP leadership was being tracked and apprehended by Syrian security forces. Saadeh himself had to move to an undisclosed location. It is unclear why in the midst of these changes the SSNP continued on the path to declare an insurgency in Lebanon. It is likely that its leadership realized that a negotiated settlement with the Lebanese government was the only path forward and sought to create facts on the ground to force such a settlement.

---

32 Letter to Juliette, June 30, 1949. *Rasa'il ila Dia'*, pp. 230.

The Uprising

Indeed, the SSNP was faced with impossible choices. It could not accede to the demands of Solh and denounce its leader for alleged treasonous acts for that would be suicidal and a worse undertaking than the "National Party" initiative of Thabit, which meant to exclude Saadeh and readjust the scope of the Party ideology, but not condemn him. Further, the SSNP could not observe the systematic dismantling of its organization in Lebanon, and the targeting of its constituency, and remain passive. Such a course would inevitably result in the loss of the largest base for the Party, demoralization, and certain demise. The largest constituency of the SSNP was in Lebanon and its leadership was predominantly Lebanese. A surrender in Lebanon was not compatible with the survival of the Party. Confrontation with a more powerful foe has always been the bane of national liberation movements, and asymmetrical wars their hallmark. Even small gains by an insurgency can be translated into a political solution compatible with the survival of the Party. While militarily more powerful than the SSNP, the Lebanese government had its vulnerabilities. The fall of the Khoury government 3 years hence in the face of an opposition coalition of which the SSNP was a significant member attests to this possibility.

When the government's campaign against the SSNP did not abate, but rather continued gathering momentum, Saadeh declared on July 4, 1949 a popular uprising calling for the overthrow of the Lebanese government and the institution of a Social Nationalist order in Lebanon. Members of the SSNP started organizing popular revolt and occupying government outposts in the villages and plains of Lebanon. Most commentators on the events of July 1949 are so preoccupied with the tragic conclusion of the revolution and the shortcomings in its execution that they fail to realize or understand the grand plan of the revolution. The revolution's *maximal* goal was to overthrow the Lebanese government, and its *minimal* goal was to force the government into a negotiated settlement, albeit the rhetoric of the era makes the latter sound unworkable. To achieve either goal, the revolution needed to reduce the territorial control of the government, or at least disrupt its ability to govern or control large areas in which the revolution would establish its own rule. The most expedient way to achieve this end was to gain rapid control of areas where government control was already tenuous such as the Bekaa valley as well as the Northern and Southern districts of the country. In parallel, the government hold over the central sectors of Beirut and the mountain would be challenged by widespread insurgency.

To gain control of the northern Bekaa, the SSNP had forged an alliance with the Dandash clans who were armed and capable of achieving the task. The central and southern parts of the Bekaa valley were to be secured by two SSNP task forces that would enter Lebanese territory from the Syrian Republic side. After securing their assigned territory, the two task forces, joined by additional SSNP recruits from the local branches, would then proceed to control the south of Lebanon. The northern districts of Lebanon would be the target of another task force that would advance along the Syrian coast. Finally, SSNP branches throughout Lebanon would launch insurgent activities against police stations and government offices with the intent of keeping government forces occupied in Beirut and the surrounding mountains. The government would keep the bulk of its forces to secure the capital and the surrounding areas, which would facilitate the control of all peripheral sectors by the revolution forces.

The strategic plan was vulnerable, however, to treachery. The various components were interdependent and the failure of any crucial part of the plan would jeopardize other components. Hence, the defection of the Dandash clans who were swayed to renege on their commitments left large segments in government control and exposed the flank of the task forces entering from the

The Uprising

Meeting of Bichara Khoury, President of Lebanon, and Husni Zaim, ruler of Syria, a few days before the deportation of Saadeh.

east. Further, Syrian betrayal exposed the routes and operational plans of these task forces to the Lebanese government forces, and allowed the latter to ambush and disperse the two advancing groups. The defective weapons and ammunitions delivered by the Syrian forces meant that these task forces were even more vulnerable to attack by well-equipped professional government forces. The task force entrusted with entering Lebanon from the north was thwarted by the Zaim's regime through widespread arrests of SSNP members, intimidation and sealing of the borders. Insurgent activities in other areas would thus become futile as they could be either ignored by the government or readily contained after defeat of the major task forces.

The factors that facilitated the counter insurgency efforts of the government do not excuse the failures of execution by the SSNP. The low response rate by SSNP constituency, the lack of diligence in inspecting weapons obtained from the Syrian army, and the amateurism of some SSNP cadres bear a significant degree of blame for the failure.

The Syrian Social Nationalist Party

Treachery, Trial and Martyrdom

On July 6, Zaim invited Saadeh to the presidential palace to meet with him, had him arrested and delivered to the Lebanese police. Saadeh had been warned about Zaeem's treachery. His visit to the presidential palace was determined by two factors: primarily, he wanted to face up to his responsibilities as a leader of a national movement. In the face of danger, he was not going to seek personal safety while his followers were espousing death for the cause. Not appearing for his appointment would have meant inviting the scourge of a military dictator on the SSNP membership. Secondly, he hoped that he could still elicit some national fervor in Husni Zaim. The latter's treachery and callous pursuit of personal glory were irremediable, and Saadeh was surrendered to the Lebanese police by his host the President of the Syrian Republic.

Saadeh was taken to Beirut in the early hours of the 7th, summarily tried by a court that sat in camera, and he was executed at 3 am on July 8. The lawyer appointed to his defense had requested a recess to study the case. His motion was not granted and he withdrew. Thereupon Saadeh undertook his own defense. Details of the court proceedings from observers and Saadeh's defense are, however, not available. The trial was obviously a sham for the sentence was decided before the trial was even convened.[1] It was as complete a travesty of justice as a trial could be. He was deprived of his right to counsel, his right to examine the evidence against him, and his right to prepare for his defense. The court was convened at 2 pm and by 8 pm a judgment of guilty had been rendered and Saadeh was sentenced to death by a firing squad to be carried out immediately removing any chance for a stay in execution or appeal by the defendant. Just before dawn on July 8, Saadeh was taken to the army shooting range south of Beirut and the sentence carried out. Witnesses of the assassination at dawn testified uniformly to Saadeh's fortitude

---

1 Adel Beshara, *Outright assassination: the trial and execution of Antun Sa'adeh, 1949*, Reading, U.K., Ithaca Press, 2012.

Treachery, Trial and Martyrdom

Saadeh during his final trial by a Lebanese Military Court a few hours before his execution.

and dignity in the face of imminent death. The police hurried the clandestine burial fearing popular reaction to the execution, increased security measures, and continued to pursue SSNP members with renewed ferocity. On July 22, six SSNP members were executed as well. Ironically, these six were chosen each from a different religious sect.

The martyrdom of Saadeh was a momentous event in the history of the SSNP. It created a new spirit in the Party and established militancy, self-denial and self-sacrifice as virtues to be embraced. Scores of SSNP members derived courage and spiritual sustenance from the example of their leader who remains the most towering symbol of Syria's will to life.

Epilogue

Within days of Saadeh's execution, the Lebanese Military Tribunal meted death sentences to twelve SSNP members in custody and harsh prison sentences to other members either in custody or in absentia. Six Party members were executed by firing squad promptly. Their courage and dignity while facing their executioners paralleled those of their leader and contrasted with mentality of the government that chose those six based on their religious affiliation to maintain sectarian balance even in injustice.

The ferocity of the actions of the Lebanese and Syrian governments were meant to subdue and intimidate. They underestimated the tenacity and resolve of the SSNP constituency. The betrayal of Saadeh by Husni Zaim only added to the mounting resentment against his megalomaniac dictatorship. On August 14, 1949, SSNP sympathizers in the Syrian army joined with others to overthrow Zaim and execute him and his prime minister immediately.[1] The Lebanese Prime Minister Riad Solh fared no better. While on a visit to Jordan in July 1951, three SSNP members approached his convoy and shot him fatally. Two of the Party members lost their lives in the successful attempt. These actions, while not sanctioned by the Party leadership, were nevertheless embraced by the SSNP constituency and their perpetrators acquired a heroic stature within the Party. They also created an aura around the SSNP as being capable of exacting retribution. As alliances and political views shifted in Lebanon, the SSNP, while banned and operating clandestinely, joined with other opposition forces to bring down President Khoury in September 1952. The newly elected president Camille Chamoun duly acknowledged the SSNP's contribution by allowing the Party to operate relatively freely.

---

1 Finer, S. E. *The man on horseback; the role of the military in politics.* Praeger, New York, 1962.

The Syrian Social Nationalist Party

Soon after the overthrow of Zaim, SSNP leaders convened in Damascus and established a new leadership structure and team. The leadership team, however, was wrought with factionalism and tendency to monopolize power. It had very narrow political horizons and naïve notions about leading a political organization. It did succeed, however, in rallying the constituency around the symbol of the martyred Saadeh and re-establishing the organizational structure of the SSNP. In the somewhat permissive atmosphere of the new regimes in Syria between 1949 and 1955, the SNP prospered and embarked on wide ranging activities. It secured very modest representation in the Syrian parliament and introduced legislation for secularization and modernization of the state that was not embraced by the majority. It opened a series of schools throughout Syria, particularly in rural areas, staffed by SSNP teachers to put in effect a model of its educational policies. Intellectuals, poets, writers, and artists gravitated towards the SSNP circles and its publications. On the political front, the SSNP had an uneasy alliance with the Syrian government, dominated during that period by President Shishakli, an ex-military officer and ex-SSNP member who separated from the Party to build his personal political fiefdom.[2]

The ascendency of the SSNP in Syria was paralleled by that of the Pan-Arab Baath Party, the Soviet-backed Communist Party, and pro-Nasserist elements. With the overthrow of Shishakli in February of 1954, anti-SSNP groups gained significant advantage in the control of government functions.[3] Fierce competition for positions of power presaged a conflagration, which materialized in the spring of 1955. The coalition of anti-SSNP groups, with strong support from the regime of Nasser in Egypt, used the pretext of the assassination of Adnan Maliki, the Deputy Chief of Staff of the Syrian armed forces on April 22, 1955, to unleash

---

2   Joshua Landis: Early US policy toward Palestinian refugees: The Syria option. In *The Palestinian Refugees: Old Problems--new Solutions*, edited by J. Ginat, Edward Joseph Perkins, University of Oklahoma Press, 2001.

3   Sami M. Moubayed, *Steel & Silk: Men and Women who Shaped Syria 1900-2000*, Cune Press, Seattle, 2006.

Epilogue

a fierce campaign against the SSNP, accusing it of plotting against the government and being responsible for Maliki's death. The coalition brought the full force of the government in a brutal attempt to extirpate the SSNP from the Syrian political scene, much as the Lebanese government had done in 1949, but with greater ferocity. Scores of SSNP members were hunted down, assassinated, imprisoned, tortured, had their livelihood destroyed, properties confiscated, and were subjected to every form of imaginable oppression.[4] The SSNP fought back, but its attempts at regime change in Syria were not successful and it had to retrench to Lebanon where the Chamoun regime was more permissive. Thus, the political role of the SSNP in Syria entered a long hiatus until the latter parts of the presidency of Hafez Assad and the advent of the Syrian civil war when it re-emerged as a visible political force. During the long hiatus, the SSNP continued to operate clandestinely in Syria perpetuating its presence and maintaining the seeds of activists and organizers that will facilitate its recent re-emergence.

The debacle in Syria precipitated a leadership crisis and a schism in the SSNP into two parallel but unequal organizations. The smaller of the two branches supported the outgoing president of the Party under whose watch the Syrian events transpired. It was a rigidly doctrinarian group, removed from any political involvement, and a faithful custodian of the older SSNP traditions. The larger group was more politically dynamic and more open to experimentation and new approaches. Consequently, however, it was more vulnerable to infiltration by agents of Western intelligence agencies and political adventurers. This group dominated the political history of the SSNP for the following decades.

---

4   "The political atmosphere of Syria now assumed a pathological character. Under the direction of Abdul Hamid al-Sarraj, chief of military intelligence, treason trials, arrests, plots, and counterplots became the normal order of the day. Conspiracy hunts, long-term imprisonments without formal charges, and the use of torture to obtain confessions became ordinary procedures of security. Hundreds of political refugees flocked to Lebanon and neighboring countries." Sharabi, Hisham, *Governments and politics of the Middle East in the twentieth century*. Princeton, N.J., Van Nostrand [1962], page 130.

The Syrian Social Nationalist Party

The political exodus from Damascus to Beirut was accompanied by a wave of displacement of intellectuals, poets, and artists that changed the cultural landscape of Beirut and consequently that of the Arab east. From this concentration of creative people many of the Avant-guard movements in poetry, theater, and other intellectual pursuits were born.[5] In its political defeat in Damascus, the SSNP scored a cultural victory in Beirut!

Confined in its visible political activity to Lebanon, the SSNP became embroiled in an array of pro-Western alliances to resist pro-Nasserist expansion. Several elements influenced this course. The Nasser regime and its supporters in Syria and Lebanon were on a warpath against the SSNP and the Party reacted in self-defense. Further, the SSNP ideologically was against ad hoc unification schemes as promoted by the pro-Nasser groups. Finally, some SSNP leaders were looking for expedient ways to gain political power in Lebanon. When the 1958 disturbances in Lebanon erupted between President Chamoun (who was seeking an extension of his term as president) and the pro-Nasser groups in Lebanon clamoring to join the United Arab Republic formed by the union of Egypt and Syria under the leadership of Nasser, the SSNP sided with Chamoun. In a way, the battles in Lebanon against the pro-Nasser groups were a continuation of the events of 1955 in Syria.

The resolution of the conflict after the US military intervention,[6] the election of a new president, Fuad Chehab, and an understanding with Nasser to curb his supporters from seeking immediate union, left the SSNP with no political gains for the sacrifices and efforts it expended in the events of 1958. Mounting frustration with the corruption and chaos

---

5   Yusuf al-Khal, Adonis and Khalil Hawi are three SSNP-affiliated poets that played a leading role in modernizing poetry in Arabic since the middle of the 1950s. Robyn Creswell: The Man Who Remade Arabic Poetry, *The New Yorker*. December 18 & 25, 2017.

6   Erika G. Alin, *The United States and the 1958 Lebanon Crisis: American Intervention in the Middle East*. University Press of America, 1994.

Epilogue

in the affairs of Lebanon and the sidelining of the Party led the SSNP leadership to embark on planning for a coup d'état in Lebanon.[7] Agents of the Lebanese intelligence services had infiltrated the SSNP ranks and knowledge of the preparations had reached the government so when on December 31, 1961 the SSNP launched its attempt, the government forces were ready to suppress it. There followed another cycle of persecution, arrests, and assassination to which the SSNP constituency was subjected. Dozens of SSNP members died under torture, scores were maimed, and all were summarily dismissed from government employment, prevented from travel, and subjected to humiliations and destructive house searches. Another dark cycle in the life of the Party was at hand. The mere suspicion of being a member, or the possession of any Party literature was an automatic sentence to jail. It was an age of terror the likes of which Lebanon had not encountered before.

It took almost a decade, two presidential elections, the Arab-Israeli war of 1967, and major cataclysms in the Middle East before the SSNP could resurface in Lebanon without fear of overt persecution. Divergent views between the leaders released from jail and new cadres that emerged during the long clandestine period, and the need to review the SSNP's political and ideological platform in view of current events necessitated a series of congresses and amendments to the constitution that only exacerbated internal discord within the Party and the struggle for power and eminence. While politically the SSNP may have deviated from its ideological base, questioning the tenets of its ideology during this period was a new phenomenon born of the pervasive activities of Marxist groups and effects of the cold war. The ascendency of Israel and the unbridled Western support of its aggression and expansionism was giving leftist ideologies fresh appeal and some SSNP intellectuals were not immune to its influence.

---

7   Adel Beshara, *Lebanon: The Politics of Frustration - The Failed Coup of 1961*, Routledge, London, 2005.

THE SYRIAN SOCIAL NATIONALIST PARTY

The internal unrest was further accentuated by the infiltration and influence of agents of the Palestine Liberation Organization and the Syrian regime leading to conflicting loyalties. This led to further splintering of the SSNP. It was with a troubled body and soul that the SSNP confronted the Lebanese civil war. Its traditional right-wing enemies in the Christian militias exerted every effort to expunge the Party from their areas of control.[8]

The political platform of these militias to create a Christian enclave allied with the Jewish state was in striking opposition to the ideology of the SSNP aiming at national unity and the relentless opposition to the state of Israel. Thus, the SSNP was ideologically driven to oppose the alliance of Christian militias, but the so-called Patriotic Front with which it allied itself was no less sectarian with its Druze Chief and Muslim militias. It also suffered at the hands of its allies the killing of some of its leading figures.[9] Until the Israeli invasion of 1982, the SSNP played an auxiliary role in the war except for a few geographal areas where its constituency was influential. After the Israelis occupied Beirut and forced the election of the Christian warlord Bashir Gemayel as President of Lebanon, the SSNP delivered the two most decisive events in the history of that period.

Israeli military might had crushed the Palestine Liberation Organization and forced its evacuation to North Africa. All other factions were subdued and the Israelis felt comfortably in control. On September 24, 1982, a lone SSNP member walked into a sidewalk café in the fashionable area of Hamra in Beirut in broad daylight and emptied his revolver into a gathering of Israeli soldiers. That single heroic act is credited

---

8   On March 26, 1976, the Christian militias massacred unarmed SSNP members and their families in the village of Aintoura northeast of Beirut, a phenomenon that will repeat itself throughout the war.

9   Muslim militias and rogue elements allegedly were responsible for the death of the leading figures Bashir Obeid (senior SSNP leader) and Kamal Kheir Bek (poet and prominent anti-Israel activist) on November 5, 1980 and Habib Keyruz (senior SSNP leader) on October 22, 1987.

EPILOGUE

16th September 1982, Phalange militants massacre Palestinians in the refugee camps at Sabra and Shatila, Lebanon.

in inspiring and launching the Lebanese resistance movement that ultimately forced the Israelis to withdraw from Lebanon. SSNP members, men and women, were responsible for some of the most spectacular attacks on the occupying Israeli forces and their local allies for the next decade. Their courage and heroism served as a role model for other factions of the Lebanese resistance movement.

The other decisive event was the elimination of the Phalange warlord, and President-elect Bashir Gemayel on September 14, 1982, before his swearing-in ceremony. This was accomplished by installing a bomb in the building in which Gemayel held meetings of the leadership of his militia. The blast killed Gemayel and scores of his closest advisors and lieutenants, gravely disrupting the Christian-Israeli political agenda.[10] While

---

10 Immediately following Gemayel's death, his militia forces attacked the Palestinian refugee camps of Sabra and Shatila on the outskirts of Beirut, and between September 16 and September 18, 1982, massacred thousands of unarmed civilians of all ages and gender while the Israeli Defense Force watched but did not interfere. While the massacre was depicted as a reaction to the assassination of Bachir, it represented a continuation of a policy of ethnic cleansing that the Christian militias had repeatedly exercised during

Bashir's older brother Amin was hastily voted in as president, he was too corrupt and ineffectual to carry forth his brother's agenda.

The SSNP emerged from the Lebanese civil war with a narrative of heroism and a decisive role in disrupting and preventing the Israeli blue print for a truncated Lebanon. Nevertheless, it was saddled by accusations of being a client of the Syrian government that allegedly secured it parliamentary and ministerial seats. Internal discord and factionalism also continued to plague the SSNP including occasions of internecine fighting. As the guns went silent, SSNP affiliated intellectuals were again engaging the cultural stage in Beirut, Damascus and Amman. SSNP branches among Palestinians in occupied Palestine and the diaspora remerged. The advent of the PLO had completely eclipsed them, but the disenchantment with the PLO after Oslo was making room for a new generation of SSNP adherents among the Palestinians. The SSNP resumed its proselytizing activities and while its strict membership did not grow dramatically, its halo effect was substantial. Indeed, internal discord has always created a barrier to the growth in active membership, but adherents to the ideology of the SSNP have always outnumbered card-carrying members by several folds.

Baathist regimes have been particularly unsympathetic to the SSNP perpetrating the antagonism born in the bloody battles of the 1950s. By the mid to late 1970s, tentative friendly relationships between limited circles in the Syrian government and some SSNP groups emerged. In the course of the Lebanese civil war, particularly in the wake of the Israeli invasion of Lebanon in 1982, these tentative relationships were cemented by the struggle against a common enemy. Supporting the SSNP in Lebanon and allowing it to operate freely in Syria are two different things. The

---

the Lebanese civil war. Massacre of large numbers of civilians had been done by Bashir forces in 1976 in the shanti-town of Qarantina in Beirut, and the captured Palestinian refugee camp of Tel-Zaatar. PLO forces were guilty of similar acts in the town of Damour south of Beirut in 1976.

SSNP Fighters break through ISIS lines in Palmyra, Syria.

former predates the latter by decades. While censorship of SSNP core literature was slightly relaxed, organization of a distinct constituency was still frowned upon, and public displays of SSNP emblems was generally discouraged. All of this changed with the advent of the Syrian civil war. Again, the position of the SSNP in its various factions was an intersection between ideologically driven positions and political necessity. The sectarian groups that dominated the insurgency were a grave threat to the concept of Syrian nationhood and the survival of a Syrian entity. Whatever the grievances against the Syrian regime, the SSNP was bound ideologically to resist the ferocious political-religious agenda of the various factions of the insurgency. This was also consonant with the rapprochement that had been building over a few decades between the SSNP and the Syrian regime.

The Syrian regime recognized that the SSNP constituency was a natural ally against the Islamic military groups and their narrative of a future Islamic state. This ally, however, could not under the circumstances, fight anonymously. Its emblems and symbols were a necessary component of the counter-narrative of a secular resistance to religious fanaticism. No example in the entire Middle East could compare to the secularism of the SSNP. After half a century of absence, the flags and emblems of the SSNP were again visible in Syria. They were carried into battle by the men and women of the "Nusur az-Zawba'a" (the Eagles of the Hurricane or Whirlwind), the military organization of the SSNP in Syria,[11] and draped the coffins of the fallen martyrs and lined the paths to their funerals. Official branch offices were opened publicly throughout Syria where the SSNP had a constituency. Training camps for youth and fighters were organized and traditional SSNP celebrations commemorating the founding of the SSNP and the martyrdom of Saadeh, where the flag of the SSNP waved side by side with the state flag, were attended by Syrian regime officials. The leader of one of the SSNP factions was appointed as reconciliation minister in the Syrian cabinet. While these developments are felicitous from the perspective of the SSNP, it is difficult to predict how far the regime will allow the growth of its ideological rival.

The SSNP is in the ninth decade of its existence. It is widely spread in the homeland and the diaspora. It has more adherents to its ideology than active members, a reservoir of support it can readily draw upon when it resolves its internal discord and reunite its factions. It has been persecuted by each and every government in Greater Syria, its literature banned, its leaders imprisoned and killed, its members incarcerated and tortured, their livelihoods destroyed, their life plans shattered. Through nine decades of incomparable strife, the SSNP continues to re-emerge as the mythical Phoenix. Observers can agree that some of the woe that befell the SSNP is of the making of its leaderships, their errors, adventurism and naïve assumptions. Indeed, two of the most damaging waves of persecution in 1955 and 1962 were precipitated by inopportune acts by the SSNP leadership. Despite it all, it survives. Why?

---

11   The organization first emerged in 1976-1978, during the Lebanese civil war, and gained visibility for some limited activity against Israel. The label, however, was dormant for a few decades and resurfaced during the Syrian civil war.

Epilogue

Saadeh described the SSNP as consisting of "an idea and a movement concerned with the life of the nation." It is in the details of the idea and the characteristics of the movement that we need to seek the answer to our question.

Despite repeated reversals, waves of suppression, assassinations, executions, and the attempts of French and British occupation forces and the various governments of Greater Syria to eradicate it, the SSNP continues to re-emerge because its ideology must have resonated with the needs and aspirations of a perpetual constituency. In its core, this ideology rests on three complementary components: an assertion of the existence of a Syrian nationhood, a declaration of the rights of this nationhood, and a vision of the future for this nationhood.

In its ideology, the SSNP institutionalized a pre-existing belief in Syrian nationhood and provided a framework for its survival. The SSNP's vision of the course of Syrian history is continuously validated and reinforced by historical and archeological research and studies. Its interpretation of the Syrian past has proven to be more robust than any of the alternatives. The ideological framework addresses the various dangers that threaten this Syrian nationhood and as these dangers mount and intensify the SSNP ideology becomes more relevant. Indeed, during the life span of the SSNP these dangers have never abated, but indeed intensified. National strife, sectarians discord, divisive tendencies, loss of national territories, and ferocious colonialism are worse today than at the time of the founding of the SSNP, and the political program delineated to combat them remains at its core sound, relevant, and necessary.

The ideology of the SSNP also defines the rights of the Syrian nation and the rights of Syrians communally and individually. This twin championing of national rights and individual rights is perpetually relevant particularly when both are endangered and threatened. National rights are threatened by the territorial encroachments of neighboring states (Turkey for example), an aggressive settler colonialism (Israel), and great imperialist powers. No political group has offered a more cogent framework for the definition of national rights, alertness to the real dangers, and firmness in how to confront these dangers than the SSNP. Individual rights are threatened by constitutions and laws framed by religious dogma, archaic traditions, patriarchal social structures, and the corrupt political elite. No political group is more determinedly secular, modern, and progressive in its approach to equality of all citizens, and justice for all citizens than the SSNP. Finally, the ideology of the SSNP offers a vision for the future of the Syrian nationhood that is never anachronistic or dated because it is open to the agency of human intellect in its finest iterations.

As a movement, the SSNP has suffered from the inadequacy of its leadership, the dissipation of its human resources, and blind adherence to antiquated forms in its discipline, all endangering its survival. Yet all observers agree that the Party has created within its ranks a unique social model of the elimination of sectarian and ethnic ailments that plague Syria. The SSNP is proof that the religious and ethnic divisions of Syria can be eliminated with the agency of its ideology, a sustained experiment of progressive social transformation with no equal in the modern Middle East. In a society where religious and ethnic divisions are perpetually roiling the masses, the success of the SSNP in creating a modern equalitarian community within its ranks and in the broader context of the more numerous adherents to its ideology must represent a powerful draw.

Another aspect of the movement that has contributed to its longevity is that it has inaugurated in Syria the age of ideologically committed heroism. The noble heroism of the SSNP founder and leader in his life and his martyrdom remains an inspiring symbol that draws new elements into the constituency. Antoun Saadeh the man was easy to kill, but his death made Antoun Saadeh the symbol, the noble hero, the martyr, nearly invincible. Critics could attack his ideas and policies, but his integrity and devotion to the cause are unassailable as they are stamped with his blood. The emulation of the noble heroism of the leader has created an ethos in the SSNP that is difficult to squash. It permeates the image of the Party of itself and informs its indoctrination policies and literature.

An additional factor of possibly lesser importance than the above but of complementary effect is the intellectual school that Saadeh founded and SSNP intellectuals developed. It would not be superlative to state that this intellectual school has influenced friend and foe across the entire spectrum of cultural activities in Syria, the former by creating the impetus to innovate and the latter by challenging their notions and driving them to attempt to refute it.

Saadeh once stated that if he were to be abandoned by all his comrades and the community he created disbanded, he would carry the message to generations yet unborn. Many such generations seem to have heeded his call.

Appendix

The Principles and Aim of the SSNP

by Antoun Saadeh, based on the fourth edition, 1947

The Basic Principles

The First Basic Principle

Syria is for the Syrians and the Syrians are a complete nation.

When I began to give serious thought to the revival of our nation and observe the irresponsible political movements rampant in its midst, it became forthwith certain to me that our most urgent problem was the determination of our national identity. Although there was no consensus of opinion concerning this problem, I became convinced that the starting point of every correct national endeavor must be the raising of this fundamental philosophical question: Who are we? After extensive research, I arrived at the following conclusion: We are Syrians and we constitute a distinct national entity.

The confused conceptions of our nation implied in the statements such as 'we are Lebanese,' 'Palestinians,' 'Syrians,' 'Iraqis,' or 'Arabs' have contributed to the breaking up of our national identity and cannot serve as the basis of a genuine national consciousness or of our national revival. Thus, the assertion that the Syrians constitute a nation complete in itself is a fundamental doctrine, which should put an end to ambiguity and place the national effort on the basis of clarity without which no national revival in Syria is possible. The realization of the complete nationhood of the Syrians and the active consciousness of this nationhood are two essential prerequisites for the vindication of the principle of national sovereignty. For, were the Syrians not a complete nation having right to sovereignty and to the establishment of an independent state, Syria would not be for the Syrians in the full sense, but might be subject to claims of sovereignty by non-Syrian entities pursuing interests conflicting with, or that likely to conflict with, the interests of the Syrian people.

This principle is intended to safeguard the unity of the Syrian nation, the integrity of its homeland, and the elimination of any ambiguity from a legal perspective. The Syrians are a nation upon whom alone devolves the right to own, dispose of, and make decisions concerning every inch of Syrian territory. The homeland belongs to the nation as a whole and no one, not even individual Syrian citizens, may dispose of any part of its territory in such a way as to destroy or endanger the integrity of the country, which integrity is a necessary condition for preserving the unity of the Syrian nation.

Every Syrian who wants to see his nation free, sovereign and advanced should inscribe this principle deeply in his heart.

Those who deny that Syria is for the Syrians and that the Syrians are a complete nation are committing a crime that deprives Syrians of their sovereignty over themselves and their homeland. The Syrian Social Nationalist Party declares them criminals in the name of millions of Syrians yearning for freedom, life, and progress.

The Second Basic Principle

The Syrian cause is an integral national cause completely independent from any other cause.

This principle signifies that all the legal and political questions that relate to any portion of Syrian territory, or to any Syrian group, are part of one indivisible cause distinct from, and unmixed with, any other external matter which may nullify the conception of the unity of Syrian interests and of the Syrian will. This principle follows from and is complementary to the first principle. Since Syria is for the Syrians and the Syrians are a complete nation endowed with the right to sovereignty, it follows that this nation's cause, that is its life and destiny, belongs to her alone and is independent from any other cause that involves interests other than those of the Syrian people.

This principle reserves to the Syrians alone the right to expound their own cause and to be their sole representatives, determine their own interests, and shape their own destiny. It renders theirs an all-inclusive and indivisible cause.

From the spiritual point of view, this principle entails that the will of the Syrian nation, which represents its interests, is a general will and that the ideals that the Syrians seek to realize emanate from their own character, temperament, and talents. The Syrian nation cannot tolerate the disintegration of these ideals, or its dissociation from them or their mingling with other aims in which they may be forfeited. These ideals are Freedom, Duty, Discipline, and Strength, abounding with Truth, Good, and Beauty in the most sublime form to which the Syrian spirit can rise and which the Syrians must attain through their own endeavors, since no one else but themselves can represent or realize those ideals for them.

In accordance with this principle, the Syrian Social Nationalist Party declares that it does not recognize the right of any non-Syrian person or organization to speak on behalf of Syria and its interests either in internal or international matters. The Party does not recognize the right of anybody to make the interests of Syria contingent on the interests of other nations.

The millions of farmers, workers, artisans, and professionals in trade and industry, which comprise the Syrian nation, have a will and an interest in life that must remain their own.

The Syrian Social Nationalist Party

The Syrian Social Nationalist Party does not recognize the right of any non-Syrian person or organization to thrust its own ideals upon the Syrian nation in substitution for its own.

The Third Basic Principle

The Syrian cause is the cause of the Syrian nation and the Syrian homeland.

This principle unequivocally defines the Syrian cause and emphasizes the indissoluble bond between the nation and its territory. Nations arise in distinct territories that sustain their lives and national character. The concept of the unity of the nation and its homeland embodied in this principle enables us to understand the nation as a social reality and frees the concept of nationhood from such historical, racial, or religious misconceptions as are contrary to the nature of the nation and its vital interest.

The interdependence between the nation and its homeland is the only principle whereby the unity of life can be achieved. It is within a national territory that the unity of national life and participation in its activities, interests and aims are attained. The national territory is vital for the development of the social character of the nation and forms the basis of its life.

The Fourth Basic Principle

The Syrian nation is the unity of the Syrian people which developed through a long history.

This principle defines what constitutes the nation mentioned in previous articles and requires close examination from an ethnological perspective. The purpose of this principle is to negate the concept of a single ethnic origin for the Syrian nation and to declare the reality of the nation, as the outcome of the long history of all the people that have settled in Syria, inhabited it, interacted with each other, and finally became fused in one people. This process started with the people of the Neolithic age who preceded the Canaanites and Chaldeans in settling this land, and continued through to the Akkadians, the Canaanites, the Chaldeans, Assyrians, Arameans, Amorites, and Hittites and led to the emergence of one people. Thus, the principle of Syrian nationhood is not based on race or blood, but rather on the natural social unity derived from homogeneous intermixing. Through this principle the interests, the aims and the ideals of the Syrian nation are unified and the national cause is guarded against disharmony, disintegration, and strife that result from primitive loyalties to blood ties.

The alleged racial purity of any nation is a groundless myth. It is found only in savage groups, and even there it is rare. All existing nations are composed of ethnic mixtures. The Syrian nation consists of a mixture of Canaanites, Akkadians, Chaldeans, Assyrians, Arameans, Hittites, and Mitanni as the French nation is a mixture of Gauls, Ligurians, Franks, etc. . . and the Italian nation of Romans, Latins, Etruscans, etc. . . the same being true of every other nation.

The Syrian nation denotes this society unified in life. Though of mixed origins, this nation has come to constitute a single society living in a distinct territory known historically as Syria or the Fertile Crescent. The common origins, Canaanites, Chaldeans, Arameans, Assyrians, Amorites, Hittites, Mitanni, and Akkadians etc. whose existence and mixing are an indisputable historical fact constitute the ethnic-historical-cultural basis of Syria's unity, whereas the Syrian Fertile Crescent constitutes the geographic-economic-strategic basis of this unity.

This ethnic and geographical reality was distorted and lost due to successive historic events which destroyed documentation and led to the substitution of various foreign accounts for authentic facts and distorted through various interpretations of our national history. A large number of historians have confined their definition of Syria to Byzantine or late Hellenistic Syria, whose boundaries extended from the Taurus range and the Euphrates to the Suez, thus excluding the Assyrians and Chaldeans from Syrian History. Other historians have further confined this definition to the region between Cilicia and Palestine, thus leaving out Palestine. All these historians were foreigners who were unable to grasp the reality of the Syrian nation and its environment and the process of its development. Moreover, most of the Syrian historians who derived their information from foreign sources without adequate criticism, have followed their lead. Thus, the truth was falsified and our genuine cause was lost.

The history of the ancient Syrian states (Akkadian, Chaldean, Assyrian, Hittite, Canaanite, Aramean, Amorite) indicates the same trend: the political, economic, and social unity of the Syrian Fertile Crescent. This fact should enable us to view the Assyrian and Chaldean wars, aimed at dominating the whole of Syria, in a new light. These were internal wars, a struggle for supremacy among the powerful groups and dynasties within the nation which was still in the making and which later attained its full formation.

This principle is not in the least incompatible with the fact that Syria is one of the nations of the Arab World, or one of the Arab nations, nor is this latter fact at variance with the statement that Syria is a complete nation with sovereign rights over its territory and consequently with a distinct and independent national cause. It is the neglect of this principle that has given the religious sects in Syria the means of disuniting the country into a Muslim-Arab faction on the one hand and a Christian-Phoenician one, on the other, so that the unity of the nation is thereby destroyed and its energies dissipated.

This principle would redeem Syria from the blood bigotries which are apt to cause the neglect of national interests. For those Syrians who believe or feel that they are of Aramaic extraction would no longer be driven to fan Aramaic blood loyalty, so long as the principle of Social Nationalist unity and the equality of

APPENDIX

civic, political, and social rights and duties are guaranteed, and no ethnic or racial discrimination in Syria is made. Similarly, those Syrians who claim to descend from a Phoenician (Canaanite), Arab, or Crusader stock would no longer have allegiance but to their Syrian community. Thus, would genuine national consciousness arise. The unity of the Syrian nation arose from the mixing of multiple elements which have formed in the course of history the Syrian people and the character and traits of the Syrian nation.

This principle cannot be said to imply that Jews are a part of the Syrian nation and equal in rights and duties to the Syrians. Such an interpretation is incompatible with this principle, which excludes the integration in the Syrian nation of elements that maintain exclusive racial loyalties. Such elements are not part of the unified people.

There are large settlements of immigrants in Syria, such as the Armenians, Kurds, and Circassians, whose assimilation is possible given sufficient time. These elements may dissolve in the nation and lose their special loyalties. However, there is one large settlement which cannot in any respect be reconciled to the principle of Syrian nationalism, and that is the Jewish settlement. It is a dangerous settlement, which can never be assimilated because it consists of a people that, although it has mixed with many other peoples, has remained a heterogeneous mixture, with strange stagnant beliefs and aims of its own, essentially incompatible with Syrian rights and sovereignty. It is the duty of the Syrian Social Nationalists to repulse the immigration of this people with all their might.

THE FIFTH BASIC PRINCIPLE

The Syrian homeland is that geographic environment in which the Syrian nation evolved. It has distinct natural boundaries and extends from the Taurus range in the northwest and the Zagros mountains in the northeast to the

Suez canal and the Red Sea in the south and includes the Sinai peninsula and the gulf of Aqaba, and from the Syrian sea in the west, including the island of Cyprus, to the arch of the Arabian desert and the Persian gulf in the east. (This region is also known as the Syrian Fertile Crescent).

These are the natural boundaries of the Syrian homeland, which has housed the elements of the Syrian nation and provided them with the basis of their lives and the opportunity of contact and collision, then mixture and fusion, which resulted in the formation of the distinct character of the Syrian nation. The Chaldeans and Assyrians were alive to the internal unity and integrity of this country and sought to unify it politically, interested as they were in the idea of the territorial state. Similarly, all the other people who inhabited this region were conscious of the internal unity of the country and sought to build up confederations between decentralized governments to avoid internal dissension and for protection from external incursions.

The secret of Syria's persistence as a distinct nation despite the numerous invasions to which it succumbed lies in the geographic unity of its homeland. It was this geographic unity that ensured the political unity of this country even in ancient times when it was still divided among the Canaanites, the Arameans, the Hittites, the Amorites, the Assyrians, and the Chaldeans, a political unity that manifested itself in the formation of alliances in the face of threats from Egyptians and other invasions. That unity reached its culmination with the formation of a Seleucid Syrian state which grew into a powerful empire, dominated Asia Minor, and extended as far as India.

Syria's loss of sovereignty because of the major foreign invasions resulted in its partition into arbitrary political units. In the Byzantine-Persian period, the Byzantines extended their rule over western Syria and applied the name "Syria" to that part only, while the Persians dominated the eastern part, which they called "Irah", later Arabicized as Iraq. Similarly, after the First

World War the condominium of Great Britain and France over Syria resulted in the partition of the country according to their political aims and interests and gave rise to the present political designations: Palestine, Jordan, Lebanon, Syria, Cilicia, and Iraq. Natural Syria consists of all those regions, which constitute one geographic-economic-strategic unit. The Syrian Social Nationalist cause will not be fulfilled unless the unity of Syria is achieved.

The partitioning of Syria between the Byzantines and the Persians into Eastern and Western Syria and the creation of barriers between them retarded considerably, and for a long period, the national growth and the development of the social and economic life cycle of the country. This division resulted also in distorting the truth about the borders of Syria. Additional factors contributing to this distortion were: the incursion of the desert upon the lower arch of the Fertile Crescent, the decrease in population, the recession of urban areas (by virtue of constant wars and invasions), and deforestation, all of which made vast areas of the country desolate. The lack of reliable studies pertaining to the cause of this ever increasing drought, which has caused deepening of the arch, has contributed to the view that the expansion of the desert has been a permanent phenomenon. In my studies, I have demonstrated the indisputable unity of the country and examined the arbitrary grounds for its present condition and its partitioning and established that all the territory to which the term Mesopotamia refers, as far as the Zagros Mountains that form the natural boundary separating Eastern Syria from Iran, falls within Syria.

The Syrian homeland is an essential factor in Syrian nationalism. Every Syrian Social Nationalist must be conversant with the boundaries of his beautiful country and keep its image in his mind. In order to safeguard his right and the rights of his descendants in this wonderful country, he should grasp well the unity of his nation, the community of its rights, and the indivisible unity of its country.

The Syrian Social Nationalist Party

I have indicated in Book One of *The Emergence of Nations* that the dynamism and vitality of a nation may lead to adjustments of its borders. A strong and ever-growing nation will transcend its frontiers and expand beyond them, whereas a weak and weathering nation will shrink within those frontiers. After the decline and fall of the great Syrian states, the Syrian nation was reduced to impotence and recession. It lost the Sinai Peninsula to Egypt and Cilicia to Turkey, and shrank within its own natural boundaries, and was finally broken up by the powers which invaded and occupied its territory in whole or in part.

The Syrian Social Nationalist Party symbolizes the resurgence of the Syrian nation, which is determined on recovering its power and vitality and reclaiming its dismembered parts.

The Sixth Basic Principle

The Syrian nation is one society.

On this fundamental principle are based some of the reform principles to be expounded later, such as the separation of religion and state and the elimination of social barriers between the various sects and creeds. This principle is the basis of genuine national unity, the mark of national consciousness, and the guarantee of the life and endurance of the Syrian character. One Nation-One Society. The unity of society is the basis of the community of interests and consequently the basis of the community of life. The absence of social unity entails the absence of common interests, and no resort to temporary expediency can make up for this loss. Through social unity, the conflict of loyalties and negative attitudes will disappear to be replaced by a single healthy national loyalty ensuring the revival of the nation. Similarly, all religious bigotries and their nefarious consequences will cease and in their stead national collaboration and toleration will prevail. Moreover, economic cooperation and a sense of national concord and unity will be fulfilled and pretexts for foreign intervention will be abolished.

Real independence and real sovereignty will not be fulfilled and will not endure unless they rest upon a genuine social unity that is the only sound basis for a national state and Social Nationalist civil legislation. This unity forms the basis for citizenship and the guarantee of the equality of rights for all citizens.

The Seventh Basic Principle

The Syrian Social Nationalist movement derives its inspiration from the talents of the Syrian nation and its cultural political national history.

This principle asserts the spiritual independence of the nation in which its national character, ideals, and aims are grounded. The Party believes that no Syrian revival can be affected save through the agency of the inborn and independent Syrian character. Indeed, one of the major factors in the absence of Syrian national consciousness or its weakness is the overlooking of the genuine character of the Syrian nation as manifested in the intellectual and practical contributions of its people and their cultural achievements, such as the enactment of the first civilized code of law and the invention of the alphabet, the greatest cultural intellectual revolution in history; let alone the material-spiritual effects of Syrian colonization and culture and the civilizing influence Syria exercised over the whole of the Mediterranean, and the immortal achievements of such great Syrians as Zeno, Bar Salibi, St John Chrysostom, Ephraim, al-Maari, Deek-el-Jin of Emessa, al-Kawakibi, Gibran, and other great figures of ancient and modern times. To this list way be added the names of Syria's great generals from Sargon the Great to Esarhaddon, Sennecharib, Nebuchadnezzar, Assurbanipal, and Tiglat-pilasser; from Hanno the great to Hannibal (the greatest military genius of all times) and Yusuf Azmeh, the hero of Meyselun.

We derive our ideals from our own character and we declare that in the Syrian character are latent all science, philosophy, and art in the world. Unless the Syrian ethos is strengthened, and unless it is freed from dominating alien influences, the elements of real independence will be wanting and Syria will fall short of its ideals.

The Eighth Basic Principle

Syria's interest supersedes every other interest.

This is the most important principle in national action for, in. the first place, it provides the clue to the sincerity and integrity of national militants, and, in the second place, it directs their energies towards the real purpose of national action, which is the interest of the Syrian nation and its welfare. It is the criterion by which all national movements and actions are judged. Through this criterion, the SSNP excels all other political factions in Syria, to say nothing of its obvious excellence in other respects. The SSNP aims at serving the concrete and tangible interests of the Syrians and at meeting their common needs and aims. There is no longer a need to seek in vain the definition of national endeavor in the domain of the abstract and the impracticable. This principle centers all other principles round the interest of the nation so that Syrians are no longer misled by the propaganda of those who would serve contrary interests.

The life of the nation is a concrete reality and so are its interests. The success of the SSNP in bringing about this remarkable national revival in our country is due, in great measure, to the fact that the Party seeks to serve the genuine interests of the Syrian nation and assert its will to life.

Syria embodies our social character, faculties, ideals, our outlook on life, art, and the universe. It is the symbol of our honor, dignity, and destiny. That is why our loyalty to Syria must transcend all personal interests and considerations.

Appendix

The Reform Principles

The First Reform Principle

Separation of religion and state.

The greatest obstacle to the achievement of our national unity and our national progress has been the pretension of ecclesiastical bodies to political power and their actual possession of such power in varying degrees. Indeed, the great battles of human emancipation were those that took place between the interests of nations and the interests of religious institutions, which clung to the principle of divine truth and divine law for dominion and control of people. It is a dangerous principle that enslaved people to religious institutions. Religious institutions were not the only ones using the principle of divine truth and divine will. It is also inherent in "Divine Kingship", where rulers claimed to derive their authority from the will of God.

Theocracy or the religious state is incompatible with the concept of nationhood because it stands for the domination of the whole community of believers by an ecclesiastical authority. Religion recognizes no national interests because it is concerned with a community of believers dominated by a central religious authority.

This is the aspect of the issue that the SSNP is opposed to not the philosophical or theological ideas concerning the mysteries of the soul, immortality, the creator, and metaphysical matters.

The concept of a religious-political bond is contrary to nationalism in general and to Syrian Social Nationalism in particular. The adherence of Syrian Christians to such a concept would set them apart from other religious groups within the nation and would expose their interests to the danger of being submerged in the interests of other groups with whom they happen to share a religious bond. Similarly, the adherence of Syrian Moslems to the concept of a religious bond would bring their interests also to possible conflict with those of their non-Muslim compatriots and would submerge those interests in those of the greater religious community. The inevitable outcome of the concept of a religious bond is the disintegration of national unity and the decline of national life.

We cannot achieve national unity by making the state a religious one because in such a state rights and interests would be denominational in nature pertaining exclusively to the dominant religious group. Where such rights and interests are those of a religious group, common national rights and interests will not obtain. Without the community of interests and rights there can be no unity of duties and no unified national will. Based on this legal philosophy, the SSNP has succeeded in laying down the foundations of national unity and in actually realizing it within its ranks.

THE SECOND REFORM PRINCIPLE

Debarring the clergy from interference in political and judicial matters.

The rationale for setting forth this principle in a separate article is that religious bodies attempt to acquire or retain civil authority even where the separation of religion and state has been conceded. This principle puts an end to the indirect interference of ecclesiastical bodies in civil and political matters. This principle defines precisely the meaning of the separation of religion from the state for reform must not be confined to the political sphere but must extend to the legal-judicial sphere as well.

In a country where judicial function is based on the diversity of religious sects, equality in civic and political rights will not be possible nor will general national unity for the latter is conditional on the unity of laws. The Social Nationalist state must have a uniform judiciary and a unified system of laws.

Citizens must all be equal before the one law of the state. There can be no unity of character where the basis of life is in conflict with the unity of the nation.

The Third Reform Principle

Removal of the barriers between the various sects and confessions.

There exists in Syria age-old barriers between the various sects and denominations that are not of the essence of religion. There are conflicting traditions derived from the structure of religious and denominational institutions that have exerted an enormous influence on the social and economic unity of the people, weakened it and delayed our national revival. As long as these barriers remain, our call for freedom and independence will remain futile.

Every nation that seeks a free and independent life in which it can realize its ideals must possess strong spiritual unity. Such spiritual unity is not possible in a country in which each group lives in isolation from other groups and has particular social and legal systems, which set it apart from other groups. This would result in differences in character and disharmony in aims and aspirations.

National unity will not be achieved unless the causes for dissension are removed. The socio-legal barriers separating the sects and denominations of the same nation constitute a major obstacle to the realization of the unity of the nation.

Unity is something real and not fictitious, so let us not surrender reality and cling to illusion. We must stand together before the world as one united nation rather than a conglomeration of heterogeneous elements of conflicting attitudes. The existence of the present social and legal barriers which separate the various sects entails the persistence of obnoxious religious bigotries.

Those barriers must be demolished so that the unity of the nation might become a reality and the Social Nationalist order, which will restore the nation to health and energy might be established.

THE FOURTH REFORM PRINCIPLE

The abolition of feudalism, the organization of national economy on the basis of production and the protection of the rights of labor and the interests of the nation and the state.

Although feudalism is not legally recognized in Syria, there exists in certain parts of the country a number of economic and social feudal conditions that threaten the economic and social welfare of the nation. The Syrian Social Nationalist Party considers that it is of the utmost importance to put an end to this state of affairs to safeguard national unity and sovereignty.

The organization of the national economy on the basis of production is the only means for the attainment of a sound balance between the distribution of labor and the distribution of wealth. Every citizen should be productive in one way or another. Moreover, production and producers must be classified in such a way to assure coordination, participation and cooperativity in the widest extent possible and to regulate the just share of laborers in production and to insure their right to work and to receive just compensation for their labor. This principle will put an end to absolute individualism in production because every form of production in society in genuinely a collective or a cooperative one. Grave injustices can be perpetrated against labor and laborers were individual capitalists to be given absolute control. The public wealth of the nation must be controlled in the national interest and under the superintendence of the national state. Progress and strength of the national state cannot be achieved save with this policy.

The aim of the Syrian Social Nationalist Party is the achievement of a sound national unity which enables the Syrian nation to excel in the struggle for existence. This unity cannot be realized if either the economic or the social order is not sufficiently wholesome. Justice in the social and economic spheres is an essential condition for the triumph of the Syrian Social Nationalist Movement.

Collective production is a public not a private right. Capital which is the guarantee of the continuity of production and its growth, and in so far as it represents the resultant of production, is consequently, in principle a public national possession. Individuals acting as trustees may dispose of it and utilize it for further productivity. Active participation in the process of production is the necessary condition for the enjoyment of public rights. With this economic organization, we guarantee our economic growth, the improvement of the lives of millions of workers and farmers, the increase of public wealth, and the strength of the social nationalist state.

The Fifth Reform Principle

Formation of strong armed forces that will be effective in determining the destiny of the nation and the homeland.

In international competition of national interests, national right is recognized only to the extent it is supported by the power of the nation. The vital interests of a nation in this struggle cannot be protected except by force in its material and intellectual aspects. Force is the decisive factor in affirming or denying national rights.

By the armed forces, we understand the army, the navy, and the air force. The art of war has reached such an advanced level that it is incumbent upon us to be always in a state complete military preparedness. The entire Syrian nation must be well armed and prepared. We have witnessed with distress parts of our country taken away and annexed to foreign countries because we have lost our military power. We are resolved not to let this state of helplessness continue. We are determined to turn the tide so that we may regain all our territory and recover the sources of our strength and vitality. It is on our own strength that we wish to depend in securing our rights and protecting our interests. We are mobilizing and preparing for our survival and preeminence in the struggle for existence. Survival and victory shall inevitably be our lot.

The Aim of the SSNP

The aim of the Syrian Social Nationalist Party is the creation of a Syrian Social Nationalist renaissance that ensures the realization of its principles and return the Syrian nation to vitality and strength; the organization of a movement leading to the complete independence of the Syrian nation and the vindication of its sovereignty; the establishment of a new order to protect its interest and raise its standard of living; and the endeavor to form an Arab front.

It is clear from this article that national revival is the central theme in the program of the Syrian Social Nationalist Party. National revival involves the establishment of the concept of nationhood in Syria and securing the very life of the Syrian nation and the creation of the conditions necessary for its progress and unity, as well as the establishment of a new social-national order. This far reaching aim of the Party is of the utmost importance because it is not restricted to the treatment of a particular political form but affects the very foundations of nationhood and the basic principles of national life. The purpose of the Party is to direct the Syrian nation towards progress and prosperity and the activation of the elements of national energy latent in Syria. This national energy once fully developed will free the nation from apathy and adherence to antiquated beliefs and stand as a deterrent against foreign ambitions threatening the interests of the millions of Syrians and their very existence. The Party also aims at dissemination of new ideas expressing our new outlook on life and our Social Nationalist doctrine.

APPENDIX

The aim of the Syrian Social Nationalist Party is a comprehensive undertaking directed towards the examination of the foundations of national life in all its aspects: economic, social, political, spiritual, and moral. It embraces national ideals, the significance of independence and the establishment of a genuine national society. This entails a new ethical outlook and a new theory of values as embodied in the basic and reform principles of the Party which contain a new and complete philosophy of life.

A complementary part of the foreign policy of the Party is the creation of an Arab Front from the Arab nations. This front should serve as a bulwark against foreign imperialistic ambitions and prove of considerable moment in deciding major political questions.

Syria is one of the Arab nations and indeed is the nation qualified to lead the Arab world as the Syrian Social Nationalist Party proves conclusively. It is obvious that a nation with no internal cohesiveness to insure its unity and progress cannot help revive other nations and lead them along the path of progress and success. Syrian nationalism is the only genuine practical way, the first prerequisite for the awakening of the Syrian nation and its ability to work for the Arab Cause.

Those who believe that the Syrian Social Nationalist Party seeks Syria's withdrawal from the Arab World because they do not distinguish between Syrian national awakening and the Pan-Arab cause are grossly mistaken.

We shall never relinquish our position in the Arab World, nor our mission to the Arab World. We want first and foremost to be strong in order to accomplish our mission more adequately. Syria must forge ahead in its national revival so that it can fulfill its great mission.

This comprehensive outlook of the Syrian Social Nationalist Party represents an ideal conception of national life. The

Party does not intend to confine this broad outlook with its far-reaching consequences to Syria alone, but it intends to pass it on to our sister Arab nations through cultural activities, mutual understanding and exchange of opinions, not by means of the abolishing of the identity of those Arab nations and the imposition of those principles on them by force.

As to the political aspect of the Party's aims, the Party considers that from the internal point of view the Lebanese question arose from subsidiary reasons, which were valid at a time when the concept of the state was still a religious concept. However, the principles of the Syrian Social Nationalist Party affirm the national social-legal basis of statehood. Through the realization of the principles of the Syrian Social Nationalist Party, those reasons for Lebanese isolation would cease to be justified.

As regards to the Arab World, the Party favors recourse to conferences and alliances, as the only practical way to cooperation between Arab nations. The Party favors the formation of an Arab Front of definite moment in international politics. National sovereignty, however, should not be surrendered in such pacts and alliances.

Bibliography

1. Abu Nowar, Maan: *The Jordanian-Israeli War, 1948-1951: A History of the Hashemite Kingdom of Jordan*. Garnet and Ithaca Press, NY, 2002.

2. Aḵl, Jurjī: *The black book of the Lebanese elections of May 25, 1947*, Phoenicia Press, NY, 1947.

3. Alin, Erika G., *The United States and the 1958 Lebanon Crisis: American Intervention in the Middle East*. University Press of America, 1994.

4. Baker, Randall: *King Husain and the Kingdom of Hejaz*. The Oleander Press, 1979.

5. Benvenisti, Meron: Maxine Kaufman Nunn: *City of Stone: The Hidden History of Jerusalem*, University of California Press, Berkley, CA, 1996.

6. Beshara, Adel: *Antun Saadeh the man, his thought: an anthology*, Ithaca Press, Reading, UK, 2007.

7. Beshara, Adel, *Lebanon: The Politics of Frustration - The Failed Coup of 1961,* Routledge, London, 2005.

8. Beshara, Adel: *Outright assassination: the trial and execution of Antun Sa'adeh*, 1949, Ithaca Press, Reading, U.K., 2012.

9. Beshara, Adel: *Syrian Nationalism: An Inquiry into the Political Philosophy of Antun Sa'adeh*, Melbourne phoenix Publishing, 2011.

10. Beshara, Adel: *The Intellectual Legacy of Antun Sa'adeh: Philosophy, Culture and Society*, Kutub,Beirut, Lebanon, 2017.

11. Biger, Gideon: *The Boundaries of Modern Palestine, 1840-1947*. Routledge, NY, 2004.

12. Bogle, Emory: *The Modern Middle East: from Imperialism to Freedom*, 1800-1958, Prentice Hall, NJ, 1996.

13. Cohen, Hillel: *Army of Shadows: Palestinian Collaboration with Zionism, 1917-1948*, University of California Press, Berkley, 2008.

14. Commins, David Dean: *Historical Dictionary of Syria*, Scarecrow Press, 2004.
15. Dayyeh, Jean: *Muhakamat Antoun Saadeh* (The Trial of Antoun Saadeh). Fajr an-Nahdah, Beirut, 2002.
16. Dayyeh, Jean: *Saadeh wal-Naziyah* (Saadeh and Nazism). Fajr al-Nahda, Beirut, 1994.
17. Dayyeh, Jean: *Tajribat Fakhry Maaluf*, Dar Nelson, Beirut, 2004.
18. Fieldhouse, David Kenneth: *Western Imperialism in the Middle East 1914-1958*, Oxford University Press, Oxford, 2006.
19. Finer, S. E. *The Man on Horseback; The Role of The Military in Politics.* Praeger, New York, 1962.
20. Firro, Kais: *The Attitude of the Druzes and Alawis vis-à-vis Islam and Nationalism in Syria and Lebanon*, in *Syncretic Religious Communities in the Near East*, edited by K Kehl-Bodrogi, B Kellner-Heinkele, and A Otter-Beaujean, Brill, Leiden, 1997.
21. Fischbach, Michael R.: *State, Society and Land in Jordan*. Brill, Leiden, 2000.
22. Friedman, Isaiah: *Palestine, a Twice-Promised Land*. Transaction Publishers, New Brunswick, NJ, 2000.
23. Hadawi, Sami: *Bitter Harvest; Palestine Between 1914-1967*, New World Press, 1967.
24. Hourani, Albert: *Syria and Lebanon: A Political Essay*, Oxford University Press, London, 1946.
25. al-Husari, Sati: *al-Uruba bayn Du'atiha wa Mu'aridiha* (Arabism between its proponents and opponents), Complete Works, part 1, Center of Arab Unity Studies, Beirut, 1990.
26. Jeha, Shafiq: *Ma'rakat Masir Lubnan fi 'Ahd al-Intidab al-Faransi* (The Battle for Lebanon's Destiny during the French Mandate), Maktabat ras Beirut, Beirut, 1995.
27. Jureij, Gibran: *Min al-Ju'bat* (From my Files), Volume 1 (1985), Volume 2 (1986), Volume 3 (1988), Volume 4 (1993), Volume 5 (in press), Beirut.
28. Karpat, Kemal: *Political and social thought in the contemporary Middle East*, Praeger, NY, 1982.

Bibliography

29. Karsh, Efraim and Inari Karsh: *Empires of the Sand: The Struggle for Mastery in the Middle East*. Harvard University Press, 2001.

30. Katibah, Habib Ibrahim: *Syria for the Syrians, under the guardianship of the United States*. Syrian National Society, Boston, 1919.

31. Khalidi, Rashid: *The Iron Cage: The Story of Palestinian Struggle for Statehood*. Beacon Press, Boston, 2006.

32. Khoury, Philip: *Syria and the French Mandate*. Princeton University Press. New Jersey, 1989.

33. Kurht, Ameli and Susan Sherwin-White (editors): *Hellenism in The East*. University of California Press, Berkley, CA, 1987.

34. Landis, Joshua: Early US policy toward Palestinian refugees: The Syria option. *The Palestinian Refugees: Old Problems--new Solutions,* edited by J. Ginat, Edward Joseph Perkins, University of Oklahoma Press, 2001.

35. Longrigg, Stephen Hemsley: *Syria and Lebanon under French Mandate*. Oxford University Press, London, 1958.

36. Maalouf, Kamal: *Memoirs of Grandma Kamal: Unique Personal Experiences and Encounters*. World Book Publishing, Beirut, 1999.

37. Mackey, Sandra: *Lebanon: death of a nation*, Anchor Books, NY, 1991.

38. Mandel, N.J.: *The Arabs and Zionism before World War I*, University of California Press, Berkley, 1976.

39. Mansfield, Peter: *The Arabs*, Harmondsworth, New York, 1978.

40. Massad, Joseph: *Colonial Effects: The Making of National Identity in Jordan*. Columbia University Press, NY, 2001.

41. Melhem, Edmond: *Antun Saadeh, national philosopher: an introduction to his philosophical thought*, Dar Fikr, Beirut, 2011.

42. Moore, J.N. (ed.): *The Arab-Israeli Conflict, vol III: Documents*, Princeton University Press, Princeton, NJ, 1974.

43. Morris, Benny: *Righteous Victims: A History of the Zionist-Arab Conflict, 1881-1999*, Knopf, 1999.

44. Morris, Benny: *The Birth of the Palestinian Refugee Problem Revisited*, Cambridge University Press, Cambridge, 2003.

45. Mossek, Moshe: *Palestine Immigration Policy Under Sir Herbert Samuel: British, Zionist and Arab Attitudes*, Routledge (UK) 1978.

46. Moubayed, Sami M., *Steel & Silk: Men and Women who Shaped Syria 1900-2000*, Cune Press, Seattle, 2006.

47. Mujais, Salim: *Antoun Saadeh: a Biography*, Kutub Publishing, Beirut, volume 1 (2004), volume 2 (2009), volume 3 (2018).

48. Mujais, Salim: *Saadeh wa al-Ikliruss al-Marouni* (Saadeh and the Maronite Ecclesiasts), Beirut, 1993.

49. Muslih, Muhammad: *The Origins of Palestinian Nationalism*. Columbia University Press, NY, 1989.

50. Nebenzahl, Kenneth: *Maps of the Holy Land*. Abbeville Press, N.Y., 1986.

51. Paris, Timothy: *Britain, the Hashemites and Arab Rule, 1920-1925*. Routledge, London, 2003.

52. Saadeh, Antoun: *al-Aamal al-Kamilah* (Complete Works). Saadeh Cultural Foundation, Beirut, 2001.

53. Saadeh, Antoun: *Rasa'el ila Dia'* (Letters to Dia'), Folio, Beirut, no date.

54. Saadeh, Antoun: *Sadar an Maktab az-Zaim* (From the Desk of the Leader), al-Rukn, Beirut, 2005.

55. Saadeh, Safia Antoun: *Antun Saadeh and democracy in geographic Syria*, London, Folios, 2000.

56. Salibi, Kamal: *A House of Many Mansions: The History of Lebanon Reconsidered*, University of California Press, 1988.

57. Salibi, Kamal: *The Modern History of Jordan*. I.B. Tauris publisher, 1998.

58. Sanders, Ronald: *The High Walls of Jerusalem: a history of the Balfour declaration and the birth of the British Mandate for Palestine*. Holt, Rinehart and Winston, NY, 1983.

59. Seikaly, May: *Haifa: transformation of a Palestinian Arab society 1918-1939*, I.B.Tauris, London, 2002.

Bibliography

60. Shambrook, Peter A.: *French Imperialism in Syria, 1927-1936.* Garnet & Ithaca Press, Reading, 1998.

61. Sharabi, Hisham, *Governments and Politics of the Middle East in the Twentieth Century.* Princeton, N.J., Van Nostrand [1962], page 130.

62. Shehadi, Nadim, Dana Haffar Mills (editors): *Lebanon: A History of Conflict and Consensus.* I.B. Tauris, London, 1988.

63. Shorrock, W.: *French imperialism in the Middle East*, The University of Wisconsin Press, Madison 1976.

64. Sicker, Martin: *Reshaping Palestine: From Muhammad Ali to the British Mandate, 1831-1922.* Praeger/Greenwood publishers, Westport, CT, 1999.

65. Simon, Reeva Spector, Lisa Anderson, Muhammad Y Muslih, Rashid Khalidi (editors): *The Origins of Arab Nationalism.*, Columbia University Press, NY, 1993.

66. Spyer, Jonathan: *The rise of nationalism: the Arab World, Turkey, and Iran*, Mason Crest Publishers, Philadelphia, 2008.

67. Stein, Leonard: *The Truth about Palestine: A Reply to the Palestine Arab Delegation.* Zionist Organization, London, 1922.

68. Tauber, Eliezer: *The formation of Modern Syria and Iraq*, Translated by J.A. Reif, Routledge, London, 1995.

69. Troen, Selwyn Ilan: *Imagining Zion: dreams, designs, and realities in a century of Jewish settlement*, Yale University Press, New Haven, 2003.

70. Yamak, Labib Zuwiyya: *The Syrian Social Nationalist Party: An Ideological Analysis.* Harvard Middle Eastern Monograph Series, Harvard University Press, Cambridge MA, 1969.

71. Zamir, Meir: *The formation of Modern Lebanon*, Cornell University Press, Ithaca, N.Y., 1985.

About the Author

Salim Mujais is a physician and a writer. Born in Shweir (Lebanon) and educated at the American University of Beirut and the University of Chicago, his work focuses on the intellectual history of the Near East and its luminaries. He has produced multi-volume biographies of Antoun Saadeh (the founder and leader of the SSNP), Kahlil Gibran (the Syrian-American painter and writer) and the celebrated Syrian feminist May Ziadeh.

www.ingramcontent.com/pod-product-compliance
Lightning Source LLC
Chambersburg PA
CBHW050136170426
43197CB00011B/1854